Tasso's Dialogues

Tasso's Dialogues

A Selection, with the *Discourse on the Art of the Dialogue*

TRANSLATED WITH
INTRODUCTION AND NOTES
BY CARNES LORD
AND DAIN A. TRAFTON

UNIVERSITY
OF CALIFORNIA
PRESS

———

BERKELEY
LOS ANGELES
LONDON

Publication of this volume has been
supported by grants from
the Università degli Studi di Padova
and the University of California.

University of California Press
Berkeley and Los Angeles

University of California Press, Ltd.
London, England

Library of Congress Cataloging in Publication Data
Tasso, Torquato, 1544-1595.
Tasso's dialogues.

(Biblioteca italiana)
Bibliography: p.
I. Lord, Carnes. II. Trafton, Dain A. III. Title.
IV. Series.
PQ4642.E2 1982   195   81-12937
ISBN 0-520-04464-9   AACR2

Printed in the United States of America

1   2   3   4   5   6   7   8   9

To our parents and Vera

Contents

Acknowledgments

Every student of Tasso's dialogues owes a large debt to the editorial labors of Ezio Raimondi. We wish to acknowledge both this debt and the promptness with which Professor Raimondi and his colleague at the University of Bologna, Bruno Basile, responded to several requests for aid as we were preparing this volume. No less prompt and helpful were A. Lowell Edmunds of Boston College and James A. Gherity of Northern Illinois University. The former's deep understanding of ancient literature and the latter's knowledge of Renaissance economic history have made the translations and the notes more accurate and useful than they might have been otherwise.

Professor Trafton's translation of *Il Malpiglio overo de la corte* first appeared in *Tasso's Dialogue on the Court*, English Literary Renaissance Supplements no. 2 (1973). We wish to thank the editors of *English Literary Renaissance* for their permission to reprint the translation (with slight alterations) here. Professor Trafton's early work on Tasso's dialogues began during time made free from teaching and other duties by a National Endowment for the Humanities Fellowship for Younger Humanists. In addition, our work has been supported by several grants from the Mary Ashby Cheek Fund of Rockford College. Barbara Jones was an especially careful and helpful typist, and Vera Trafton read the entire manuscript with her acutely critical eye.

Finally we wish to express our gratitude to Louise George Clubb, General Editor of Biblioteca Italiana. Her editorial judgment and encouragement were essential to the making of this book.

Introduction

The Dialogues in
Tasso's Life and Work

TORQUATO TASSO'S extant dialogues date from the last eighteen years of his life. Between 1578, when he began work on the *Forno, or On Nobility*, and his death in 1595, Tasso completed twenty-five works in the form—many of them lengthy and intricate—and composed his *Discourse on the Art of the Dialogue*.[1] Behind this sudden and important development in the latter part of the poet's career lies a complex of interests and influences. Tasso's long-standing interests in philosophy and in the dialogue as a means of philosophical expression matured under the pressure of events in the late 1570s and flourished in the adversity that afflicted his life thereafter.[2]

Tasso's first serious contact with philosophy and the dialogue probably occurred at the University of Padua, where he went in 1560, at the age of seventeen.

1. On the chronology of Tasso's dialogues, see Ezio Raimondi, "Il problema filologico e letterario dei *Dialoghi* di T. Tasso," in *Torquato Tasso*, ed. Comitato ferrarese per le celebrazioni di Torquato Tasso (Milan: Marzorati, 1957), pp. 479–89, and Torquato Tasso, *Dialoghi*, ed. Ezio Raimondi, 3 vols. (Florence: Sansoni, 1958), 1:8–192. Although the dating of many dialogues remains conjectural, Raimondi's careful arguments are generally persuasive.

2. The account of Tasso's life given here depends heavily on Angelo Solerti, *Vita di Torquato Tasso*, 2 vols. (Turin-Rome: Loescher, 1895). The main sources of biographical information about Tasso are his letters (Torquato Tasso, *Lettere*, ed. Cesare Guasti, 5 vols. [Florence: Le Monnier, 1854–55]). Solerti's *Vita* refers the reader to most of the relevant material in the *Lettere*.

hat the young Tasso would study
o evidence that he applied himself
ce to that field. Instead, he devoted
—his romance *Rinaldo* appeared in
osophical studies. Recalling this pe-
iter as he was writing the dialogue
otic Disputations, Tasso represented
it who was "not content to have ac-
quired great praise for poetry at a young age," but was
also eager "to engage in philosophical debates with the
philosophers themselves."[3] Among Tasso's most influential teachers at Padua was the philosopher Sperone
Speroni, who had been a student of the great Pietro
Pomponazzi. Speroni himself was the author of several
dialogues as well as of an *Apologia dei dialoghi* (not published until 1596), and he evidently stimulated Tasso's
interest in philosophy and in Plato, the greatest practi-
tioner of the dialogue. In the *Discourses on the Poetic
Art*, Tasso wrote of Speroni: "While I was studying in
Padua I was in the habit of frequenting his private
room not less often and less willingly than I frequented
the public schools, for it seemed to me to present a
likeness of that Academy and that Lyceum in which
the Socratics and the Platonists used to dispute."[4] Another professor at Padua who had a hand in turning
Tasso's attention to the possibilities of the dialogue was
Carlo Sigonio. His *De dialogo liber* appeared in 1562,
while Tasso was still at Padua, and its influence on
Tasso's *Discourse on the Art of the Dialogue* is unmistak-
able. In the preface to the *Rinaldo*, Tasso pays tribute to
the excellence of Sigonio's teaching, and when Sigonio

3. Tasso, *Dialoghi*, 2:797. All translations are our own unless otherwise indicated.
4. Torquato Tasso, *Discorso dell'arte poetica e del poema eroico*, ed.
Luigi Poma (Bari: Laterza, 1964), p. 15.

moved to Bologna in 1562, as the result of a dispute with another professor, Tasso followed.[5]

That such teachers and such an environment might have stimulated Tasso to try his hand at writing philosophy in the form of dialogues would not be surprising. In fact, we know that he began to do so soon after leaving Padua in 1565: a letter of 1566 informs us, "I have reached the sixth canto of the *Gottifredo* [the *Jerusalem Delivered*], and I have finished some dialogues and orations."[6] Nevertheless, Tasso was not yet ready to make either philosophy or the dialogue a central focus of his activity. The dialogues of 1566 were never published, and no further references to them occur. The decade of Tasso's career from 1565 to 1575 belongs to poetry. It was during these years, mostly spent in Ferrara, where he enjoyed the patronage of the Este family, that Tasso accomplished his greatest works: his pastoral drama *Aminta*, produced with acclaim in 1573, and the *Jerusalem Delivered*, completed in 1575 after more than ten years of labor. Ironically, however, the successful conclusion of this latter project seems to have precipitated an intense personal crisis, and it was in the midst of this crisis that he turned once again to the dialogue.

As he approached the end of his work on the *Jerusalem Delivered*, Tasso grew uneasy about its reception. Before publishing, he insisted that the work be reviewed by a group of critics who could judge not only its literary merit but also its theological, moral, and political orthodoxy. Tasso seems to have been espe-

5. For some indication of Sigonio's influence on Tasso's *Discourse on the Art of the Dialogue*, see the notes to the translation in this volume and Guido Baldassarri, "L'arte del dialogo in Torquato Tasso," *Studi tassiani* 20 (1970): 11–14.

6. Tasso, *Lettere*, 1:15.

cially uneasy about offending the various authorities who might take an interest in the poem. In his letters he refers worriedly to "the strictness of the times," admits that he designed an allegory for the poem primarily in order to protect certain passages that might attract censure if read literally, and speaks of prefacing the whole work with a letter "that states fully how the poet is of service to the political man."[7] Concern for such matters was not unreasonable. The Council of Trent had ended its deliberations in 1563 after ratifying the proposals of those elements in the Church most eager for severe ecclesiastical discipline and strict definitions of orthodoxy, placing unprecedented power for the control of opinion in the hands of the pope and the papal Inquisition. Writers like Castiglione and Erasmus were included on the Index of forbidden books, and living authors who aroused the suspicions of the authorities could suffer more than censorship: as the fates of Pietro Carnesecchi, Fausto Sozzini, Giordano Bruno, Alberico Gentili, and others testify, the dangers of imprisonment, exile, and the stake were real.[8]

7. Tasso, *Lettere*, 1:185–86.

8. On the general political, religious, and intellectual conditions in the second half of the sixteenth century in Italy, see Delio Cantimori, "Italy and the Papacy," *New Cambridge Modern History*, vol. 2, ed. G. R. Elton (Cambridge, Eng.: Cambridge University Press, 1958), pp. 251–74; Cantimori, "'Nicodemismo' e speranze conciliari nel Cinquecento italiano," *Contributi alla storia del Concilio di Trento e della Controriforma*, Quaderni di Belfagor (Florence: Vallechi, 1948), pp. 14–23; Eric Cochrane, "A Case in Point: The End of the Renaissance in Florence," *Bibliothèque d'humanisme et renaissance* 27 (1965): 7–29; Luigi Firpo, "Filosofia italiana e Controriforma," *Rivista di filosofia* 41 (1950):150–73; and H. G. Koenigsberger, "Western Europe and the Power of Spain," *New Cambridge Modern History*, vol. 3 (Cambridge, Eng.: Cambridge University Press, 1968), pp. 234–63. Cochrane's essay and English versions of those of Cantimori and Firpo may be found in *The Late Italian Renaissance*, ed. Eric Cochrane (New York: Harper Torch Books, 1970), pp. 43–73, 244–65, and 266–84.

Unfortunately, the response of the chosen critics was not reassuring. Tasso soon found himself involved in a fruitless debate over a multitude of issues and became alarmed that ecclesiastical or political authorities might suppress the poem altogether.[9] At the same time, he became increasingly convinced that fellow courtiers at Ferrara and even Duke Alfonso II were intriguing to steal the manuscript of the *Jerusalem Delivered* and to denounce him to the Inquisition. He was conscious of having expressed unorthodox religious views to courtiers who he now believed could not be trusted, and he knew of Alfonso's concern to avoid any taint of heresy; ever since Alfonso's mother, Renée of France, had brought Calvin to Ferrara in 1537, the Este court had been suspect at Rome.[10] Tasso's fears multiplied. Efforts of self-justification, visits to the Inquisitors,[11] outbreaks of violence, and flights from Ferrara in search of new patrons followed. It was in fact on one of these flights, in 1578, that Tasso composed the dialogue *Forno, or On Nobility*. Back in Ferrara in 1579, he seems to have suffered a nervous collapse. During the festivities for the marriage of Alfonso to Margherita Gonzaga, Tasso burst out into such violent denunciations of the court that he had to be restrained by force. He was taken to the hospital of Sant' Anna and chained like a madman. Although his confinement lasted seven years, his chains were soon removed, and he was provided with books and material for writing. Almost immediately, he con-

9. Solerti's account of Tasso's difficulties with his chosen critics (Solerti, *Vita*, 1:210–11, 219–35) cites the relevant documents from Tasso's correspondence.

10. Ferrara's delicate political and religious situation is described by Solerti, *Vita*, 1:259–60, 578–80, and Cantimori, "Italy and the Papacy," *New Cambridge Modern History*, 2:261–62.

11. On Tasso's visits to the Inquisitors at Bologna and Ferrara, see Solerti, *Vita*, 1:210–11, 258–60; and Tasso, *Lettere*, 1:254–56, 257–62, 265–67, and 2:23–25, 74–76, 84–86.

firmed the new direction in his career signaled by the *Forno*: before the end of 1580 he had completed drafts of at least six more dialogues, including three of his longest and finest works in the form—*Nifo, or On Pleasure*, *The Messenger*, and *The Father of the Family*.

Tasso's return to the dialogue during this crisis reflects a profound shift in his view of himself and of the world in which he lived. Disputes with the critics of the *Jerusalem Delivered* apparently revived his taste for philosophical speculation, and he began to think of himself as a philosopher as well as a poet. "I am tired of writing poetry and have turned to philosophy," he writes in a letter of 1576.[12] In letters of 1579, he identifies himself "as one who is, if not fully a master of philosophy, at least eager for it and a lover of it," and proclaims his ambition to win glory in prose as well as in poetry and "to combine eloquence with philosophy in such a way that an eternal memory of me will remain in the world."[13] Elsewhere he is even more emphatic: "I am a lover of the truth, and if I am a lover of the truth, I am a philosopher."[14] Along with this view of himself as a philosopher went an intense awareness of the need for prudence: his troubles with the critics and at Ferrara only reinforced the cautious bent that moved him to delay publication of his poem in the first place. Dissimulation became a principle of his intellectual life. "Not because I hid some part of the truth," he writes soon after his confinement in Sant' Anna, "should I be considered any the less a philosopher. . . . If I denied a thing to the priest and avowed it to the prince, I did not only what was necessary according to the new and extraordinary fashions, but also what was fitting."[15] In *Malpiglio, or On the Court*, fin-

12. Tasso, *Lettere*, 2:185.   13. Tasso, *Lettere*, 2:8, 60.
14. Tasso, *Lettere*, 2:74.   15. Tasso, *Lettere*, 2:74–75.

ished in 1585, Tasso indicates that prudence is "the most important single virtue" for a man who wishes to prosper at court, and he defines it frankly as the ability to conceal qualities and opinions that might offend.[16] As a literary form, the dialogue lends itself to both of these preoccupations: it is especially congenial to a prudent expression of philosophy. Because the dialogist presents his ideas through his characters, he can indulge in a wide range of speculation without committing himself unequivocally to a single view: only through interpretation can one arrive at the author's position—and then only tentatively.

Once established in the late 1570s, Tasso's commitment to philosophy and the dialogue persisted and was especially strong during the seven years of his imprisonment. His psychological condition while in prison has been the subject of much study and speculation. That his fears of persecution worsened is undeniable, and at times he suffered from hallucinations. On the other hand, the view that he was mad, used to justify Alfonso's treatment of him, seems untenable.[17] The testimony of friends who visited him, as well as the evidence of his nearly constant philosophical and literary activity, indicates that his periods of mental and emotional disorder were brief. While in Sant' Anna he continued his revisions of the *Jerusalem Delivered*, pur-

16. See pp. 171–81 below. For a discussion of prudence in the *Malpiglio*, see Dain A. Trafton, *Tasso's Dialogue on the Court*, English Literary Renaissance Supplements no. 2 (Amherst, Mass.: Dartmouth College and *English Literary Renaissance*, 1973), pp. 1–13.

17. The main problem for all students of Tasso's life has been to determine the extent to which his own neurotic behavior caused his difficulties and the extent to which he was victimized by real intrigues and injustice. Since Solerti, most commentators have tried to find a judicious balance between the view that Tasso was simply mad and the view that he was simply a victim. Nevertheless, the tendency in the work of modern scholars has been to emphasize

sued a number of minor literary projects, and went on writing dialogues at a steady pace. Among the products of his last years in prison are *Cavaletta, or On Tuscan Poetry* (1585); *Gianluca, or On Masks* (1585); and *Cataneo, or On Idols* (1585). The *Discourse on the Art of the Dialogue* (1585) also issued from Sant' Anna. In 1586 Tasso's pleas and the good offices of numerous friends at last secured his release. The first years of freedom were expended in the revision of old work, schemes for publication, and agitated wandering from one Italian city and court to another. In 1589, however, a final surge of creativity began with a new dialogue, *Costante, or On Clemency.* As he made the final adjustments to the *Jerusalem Delivered* (the revised version, known as the *Jerusalem Conquered,* appeared in 1593) and embarked on an important new religious poem, *The Seven Days of the Created World,* he continued to give a major part of his attention to his dialogues. *Cataneo, or On Amorous Conclusions* appears to have been finished during 1591; by 1593 he had added *Manso, or On Friendship; Ficino, or On Art; Minturno, or On Beauty;* and *Porzio, or On the Virtues. The Count, or On Emblems* is the last of his dialogues; he completed it sometime in the summer of 1594. As far as we know, he began no new dialogue before his death on April 25, 1595.

Tasso is remembered today mainly as the poet of the *Aminta* and the *Jerusalem Delivered.* Nevertheless, the

---

Tasso's neuroses. See, for example, C. P. Brand, *Torquato Tasso* (Cambridge, Eng.: Cambridge University Press, 1965), pp. 3–37, especially pp. 22–24. While not wishing to obscure the undeniable evidence of Tasso's mental and emotional aberrations, we think that the genuine reasons Tasso had for his anger and fear deserve more attention than they have received in most modern studies. When reading the dialogues it is essential not to lose sight of the political and religious pressures that affected Tasso's work and indeed all artistic and philosophical endeavor in late sixteenth-century Italy.

dialogues, the philosophical works to which he devoted so much of his time and energy, have also contributed to his fame. Numerous editions and translations attest to their popularity throughout Europe during Tasso's lifetime and well into the seventeenth century, and during the eighteenth and nineteenth centuries they were regularly reprinted in the various editions of Tasso's complete works.[18] In 1858–59 they were brought together for the first time in a separate edition prepared by Cesare Guasti. Since Francesco de Sanctis's great *Storia della letteratura italiana* (1870), moreover, the dialogues have not been neglected by modern criticism and scholarship. Eugenio Donadoni and Giovanni Getto both devote long sections to the dialogues in their general studies of Tasso, and a heightening of interest in the subject has been especially apparent in the last two decades, stimulated by Ezio Raimondi's admirable critical edition published in 1958.[19] Much of the biographical, philological, and historical background from which the dialogues emerge has

18. On the early fame of the dialogues, see Solerti, *Vita*, 1:350, 396–98 (especially p. 396, n. 6), and Chandler B. Beall, *La fortune du Tasse en France*, University of Oregon Studies in Literature and Philology no. 4 (Eugene, Ore.: University of Oregon, 1942), pp. 16, 74–75, 112, 210, 277. A list of early editions of Tasso's prose works can be found in Angelo Solerti, *Appendice alle opere in prosa* (Florence: Le Monnier, 1892), pp. 9–67.

19. See Francesco de Sanctis, *The History of Italian Literature*, trans. Joan Redfern, 2 vols. (New York: Harcourt, Brace, 1931), 2:670–72; Eugenio Donadoni, *Torquato Tasso: Saggio critico* (1920–21; reprint ed., Florence: La Nuova Italia, 1936), pp. 387–511; Giovanni Getto, *Interpretazione del Tasso* (Naples: Edizioni scientifiche italiane, 1951), pp. 79–111; Ezio Raimondi, "Il problema dei *Dialoghi*," pp. 489–502; Raimondi, *Rinascimento inquieto* (Palermo: Manfredi, 1966), pp. 197–227; Baldassarri, "L'arte del dialogo in Tasso," pp. 5–46; and B. T. Sozzi, *Nuovi studi sul Tasso* (Bergamo: Centro Tassiano, 1963), pp. 121–32. A useful account of the different scholarly and critical approaches to the dialogues can be found in Giorgio Cerboni Baiardi, "I *Dialoghi* di Torquato Tasso: Linee di storia della critica," *Studi urbinati di storia, filosofia e letteratura* 42 (1968): 113–42.

been illuminated: their chronology has been defined; their texts have been established; and they have been located generally "at the center of that crucial moment which, confused between Renaissance and Baroque, is precisely Mannerism."[20] What are needed now are close readings of individual dialogues. The most thorough studies published so far—recent interpretations of *Malpiglio* and *Nifo* by the editors and translators of this volume—find in Tasso's dialogues a philosophical independence that has not been detected elsewhere in his work. These interpretations argue that Tasso exploited the dialogue's inherent obliqueness in order to protect himself while expressing heterodox political and philosophical ideas.[21] Read with an eye to their nuances as well as to their broader emphases, *Malpiglio* and *Nifo* indicate that Tasso was neither the admirer of princes nor the simply pious mouthpiece of the Counter-Reformation that most scholars have taken him to be. Politically, he seems to have recognized many of the disadvantages of monarchic government and to have been attracted to certain features of republicanism. Philosophically, he was capable of expressing a heterodox Aristotelianism owing more to Averroës and the pagan commentators than to Thomas Aquinas. In short, *Malpiglio* and *Nifo* seem to document not Tasso's orthodoxy but rather the complex strategies by which he sought to preserve his intellectual freedom amid the pressures of his time. In the light of these dialogues Tasso emerges as a noteworthy figure in the revival of ancient philosophic thought and style during the late Renaissance. His example sheds light on the special dangers that attended the pursuit of truth in that

20. Raimondi, "Il problema dei *Dialoghi*," p. 502.
21. See Trafton, *Tasso's Dialogue on the Court*, pp. 1–13, and Carnes Lord, "The Argument of Tasso's *Nifo*," *Italica* 56 (1979): 22–45.

age—as well as on the conflict or tension that has always marked the relationship of the philosopher to society. Whether other readings will confirm this line of interpretation or not remains to be seen, but until the form and substance of each of the major dialogues have been examined in detail the significance of Tasso's commitment to the dialogue cannot be grasped. We hope that this volume will help to stimulate the close critical attention that Tasso's dialogues deserve.

The Texts and Translations

Neither the *Discorso dell'arte del dialogo* nor the dialogues present serious textual problems. Readers interested in the minor variations of wording and spelling that distinguish the manuscripts and early printed versions should consult the critical editions from which the texts in this volume have been taken: Guido Baldassarri, "Il discorso tassiano 'Dell'arte del dialogo,'" *Rassegna della letteratura italiana* 75 (1971):120–34; and Torquato Tasso, *Dialoghi*, ed. Ezio Raimondi, 3 vols. (Florence: Sansoni, 1958).

The translations of the individual dialogues as well as of the *Discourse on the Art of the Dialogue* are the first in modern English. We have tried to render Tasso's words as literally as possible without violating modern English usage. His prose in the dialogues and in the *Discourse* is relatively unembellished and admirably clear; our English aims at a corresponding directness. At the same time, we have avoided an informality that would be misleading and inappropriate. We believe that Tasso's meaning is not independent of his style and choice of words, and our versions seek to maintain something of the courtly flavor that pervades his work. The English renderings of Tasso's many citations of Latin and Italian poetry are our own.

TEXTS AND TRANSLATIONS

Discourse on
the Art of the Dialogue

According to the *Discourse on the Art of the
Dialogue*, Tasso's only theoretical statement
about the dialogue's form, the writer of
dialogues "occupies a kind of middle ground
between the poet and the dialectician." In
interpreting a dialogue, the *Discourse*
indicates, one must attend not only to the
discussion but also to the characters, the
setting, and the action; a dialogue's meaning
emerges from the interplay
of all its elements.

Discorso
dell'arte del dialogo

AL MOLTO REVERENDO PADRE
IL PADRE DON ANGELO GRILLO

Voi mi pregate, Padre Molto Reverendo, nelle vostre lettere, ch'io voglia darvi alcun ammaestramento; e 'l chiedete, se non m'inganno, de lo scrivere i dialogi, perchè son quelle medesime nelle quali m'avisate d'aver ricevuti quel della *Poesia Toscana* e della *Pace*. E se propriamente ragionate, io non posso compiacervi, perchè tanto a me disdicevol sarebbe la persona di maestro quanto a voi quella di scolare; nè rifiutandola io temo di poterne esser biasimato, come Giotto; perch'egli ricusò convenevole onore, io non accetto ufficio non conveniente. Ma se volete onorarmi con questo nome, ed ammaestramento chiamate l'opinione, io la scriverò; perchè niuna cosa debbo tenervi celata, la qual possa giovar a gli altri, o pur a me stesso; ed allora stimerò buone le mie ragioni, che dal vostro giudizio saran confermate. E se delle regole aviene quel che delle leggi; sì come altre leggi hanno i Genovesi diverse da quelle de' Viniziani o de' Ragusei; così potrebbono avere altri precetti nell'artificio del bene scrivere. Ma io non gli voglio dar questo nome, nè voi gliele scrivete in fronte; perciochè io l'ho raccolte in una operetta assai breve per assomigliar alcuni dottori cortegiani, i quali non potendo sostener persona così grave vestono di corto. E s'in quest'abito potranno esser vedute dagli

Discourse on
the Art of the Dialogue[1]

TO THE MOST REVEREND FATHER
DON ANGELO GRILLO[2]

In your letters, most reverend father, you ask that I give you some instruction. Unless I am deceived, you want to learn about writing dialogues, for your requests are contained in the very letters that inform me that you have received my dialogues *On Tuscan Poetry* and *On Peace*.[3] If you reflect upon these requests properly you will understand why I cannot satisfy you: the role of teacher would be as ill-suited to me as the role of student to you. Nor do I fear that in refusing this role I shall be blamed as Giotto was; he rejected an appropriate honor, while I am refusing an office that does not suit me.[4] If you insist upon honoring me with this name, however, and want to call an opinion a teaching, I shall write mine down, because I ought to conceal nothing from you that might be useful to others, or even to myself, and I shall consider good any of my arguments that are confirmed by your judgment. Perhaps the rules of writing are rather like laws; just as the Genoese have laws that are different from those of the Venetians or the Ragusans, so the precepts in the art of good writing may vary. But I do not want to give such a title to what follows, nor should you advertise it as such. The rules that I have collected in this very brief work resemble certain scholars at court who, unable to sustain so serious a role, put off the gown and dress in the common fashion. If, thus at-

amici e da' parenti vostri, che sono usati non solamente d'udire, ma di scriver e di far nobilissime azioni, non v'incresca di leggerle.

Nell'imitazione o s'imitano l'azioni degli uomini o i ragionamenti; e quantunque poche operazioni si facciano alla mutola, e pochi discorsi senza operazione, almeno dell'intelletto, nondimeno assai diverse giudico quelle da questi; e degli speculativi è proprio il discorrere, sì come degli attivi l'operare. Due saran dunque i primi generi dell'imitazione; l'un dell'azione, nel qual son rassomigliati gli operanti; l'altro delle parole, nel quale sono introdotti i ragionanti. E 'l primo genere si divide in altri, che sono la tragedia e la comedia, ciascun delle quali patisce alcune divisioni; e 'l secondo si può divider parimente. Ed Aristide, un de' più famosi Greci, i quali scrissero e non parlorono, così parve che gli dividesse, dicendo che Platone avea comicamente rappresentato Ippia, Prodico, Protagora, Gorgia, Eutedemo, Dionisidoro, Agatone, Cinesia e gli altri; e ch'egli medesimo chiama le sue *Leggi* tragedia e si confessa ottimo tragico. Ma tra' moderni v'è chi gli divide altramente, facendone tre spezie, «l'una delle quali può montare in palco, e si può nominar rappresentativa, percioch'in essa vi siano persone introdotte a ragionare δραματικῶς, ciò è in atto, com'è usanza di farsi nelle comedie e nelle tragedie; e simil maniera è tenuta da Platone ne' suoi ragionamenti e da Luciano ne' suoi. Ma un'altra ce n'è che non può montare in palco, percioché, conservando l'autore la sua persona, come istorico narra quel che disse il tale e 'l cotale; e questi ragionamenti si possono domandare istorici o narrativi; e tali son per lo più quelli di Cicerone. E c'è ancora la terza maniera; ed è di quelli che son mescolati

thor speaks in his own voice and narrates as a historian while also introducing characters who speak δραμα-τικῶς, as is done in tragedies and comedies. Such works both can and cannot be staged; those parts in which the author speaks in his own voice and writes as a historian cannot, while those parts in which he uses dramatic characters can. Cicero also wrote some dialogues of this kind. These two divisions—one modern and the other ancient—appear distinctly different, but both perhaps express the same intention. For tragedy can be divided into the kind that is called tragedy proper and another kind in which the poet himself speaks—the kind of tragedy composed by Homer.[8] And while the ancient division is closer to perfection in that it contains two parts, the fact remains that dialogues are called tragic and comic only by analogy; tragedies and comedies, properly understood, imitate actions, but dialogues imitate discussions and participate in the tragic and the comic only insofar as they deal with actions. More than any other dialogues, the *Crito* and *Phaedo* can be called tragic. In one, Socrates has been condemned to death but refuses to escape with his friends; in the other, after a long disputation on the immortality of the soul, he drinks the poison. The *Symposium*, on the other hand, in which Aristophanes' speech is impeded by hiccuping and the drunken Alcibiades mingles with the guests, is comic. And the *Menexenus* seems to be a mixture of both of these kinds, for when Socrates is beaten by the clever Aspasia he is comic, but when he praises the dead Athenians he elevates the dialogue to the height of tragedy.[9] Even these dialogues, however, are not true tragedies or comedies; in both tragedies and comedies the debates and the discussions are described for the sake of the action, but in a dialogue the action is more or less an adjunct to the discussion. If the action were

sono accidentali più tosto ch'altramente; ma le proprie
si toranno dal ragionamento istesso, e da' problemi in
lui contenuti, ciò è dalle cose ragionate, non sol dal
modo di ragionare: perch'i ragionamenti sono o di cose
ch'appartengono alla contemplazione, o pur di quelle
che son convenevoli all'azione. E ne gli uni sono i
problemi intenti all'elezione ed alla fuga; ne gli altri
quelli che risguardano la scienza e la verità: laonde alcuni dialogi debbono esser detti civili e costumati, altri
speculativi: e 'l soggetto de gli uni e de gli altri o sarà la
quistione infinita: come la virtù si possa insegnare; o la
finita: che debba far Socrate condennato alla morte. E
perciochè gran parte de' platonici dialogi sono speculativi, e quasi in tutti la quistione è infinita, non pare che
lor si convenga la scena in modo alcuno, nè meno a gli
altri che son de' costumi, perchè son pieni d'altissime
speculazioni. Anzi più tosto non si conviene ad alcun
dialogo, se non forse per rispetto dell'elocuzione, la
quale alcuna volta pare istrionica, sì come disse il
Falereo, avegnachè nella scena si rappresenti l'azione, o
atto, dal quale son denominate le favole e le rappresen-
tazioni drammatice. Ma nel dialogo principalmente
s'imita il ragionamento, il qual non ha bisogno di
palco; e quantunque vi fosse recitato qualche dialogo di
Platone, l'usanza fu ritrovata dopo lui senza necessità.
Perchè s'in alcuni luoghi l'elocuzione pare accommo-
data all'istrione, come nell'*Eutidemo*, può leggersi dallo
scrittore medesimo, ed aiutarsi con la pronuncia. Nè

removed the dialogue would not lose its form. The distinctions that we have been making, therefore, are accidental rather than essential. The essential distinctions between types of dialogues derive from the discussions themselves and from the problems contained within them—from the things discussed, that is, not only from the modes of discussing them. Discussions can be directed toward contemplative matters or toward actions; if they are directed toward actions, they deal with choosing and avoiding, if toward contemplative matters, with knowledge and truth. Accordingly, some dialogues ought to be called civil and moral, while others should be called speculative. In either case the subject of debate can be infinite—for example, the question of how virtue can be taught—or finite—the question of what Socrates should do once he has been condemned to death.[10] Because a large number of the Platonic dialogues are speculative and because the subject of debate in almost all of them is infinite, they seem entirely unsuited to the stage. So, for that matter, do those that deal with morality, for they too are full of the most elevated speculations. Indeed, presentation on the stage seems inappropriate for any dialogue—except, perhaps, from the point of view of style, which in some dialogues appears to be histrionic, as the Phalerean points out[11]—since the things represented on the stage are actions or acts, and are therefore called plays or dramatic representations.[12] In a dialogue the principal object of imitation is a discussion, which needs no stage, and although certain of Plato's dialogues may have been recited, the custom was invented after his time, unnecessarily. For while the style of certain dialogues—the *Euthydemus*, for example—sometimes seems suitable for an actor, in fact the author could easily read them aloud by himself and help to bring out their meaning by his delivery. Furthermore, as others

gli conviene ancora il verso, come hanno detto, ma la prosa, perciochè la prosa è parlar conveniente allo speculativo, ed all'uomo civile, il qual ragioni degli uffici e delle virtù. E i sillogismi, e l'induzioni, e gli entimemi, e gli essempi, non potrebbono esser convenevolmente fatti in versi. E se leggiamo alcun dialogo in versi, come è l'*Amicizia bandita* di Ciro prudentissimo, non stimerem lodevole per questa cagione, ma per altra; e direm che 'l dialogo sia imitazione di ragionamento scritto in prosa senza rappresentazione per giovamento de gli uomini civili e speculativi; e ne porrem due spezie, l'una contemplativa, e l'altra costumata; e 'l soggetto nella prima spezie sarà la quistione infinita; nella seconda può esser l'infinita o la finita; e quale è la favola nel poema, tale è nel dialogo la quistione; e dico la sua forma e quasi l'anima. Però s'una è la favola, uno dovrebbe esser il soggetto del quale si propongono i problemi. E nel dialogo sono oltre di ciò l'altre parti, ciò è la sentenza, e 'l costume, e l'elocuzione; ma trattiam prima della prima.

Dico adunque ch'in ogni questione si concede alcuna cosa e d'alcuna si dubita: e intorno a quella di cui si dubita nasce la disputa, la qual si forma della dimanda e della risposta: e perchè 'l dimandare s'appartiene particolarmente al dialettico, par che lo scrivere il dialogo sia impresa di lui; ma 'l dialetico non dee richieder più cose d'uno, o pur una cosa di molti; perchè s'altri rispondesse non sarebbe una l'affirmazione o la negazione: e non chiamo una cosa quella c'ha un nome solo, se non si fa una cosa di quelle; come l'uomo è animal con due piedi e mansueto; ma di tutte queste si fa una sola cosa: ma dell'esser bianco, e dell'essere uomo, e del caminare, come dice Aristotele, non se ne fa uno; però

have said, dialogues should not be written in verse; they should be in prose, which is the form of speech that suits both the speculative man and the civil man who reasons about duties and virtues. And if we read some dialogue in verse, such as *Banished Friendship* by the very prudent Cyrus, we shall not deem it praiseworthy because it is in verse, but for some other reason.[13] We shall say, then, that the dialogue is an imitation of a discussion, written in prose, not intended for performance, and designed for the benefit of civil and speculative men. We shall set it down that there are two kinds—one contemplative and the other moral—and that the subject of debate in the first is infinite while in the second it can be infinite or finite. What the plot is to a poem, moreover, the subject of debate is to a dialogue: its form and, as it were, its soul. And just as a plot must possess unity, so too must the subject about which questions are raised in a dialogue. There are also other parts to a dialogue—opinions, characters, and style—but let us deal with first things first.[14]

In every debate, some points are conceded, while about others doubts are raised that lead to a disputation in the form of questions and answers. And because questioning is the particular business of the dialectician, it seems that he is the one who ought to undertake to write dialogues. He must not, however, ask one thing about several subjects or several things about one subject, for if someone else should respond, there will be no unity in the affirmation or denial. When I speak of one thing, moreover, I do not mean whatever has a single name unless its parts actually form a unity. A man, for example, is an animal, a biped, and tame, and all these qualities form a unity. On the other hand, as Aristotle points out, white, being a man, and walking do not combine into a unity, and if someone were to affirm something about them it would not consti-

s'alcuno affermasse qualche cosa, non sarebbe una affermazione ma una voce, e molte l'affermazioni. Se dunque l'interrogazione dialettica è una dimanda della risposta, o vero della proposizione, o vero dell'altra parte della contradizione; e la proposizione è una parte della contradizione; a queste cose non sarà una risposta nè una dimanda. Ma s'al dimostrativo non s'appertiene il dimandare, a lui non converrà di scriver dialogo. E par ch'Aristotele assai chiaramente faccia questa differenza nel primo delle *Prime Resoluzioni* fra la proposizion dimostrativa e la dialettica, dicendo che la demonstrativa prende l'altra parte della contradizione; perchiochè colui il qual dimostra non dimanda, ma piglia; ma la dialettica è dimanda della contradizione; nondimeno nel primo delle *Posteriori* egli dice che, s'è il medesimo l'interrogazione sillogistica e la proposizione, el le proposizioni si fanno in ciascuna scienza, in ciascuna scienza ancora si posson fare le dimande. Laonde io raccolgo che si possan fare i dialoghi nell'aritmetica, nella geometria, nella musica e nell'astronomia, e nella morale e nella naturale e nella divina filosofia; ed in tutte l'arti ed in tutte le scienze si posson far le richieste e conseguentemente i dialoghi. E s'oggi fossero in luce i dialoghi scritti d'Aristotele, non ce ne sarebbe per aventura dubbio alcuno. Ma leggendo que' di Platone, i quali son pieni di proposizioni appertenenti a tutte le scienze, potremo chiaramente conoscere l'istesso; nondimeno, sì come il dimandare è proprio al dialettico, così a lui si conviene il dialogo più ch'a tutti gli altri: laonde Aristotele nel capitolo seguente pare che faccia differenza fra le matematiche e i dialoghi, dicendo

tute a single affirmation but rather a single statement containing many affirmations. A dialectical question, then, is a request for an answer, an answer that either affirms a proposition or contradicts it—for the proposition to be discussed in a dialogue is one side of a contradiction. About a thing that does not form a unity, however, there can be no single answer or question.[15] And if the man who is skilled in logical demonstrations is not also skilled in asking questions, he ought not to write dialogues. At the beginning of the *Prior Analytics*, Aristotle distinguishes very clearly between demonstrative and dialectical propositions; he says that the demonstrative proposition asserts one side of a contradiction, because one who is conducting a demonstration does not ask but rather asserts, while the dialectical proposition treats a contradiction as a question.[16] Nevertheless, he also says, at the beginning of the *Posterior Analytics*, that if a syllogistic question is the same as a proposition, and if propositions figure in every kind of knowledge, then every kind of knowledge must admit questions.[17] From this I conclude that dialogues can be written about arithmetic, geometry, music, and astronomy, as well as about moral, natural, and divine philosophy; in all the arts and in every kind of knowledge questions can be asked and consequently dialogues can be written. Of this, perhaps, there would be no doubt at all if the dialogues written by Aristotle were extant today, but if we read those of Plato, which are full of propositions touching every kind of knowledge, we shall be able to grasp the same point clearly enough. Nevertheless, since questioning is properly the activity of the dialectician, writing dialogues is more appropriate for him than for anyone else. It is for this reason that, in the chapter that follows, Aristotle seems to stress the difference between mathematics and the dialogue. He says that if it were impossible to

che, se fosse impossibile mostrar dal falso il vero, sarebbe facile il risolvere, perchè si converterebbono di necessità. Ma si convertono più quelle che son nelle matematiche, perchè non ricevono alcuno accidente; e 'n ciò son differenti da quelle che son ne' dialogi: e dialogi chiama i parlari dialettici, i quali son composti della dimanda e della risposta. Al dialettico dunque converrà principalmente di scrivere il dialogo, o a colui che vuol rassomigliarlo. E 'l dialogo sarà imitazione d'una disputa dialettica. Ma perchè quattro sono i generi delle dispute, il dottrinale, il dialettico, il tentativo e il contenzioso; l'altre dispute ancora si possono imitare ne' dialogi. E forse in quelli d'Aristotele erano tutte quattro; ma in quelli di Platone si troverebbono similmente; perchè Socrate per via d'ammaestramento e d'essortazione parla con Alcibiade, con Fedro e con Fedone; e come dialettico disputa con Zenone e con Parmenide; e come tale riprova Ippia, Gorgia, Trasimaco e gli altri Sofisti, e talora gli tenta; ma i Sofisti son contenziosi e vaghi di gloria, come appare nell'*Eutidemo* detto altramente il *Litigioso*. Nondimeno questi quattro generi non sono così partitamente distinti dagli interpreti di Platone, i quali pongono tre maniere de' dialogi: l'una, nella quale Socrate essorta i giovanetti, nell'altra riprova i Sofisti; la terza è mescolata dell'una e dell'altra, la qual senza dubbio è più soave per la mescolanza; ma chi volesse scriver dialogi secondo la dottrina de Aristotele, ed arrichir di questo ornamento le scuole peripatetiche, potrebbe scriverli in tutte quattro le maniere. Ma principalmente son lodevoli le due prime, la dottrinale e la dialettica, l'artificio della quale consiste principalmente nella dimanda usata con molto artificio da Socrate ne' libri di Platone, come appare nel

derive the true from the false, resolution would be easy; propositions and their consequences would necessarily be convertible. In fact, however, such convertibility is more common in mathematics than in other branches of knowledge, for mathematical propositions exclude accidents and therefore differ from the propositions in dialogues—and dialogue is the name Aristotle gives to a dialectical discussion composed of questions and answers.[18] Thus it is the dialectician or the person who wants to resemble the dialectician who is most suited to compose dialogues, and dialogues themselves are imitations of dialectical disputes. Nevertheless, since there are four kinds of dispute—didactic, dialectical, probative, and contentious—the dialectical is not the only kind that can be imitated in dialogues.[19] Aristotle's dialogues may have included all four kinds, and those of Plato certainly do. With Alcibiades, Phaedrus, and Phaedo, Socrates seeks to teach and exhort. He argues dialectically with Zeno and Parmenides. In the manner of a dialectician, he sometimes reproves Hippias, Gorgias, Thrasymachus, and the other Sophists. Sometimes he probes and tests them. They, on the other hand, are contentious and eager for glory, as can be seen in the *Euthydemus*, which is also known as *The Litigant*.[20] Nevertheless, these four kinds are not distinguished in this way by the interpreters of Plato; they describe three kinds. In one, Socrates exhorts young men; in another, he censures the Sophists; and the third is a mixture of the first two and is no doubt more delightful for that reason.[21] Whoever wants to write dialogues according to the doctrine of Aristotle and enrich the Peripatetic schools by this ornament can work in all four kinds, but the most praiseworthy are the first two—the didactic and the dialectical—whose art consists principally in the kind of questioning that Socrates uses so cleverly in the books of Plato. Consider

primo dialogo, nel quale Socrate richiede ad Ipparco quel che sia la cupidigia del guadagno; e 'n tutti gli altri simiglianti, non eccettuando quelli ne' quali sotto la persona di Forestiero Ateniese dà le nuove leggi d'una città; e 'n quelli di Senofonte ancora con arte molto simile Socrate chiede a Critobulo se l'economia è nome di scienza, come la medicina e l'architettura. E nel *Tirrano*, Simonide ad Ierone, che differenza sia fra la vita reale e la privata; e dalla risposta ch'è fatta prendono occasione de insegnare. Ma da questo artificio si dipartì M. Tullio, il quale nelle *Partizioni oratorie* pone la dimanda in bocca non di quel ch'insegna ma di colui ch'impara; ed egli medesimo ci dimostra la diversità fra i Greci e i Latini in quelle parole di Cicerone figliuolo: «Vuoi dunque ch'io ti dimandi scambievolmente in lingua latina di quelle cose medesime delle quali tu mi suoli addomandare nella greca ordinatamente?». Laonde pare che la dimanda fatta dal discepolo sia derivata da Cicerone, e l'artificio sia proprio de' Romani, il quale s'usò dal Possevino e da altri nella dottrina peripatetica perchè forse è più facile; ma è non così lodevole, nè fu, ch'io mi ricordi, usata da gli antichi; e per questa ragione M. Tullio nelle *Quistioni Tusculane* più s'avvicina all'arte de' Greci, perciochegli commandava ch'alcun de' suoi famigliari ponesse quel che gli pareva, ed egli contradiceva alla conclusione in questo modo: «Auditore. La morte mi pare esser male. M. A quelli che son morti, o a quelli c'han da morire?». La quale è vecchia e socratica ragione da disputar contra l'altrui opinione; tuttavolta il por la conclusione ha dello scolastico; e però dice d'aver poste ne' cinque libri le scuole de' cinque giorni. Tanto potè l'amor della filosofia in un vecchio senator Romano padre della pa-

the first dialogue, in which Socrates asks Hipparchus what love of gain is, and all the others like it, not excluding those in which, in the guise of the Athenian Stranger, he gives new laws to a city.[22] The dialogues of Xenophon also employ this artful questioning: Socrates asks Critoboulos whether economics is the name of a science like medicine and architecture; in *The Tyrant*, Simonides asks Hiero what the difference is between a royal and a private life; and in the answers given to these questions, both Socrates and Simonides find opportunities for instruction.[23] M. Tullius, however, abandons the device in his *Oratorical Classifications* and puts the questions in the mouth of the learner rather than the teacher. And he indicates the difference between the Greeks and the Latins when he attributes to his own son the following words: "Do you, then, want me to adopt your method and ask you systematically in Latin about the very subjects upon which you usually examine me in Greek?"[24] From this remark it appears that the device of having the learner do the questioning, which Possevino and other Peripatetics use, perhaps because it is easier, derives from Cicero and is properly Roman.[25] It is not as commendable as the other device, however, and was not, as far as I can remember, used by the ancients. Thus M. Tullius is closer to the art of the Greeks in his *Tusculan Disputations*. There he invites one of his companions to speak his mind and then proceeds to contradict him in the following manner: "Auditor: Death seems to be evil. Cicero: For those who are already dead or for those who still have to die?" This is the old Socratic method of disputing another person's opinion; still, the way in which conclusions are stated in the work is rather scholastic, and therefore Cicero says that the five books contain five days' worth of lessons.[26] Such was the power of the love of philosophy in an old Roman

tria; il qual quistionava secondo il costume de' Greci, forse per ingannar se stesso in questo modo e consolarsi nella servitù. Ma non si dimenticò ne' libri dell'*Oratore* di quel ch'era convenevole a' Romani senatori; laonde Crasso ed Antonio in altra maniera introduce a favellare. Ma fra tutti dialogi greci lodevolissimi son que' di Platone, perciochè superano gli altri d'arte, di sottilità, d'acume, d'eleganza, e di varietà di concetti e d'ornamento di parole. E nel secondo luogo son que' di Senofonte; e que' di Luciano nel terzo. Ma Cicerone è primo fra' Latini, il quale volle forse assomigliarsi a Platone; nondimeno nelle quistioni e nelle dispute alcuna volta è più simile a gli oratori ch'a' dialettici. Ma nel secondo luogo non so chi se gli avicini, o chi si possa paragonare a' Greci; e nella nostra lingua coloro c'hanno scritto dialogi per la maggior parte hanno seguita la maniera men artificiosa, nella qual dimanda quel che vuole imparare, non quel che ripruova. E s'alcuno s'è dipartito da questo modo di scrivere, merita lode maggiore; e tanto basti della prima parte, ch'è la quistione.

Ma perchè, come abbiam detto, il dialogo è imitazione del ragionamento, e 'l dialogo dialettico imitazione della disputa, è necessario ch'i ragionanti e disputanti abbiano qualche opinione delle cose disputate e qualche costume, il qual si manifesta alcuna volta nel disputare; e quindi derivano l'altre due parti nel dialogo, io dico la sentenza e 'l costume; e lo scrittore del dialogo deve imitarlo non altramente che faccia il poeta; perch'egli è quasi mezzo fra 'l poeta e 'l dialettico. E niun meglio l'imitò e meglio l'espresse di Platone, che descrisse nella persona di Socrate il costume d'un uomo da bene, ch'ammaestra la gioventù, e risveglia

Senator, the father of his country, who raises questions in the manner of the Greeks, perhaps in order to beguile and console himself in servitude. In his books *On the Orator*, however, he does not forget what befits a Roman Senator, and therefore he introduces Crassus and Antony in a different manner. But of all the Greek dialogues those of Plato are the most worthy of praise, for they surpass the others in art, subtlety, insight, elegance and variety of conceit, and verbal ornament. The dialogues of Xenophon rank second, while those of Lucian are third. Cicero stands first among the Latin writers, which makes him a kind of parallel to Plato, but in fact his manner of debating and disputing is sometimes closer to the orators than to the dialecticians. Nevertheless, there is no one else among the Latin authors who approaches his excellence or who can be compared to the Greeks. And those who have written dialogues in our own language have for the most part followed the less artful manner by beginning with a request for instruction rather than by attempting to elicit a false opinion to be refuted. Any of our modern writers who have resisted this trend deserve great praise. So much for the first of the dialogue's parts: the subject of debate.

We have said that dialogues are imitations of discussions and that dialectical dialogues imitate disputations. It follows that those who are involved in discussing and disputing will reveal both their opinions and their character, and these—opinions and character—are the other essential parts of the dialogue. The writer of a dialogue must be an imitator no less than the poet; he occupies a middle ground between poet and dialectician. No one performs this imitation or expresses the art of the dialogue better than Plato. In Socrates Plato presents the character of a good man and of a teacher of youth; Socrates awakens sluggish wits, restrains the

gli ingegni tardi, e raffrena i precipitosi, e richiama gli erranti, e riprova la falsità de' Sofisti, e confonde l'insolenza e la vanità; amator del giusto e del vero; magnanimo non che mansueto nel tolerar l'ingiurie, intrepido nella guerra, costante nella morte. Ma in quella d'Ippia, e di Gorgia, e d'Eutidemo e degli altri sì fatti si descrivono gli avari, ed ambiziosi, ed amatori di gloria, i quali non hanno vera scienza d'alcuna cosa, ma parlano per opinione. In quella di Menone e di Critone descrive il buon padre e 'l buon amico; e 'n quella d'Alcibiade, di Fedro e di Carmide i costumi de' nobili giovani son descritti maravigliosamente. Oltra queste parti del dialogo ci sono le digressioni, come nel poema gli episodi: e tale è quella d'Eaco e di Minos e di Radamanto nel *Gorgia*; e quella di Teut demone de gli Egizii nel *Fedro*; e d'Ero Pamfilio ne' dialoghi della *Republica*. Ma perch'a bastanza s'è ragionato del soggetto del dialogo, e della sentenza, e de' costumi di coloro che sono introdotti a favellare, resta che paraliamo dell'ultima parte, la quale è l'elocuzione: e se crediamo ad Artemone che ricopiò l'epistole d'Aristotele, bisogna scriver co 'l medesimo stilo il dialogo e l'epistola; perch'il dialogo è quasi una sua parte. Ma Demetrio Falereo dice ch'il dialogo è imitazione del ragionare all'improviso; ma l'epistola si scrive e si manda in dono in qualche modo; però dee esser fatta e polita con maggiore studio. Tuttavolta nè Platone nè M. Tullio par che sempre avessero questa considerazione; perchè ne' dialoghi l'elocuzione dell'uno e dell'altro non è meno ornata che quella dell'epistole; e 'n tutti gli altri ornamenti i dialoghi paiono superiori; e ciò non par fatto senza molta ragione, conciosiacosachè i dialoghi di Platone e di M. Tullio sono imitazione de' migliori; e nell'imitazioni sì fatte le persone e le cose imitate deb-

rash, calls back those who have gone astray, refutes the false reasoning of the Sophists, and confounds insolence and vanity; he is a lover of the just and true, magnanimous—even meek—in tolerating wrongs, brave in war, and constant in death. In the characters of Hippias, Gorgias, Euthydemus, and others like them, Plato describes men who are avaricious, ambitious, and vainglorious, men who have no real knowledge of anything and whose discourse rests on nothing but opinion.[27] In Meno and Crito, he gives a picture of a good father and a good friend. And in Alcibiades, Phaedrus, and Charmides, he presents the habits and manners of young aristocrats in a wonderful manner. Besides these parts, there are digressions in dialogues just as there are episodes in poems. The story of Eacus, Minos, and Rhadamanthus in the *Gorgias* constitutes such a digression, as do the stories of Thoth, the daimon of the Egyptians, in the *Phaedrus*, and of Er the Pamphylian in *The Republic*.[28] Enough has been said, however, about the subject of the dialogue, the opinions, and the characters; what remains is to speak about the dialogue's last part—its style. According to Artemon, who transcribed the epistles of Aristotle, dialogues and epistles should be written in the same style because the dialogue is almost a form of epistolary literature. Demetrius of Phalerum, on the other hand, claims that the dialogue imitates improvised reasoning, while the epistle is written and sent as a kind of gift; therefore, the latter must be composed and polished with greater care.[29] But neither Plato nor Cicero takes this view; in style their dialogues are no less ornate than their epistles, and in every other respect the elaboration of their dialogues seems in fact to be superior. Indeed, this is not unreasonable, because the dialogues of Plato and Cicero imitate the better kind of men, and therefore the characters and everything else

bono più tosto accrescere che diminuire, come ci insegna Demetrio medesimo, il qual vuol che la magnificenza sia nelle cose, s'il parlare è del cielo o della terra. Oltre di ciò, là dove egli parla del periodo, ne fa tre generi, il primo istorico, il secondo dialogico, il terzo oratorio: e vuol che l'istorico sia nel mezzo dell'uno e dell'altro, non molto ritondo nè molto rimesso. Ma la forma dell'oratorio sia contorta e circolare, e quella del dialogico più simplice dell'istorico, in guisa ch'a pena dimostri d'esser periodo. I quali ammaestramenti sono stati meglio osservati da' Greci che da M. Tullio, ch'imitò Platone solamente: perch'egli così nel periodo com'in ciascun'altra parte ricercò la grandezza più di Senofonte e de gli altri; laonde usa le metafore pericolosamente in luogo delle imagini, che sono usate da Senofonte; e somiglia colui il quale camina in luogo dove è pericolo di sdrucciolare, compiacendo a sé medesimo ed avendo molto ardire, sì come è proprio delle nature sublimi. Talchè fu detto di lui ch'egli molto s'inalzava sovra il parlar pedestre; e ch'il suo parlare non era in tutto simile al verso, nè 'n tutto simile alla prosa, e ch'egli usava l'ingegno non altramente ch'i re facciano la podestà. Ed in somma niun ornamento di parole, niun color retorico, niun lume d'oratore par che sia rifiutato da Platone. Ma s'in alcuna parte del dialogo debbiamo aver risguardo a gli avertimenti di Demetrio, è in quella nella qual si disputa; perch'in lei si conviene la purità e la simplicità dell'elocuzione, e 'l soverchio ornamento par ch'impedisca gli argomenti, e che rintuzzi, per così dire, l'acume e la sottilità. Ma l'altre parti debbono esser ornate con maggiore diligenza; e dovendo lo scrittor del dialogo assomigliare i poeti nell'espressione e nel por le cose inanzi a gli occhi, Platone meglio di ciascuno ce le fa quasi vedere; il qual nel *Protagora*, parlando d'Ippocrate che s'era arrosito essendo ancora di notte, sog-

ought to be magnified rather than diminished.[30] Demetrius himself makes this point; he desires magnificence, whether heaven or earth is being discussed. In
addition, he distinguishes three types of periodic sentence: the first is historical, the second dialogic, and the
third oratorical. He argues that the historical period
lies between the other two and is neither very inflated
nor very flat. The oratorical style is complex and circu-
lar, while that of the dialogue is simpler than the historical and scarcely seems to be periodic.[31] The Greeks
observe these precepts better than Cicero. Cicero imitates only Plato, and in his periods as in everything
Plato strives for a greater elevation than is sought by
Xenophon and the other Greeks. Thus Xenophon uses
images, but Plato audaciously employs metaphors instead. Plato resembles a man taking a walk through a
dangerously slippery place; he pleases himself while at
the same time exhibiting such daring as befits a sublime nature. It is said of him that he raises himself
far above the pedestrian manner of speaking, that his
speech is neither entirely like verse nor entirely like
prose, and that he uses his wit as kings use power. In
short, Plato seems to have eschewed no verbal ornament, no color of rhetoric, and no device of oratorical
emphasis.[32] If there is some part of the dialogue to
which the advice of Demetrius might be applied, however, it is the conduct of the disputation itself; there a
purity and simplicity of style are fitting, for excessive
ornamentation impedes argument and blunts, so to
speak, insight and subtlety. But the other parts should
be diligently ornamented; in them the writer of dialogues ought to resemble the poets in his expression
and in his effort to make us see the things he describes.
Plato does this better than anyone. When he tells us in
the *Protagoras* that Hippocrates blushed in the dark,
Plato adds, "Day was already appearing, so the color

giunge: «Già appariva la luce, onde il color poteva esser veduto»; e la chiarezza, ch'evidenza è chiamata da' Latini, nasce dalla cura usata nel parlare, e dall'essersi ricordato ch'Ippocrate era a lui venuto di notte. E nel medesimo dialogo leggiamo con maraviglioso diletto che l'Eunuco portinaio, perchè i Sofisti gli erano venuti a noia, serra con ambe le mani la porta a Socrate ed al compagno, ed a pena l'apre, udendo che non erano di loro. E ci piace il passeggiar di Protagora e de gli altri, che passeggiando con tanto ordine ascoltavano il ragionare. E ci par di vedere Ippia seder nel trono, e Prodico giacere avviluppato. E con piacer incredibile leggiamo similmente che due giovanetti appoggiati sovra il gomito descrivessero cerchi ed altre inchinazioni della sfera; e che Socrate pur co 'l gomito dimandasse di che ragionavano. Nè con minor espressione ci pone inanzi a gli occhi Carmide e gli amici; e quasi veggiamo gli estremi, che sedevano da questa parte e da quella, l'uno cadere, e l'altro esser costretto a levarsi. Ma sopra tutte le cose c'empie di compassione e di maraviglia il venir di Critone alla prigione inanzi al giorno, e l'aspettar che si destasse Socrate condannato alla morte. E poi ch'il medesimo raccoglia la gamba, la quale era stata legata, e grattandosi discorra del dolore e del piacere, l'estremità de' quali son congiunte insieme; e distendendosi, e postosi a sedere sovra la lettiera, dia principio a maggiore e più alta contemplazione. E nel medesimo dialogo tempera il dolore, quando scherza con le belle chiome di Fedone, le quali dovevano il giorno tagliarsi; e nella descrizione parimente è maraviglioso. E se leggiamo i ragionamenti di Socrate sotto il platano, e quelli del Forestiero Ateniese

in his cheeks could be seen." Here the clarity—which Latin writers call evidence—comes from the care used in expression and from the fact that Socrates remembers that Hippocrates had arrived while it was still dark.[33] And in the same dialogue we read with marvelous delight about the eunuch at the door, who had been so annoyed by the Sophists that he slammed it with both hands on Socrates and his companion and would hardly open it even when he learned that they were no friends of the Sophists. Delightful too is the way in which Protagoras is shown strolling about while the others follow in such an orderly way, listening to his reasoning. We receive similarly vivid images of Hippias sitting on his throne and of Prodicus lying wrapped up.[34] And we read with incredible pleasure that two youths, leaning on their elbows, are drawing circles and various segments of the sphere, and that Socrates, also leaning on his elbow, inquires about their reasoning.[35] Nor does Plato set Charmides and his friends any less effectively before our eyes; we can almost see the youth sitting on one end of the bench fall off while the fellow at the other end is constrained to rise.[36] Nothing could fill us with more compassion and wonder than to see Crito come to the prison before daybreak to wait for the condemned Socrates to wake up,[37] then to see Socrates himself draw up his leg, which had been bound, and while scratching it discourse on pain and pleasure, whose extreme manifestations are closely connected, and finally to see him stretch himself, sit up in bed, and begin to speak about great and elevated contemplative matters.[38] In the same dialogue, he moderates the pain when he toys with the beautiful locks of Phaedo that must be trimmed that very day; the description of this scene is also marvelous. When we read, moreover, the reasonings of Socrates under the plane tree and those of the Athenian

all'ombra degli alberi frondosi, mentre co 'l Lacede-
monio e co 'l Candiano vanno all'antro di Giove, ci par
di vedere ed ascoltare quel che leggiamo. Queste son le
perfezioni di Platone, veramente maravigliose, le quali
se ben saranno considerate non ci rimarrà dubbio alcuno che lo scrittor del dialogo non sia imitatore o
quasi mezzo fra 'l poeta e 'l dialettico. Abbiam dunque
che 'l dialogo sia imitazione di ragionamento fatto in
prosa per giovamento degli uomini civili e speculativi,
per la qual cagione egli non ha bisogno di scena o di
palco; e che due sian le specie; l'una, nel soggetto della
quale sono i problemi che risguardano l'elezione e la
fuga; l'altra speculativa, la qual prende per subietto
quistione ch'appertiene alla verità ed alla scienza; e
nell'una e nell'altra non imita solamente la disputa, ma
il costume di coloro che disputano, con elocuzioni in
alcune parti piene di ornamento, in altre di purità,
come par che si convenga alla materia.

Stranger in the leafy shade, while he and the Lacede-
monian and the Cretan were on their way to the cave
of Jove, we seem to see and hear what we are reading.[39]
Such are the truly marvelous perfections of Plato. If we
consider them well we should have no more doubts
about the view that the writer of dialogues is an imitator and that he occupies a kind of middle ground between the poet and the dialectician. We have established, then, that the dialogue is an imitation of a
discussion, made in prose for the benefit of civil and
speculative men, and that it needs no stage or theater.
Furthermore, there are two kinds of dialogue: one
deals with choosing and avoiding; the other is speculative and takes for the subjects of its debates matters
that touch on truth and knowledge. In both, one imitates not only the disputation but also the characters of
those who are disputing, and in both one employs a
style that is sometimes highly ornamented and sometimes very pure, as befits the subject.

The Father of the Family

The Father of the Family, one of the best
known of Tasso's dialogues, presents a
charming portrait of Renaissance country life
and a treatise on the family. Through the
characters, the setting, and the action, as well
as through the Father's long discourse and
the discussion that surrounds it, Tasso
expresses his understanding of the family's
place within the context of nature
and politics.

Il padre di famiglia

ALL' ILLUSTRISSIMO
SIGNOR SCIPION GONZAGA

Illustrissimo mio signore,

Dedico a Vostra Signoria illustrissima questo mio dialogo per arra d'alcun'altre cose che m'apparecchio di scriverle. E le bacio le mani.

Di Vostra Signoria illustrissima affezionatissimo servitore

TORQUATO TASSO

ERA NE LA STAGIONE che 'l vindemiatore suol premer da l'uve mature il vino e che gli arbori si veggono in alcun luogo spogliati de' frutti, quando io, ch'in abito di sconosciuto peregrino tra Novara e Vercelli cavalcava, veggendo che già l'aria cominciava ad annerare e che tutto intorno era cinto di nuvoli e quasi pregno di pioggia, cominciai a pungere più forte il cavallo. Ed ecco intanto mi percosse negli orecchi un latrato di cani confuso da gridi: e volgendomi indietro, vidi un capriolo che, seguito da due velocissimi veltri, già stanco, fu da loro sovragiunto, sì che quasi mi venne a morire innanzi a' piedi. E poco stante arrivò un giovinetto d'età di diciotto o venti anni, alto di statura, vago d'aspetto, proporzionato di membra, asciutto e nerboruto, il quale, percontendo i cani e sgridandoli, la fera, che scannata avevano, lor tolse di bocca e diedela ad un villano, il qual, recatala in ispalla, ad un cenno del

The Father of the Family[1]

TO THE MOST ILLUSTRIOUS
LORD SCIPIO GONZAGA[2]

Most illustrious lord,

I dedicate to your lordship this dialogue of mine as a token of certain other things that I am preparing to write for you. And I kiss your hands.

From the most affectionate servant of your most illustrious lordship,

TORQUATO TASSO

IT WAS THE SEASON when the harvesters press the wine from the ripe grapes and when, here and there, one sees the trees picked clean of their fruit. I was riding, dressed in the clothes of an insignificant traveler, between Novara and Vercelli when the air began to grow dark and the sky overcast with rain clouds.[3] As I was spurring my horse on more rapidly I was startled to hear an uproar of dogs mingled with human cries, and turned to see a roebuck followed by two swift greyhounds. Already exhausted, the roebuck was overtaken and died almost at my feet. Moments later, a youth of eighteen or twenty years of age, tall, handsome, well-proportioned, lean, and muscular, arrived upon the scene. He beat the dogs off, scolded them, and taking the beast whose throat they had torn open, gave it to a rustic who shouldered it and, obeying a sign from the youth, departed at a rapid pace. Then the

giovinetto innanzi con veloce passo s'incaminò; e 'l giovanetto, verso me rivolto, disse: Ditemi, per cortesia, ov' è il vostro viaggio? E io: A Vercelli vorrei giungere questa sera, se l'ora il concedesse. Voi potreste forse arrivarvi, diss'egli, se non fosse che 'l fiume, che passa dinanzi alla città e che divide i confini del Piemonte da quelli di Milano, è in modo cresciuto che non vi sarà agevole il passarlo: sì che vi consiglierei che meco questa sera vi piacesse d'albergare; ché di qua del fiume ho una picciola casa, ove potrete star con minor disagio ch'in altro luogo vicino.

Mentr'egli queste cose diceva, io gli teneva gli occhi fissi nel volto, e parevami di conoscere in lui un non so che di gentile e di grazioso. Onde, di non basso affare giudicandolo, tutto ch'a piè il vedessi, renduto il cavallo al vetturino che meco veniva, a piedi dismontai e gli dissi che su la ripa del fiume prenderei consiglio, secondo il suo parere, di passar oltre o di fermarmi: e drietro a lui m'inviai. Il qual disse: Io innanzi anderò non per attribuirmi superiorità d'onore, ma per servirvi come guida. E io risposi: Di troppo nobil guida mi favorisce la mia fortuna: piaccia a Dio ch'ella in ogni altra cosa prospera e favorevol mi si dimostri. Qui tacque; e io lui, che taceva, seguitava; il quale spesso si rivolgeva a dietro e tutto con gli occhi dal capo a le piante mi ricercava, quasi desideroso di saper chi io mi fossi. Onde a me parve di voler, prevenendo il suo desiderio, in alcun modo sodisfarlo, e dissi: Io non fui mai in questo paese, perciochè altra fiata ch'andando in Francia passai per lo Piemonte, non feci questo camino; ma, per quel ch'a me ne paia, non ho ora da pentirmi d'esserci passato, perché assai bello è il paese e da assai cortese gente abitato.

young man turned toward me and said, "Tell me, please, where are you going?"

"I should like to reach Vercelli this evening, if time permits," I replied.

"You might be able to get there," he returned, "but the river that passes before the city and divides the territory of Piedmont from that of Milan is so swollen that it won't be easy to cross.[4] I advise you to put up with me tonight; I have a little house on this side of the river where you could stay with less discomfort than anywhere else in the area."

While he was saying these things I looked steadily into his face, and I seemed to recognize in it an indefinable quality of nobility and grace. Judging him, therefore, to be of gentle condition in spite of the fact that he was on foot, I dismounted, turned my horse over to the groom who was accompanying me, and told the young man that I should decide on the bank of the river itself whether to cross or not. Then I set out, walking behind him. "I shall go first," he remarked, "not because I consider myself worthy of greater honor but in order to guide you."

"Fortune has sent me a nobler guide than I deserve," I replied. "May it please God that she show herself bountiful and favorable to me in all my other affairs."

Then he fell silent, and I followed him. Many times, however, he turned and scrutinized me from head to foot as though he wanted to know who I was, so finally I decided to anticipate his request and to give him a measure of satisfaction. "I have never been in this region," I said, "for on another occasion when I was going to France I passed through Piedmont by a different route.[5] It seems to me now, however, that I have no reason to repent coming this way, for the countryside is very beautiful and the inhabitants very courteous."

Qui egli, parendogli ch'io alcuna occasione di ragionar gli porgessi, non poté più lungamente il suo desiderio tener celato, ma mi disse: Ditemi, di grazia, chi siete e di qual patria, e qual fortuna in queste parti vi conduce. Son, risposi, nato nel regno di Napoli, città famosa d'Italia, e di madre napolitana, ma traggo l'origine paterna da Bergamo, città di Lombardia; il nome e 'l cognome mio vi taccio, ch'è sì oscuro che, perch' io pur il vi dicessi, né più né meno sapreste delle mie condizioni: fuggo sdegno di principe e di fortuna, e mi riparo negli stati di Savoia. Ed egli: Sotto magnanimo e giusto e grazioso principe vi riparate. Ma come modesto, accorgendosi ch'io alcuna delle mie condizioni gli voleva tener celata, d'altro non m'addomandò. E poco eravamo oltre cinquecento passi caminati, ch'arrivammo in ripa al fiume, il qual correva così rapido che niuna saetta con maggior velocità da arco di Partia uscì giamai, ed era tanto cresciuto che più dentro alle sue sponde non si teneva; e per quel ch' ivi da alcuni villani mi fu detto, il passatore non voleva dispiccarsi dall'altra riva e aveva negato di tragittare alcuni cavalieri francesi, che con insolito pagamento avevan voluto pagarlo. Ond' io, rivolto al giovinetto che m'aveva guidato, dissi: La necessità m'astringe ad accettar quello invito che per elezione ancora non avrei ricusato; ed egli: Se ben io vorrei più tosto questo favore riconoscer dalla vostra volontà che dalla fortuna, piacemi nondimeno ch'ella abbia fatto in modo che non ci sia dubbio del vostro rimanere. Io m'andava più sempre per le sue parole confermando ch'egli non fosse d'ignobile nazione né di picciolo ingegno; onde, contento d'essermi a così fatto oste avenuto: S'a voi piace, risposi, quanto prima riceverò il favor dell'esser albergato, tanto più mi sarà grato. A queste parole egli la sua casa m'additò, che dalla ripa del fiume non era molto lontana.

Ella era di nuovo fabricata ed era di tanta altezza

At this he saw that I was offering him a chance to talk, and, unable to restrain himself longer, said: "Tell me, please, who you are, where you come from, and what fortune brings you to these parts."

"I was born," I replied, "in the Kingdom of Naples—one of the famous cities of Italy. My mother was Neapolitan, but my father's family came from Bergamo, a city in Lombardy. I shall not mention, however, my given or my family names, for they are so obscure that, even if I were to declare them, you would know nothing more or less of my situation. I am fleeing the wrath of princes and of fortune, and seeking shelter in the territories of Savoy."

"You are seeking refuge under a magnanimous, just, and gracious prince," he remarked, but since he perceived that I wished to keep part of my story hidden, he discreetly refrained from asking more. We had traveled little more than five hundred paces when we arrived at the bank of the river, which was running more swiftly than an arrow shot from a Parthian bow and was so swollen that its banks no longer contained it. From some peasants who were there I learned that the ferryman was unwilling to cast off from the opposite side and had refused to bring over some French gentlemen in spite of the fact that they had offered to pay him much more than the usual fee. Therefore I turned to the youth who had been my guide and said: "Necessity compels me to accept your invitation, which I should not have declined in any case as a result of my own choice."

"Although I should prefer to receive this favor from your will rather than from fortune," he replied, "I am glad nevertheless that fortune has removed all doubts about your staying."

From his words I was growing more and more cer-

ch'alla vista di fuor si poteva comprendere che più ordini di stanze, l'uno sovra l'altro, contenesse; aveva dinanzi quasi una picciola piazza d'alberi circondata: vi si saliva per una scala doppia, la qual era fuor della porta e dava due salite assai commode per venticinque gradi, larghi e piacevoli, da ciascuna parte. Saliti la scala, ci ritrovammo in una sala di forma quasi quadrata e di convenevol grandezza; perciò che aveva due appartamenti di stanze a destra e due altri a sinistra, e altrettanti appartementi si conosceva ch'erano nella parte della casa superiore. Aveva incontra alla porta per la quale noi eravamo entrati un'altra porta; e da lei si discendeva per altrettanti gradi in un cortile, intorno al quale erano molte picciole stanze di servitori e granai, e di là si passava in un giardino assai grande e ripieno d'alberi fruttiferi, con bello e maestrevole ordine disposti. La sala era fornita di corami e d'ogni altro ornamento ch'ad abitazion di gentiluomo fosse conveniente: e si vedeva nel mezzo la tavola apparecchiata e la credenza carica di candidissimi piatti di creta, piena d'ogni sorte di frutti.

Bello e commodo è l'alloggiamento, dissi io, e non può esser se non da nobile signore posseduto, il quale tra' boschi e nella villa la dilicatura e la politezza della città non lassa desiderare; ma sientene forse voi il signore? Io non, rispose egli, ma mio padre n'è signore, al quale piaccia Iddio di donar lunga vita: il qual non negherò che gentiluomo non sia della nostra città non del tutto inesperto delle corti e del mondo, se ben gran parte della sua vita ha spesa in contado, come colui c'ha un fratello che lungamente è stato cortigiano nella

tain that he was neither of ignoble birth nor of small intelligence, and I was happy to have chanced upon such a host. "If you please," I answered, "the sooner I receive the favor of your hospitality, the more grateful I shall be." At these words he pointed to his house, which was not very distant from the riverbank.

It was newly built, and of such a height that one could tell from outside that it contained several stories. Before it was a sort of small open square, surrounded by trees, from which the door was reached by a double flight of twenty-five broad and pleasant steps. Once inside we found ourselves in a nearly square room whose size was suitable to accommodate two apartments of rooms to the right and two others to the left, and one gathered that there were similar apartments in the upper stories. Opposite the door by which we had entered was another door, from which one could descend into a courtyard. Around this courtyard were numerous small rooms for the use of servants and for the storage of grain, and beyond it was a very large garden, with many fruit trees set out in a beautiful and skillful manner. The spacious central room was furnished with leather hangings and everything else proper for the dwelling of a gentleman. In the middle stood the table, set for dinner, and the sideboard, loaded with gleaming white earthenware plates full of fruit.

"This is a beautiful and comfortable dwelling," I said. "It could only be the property of a noble lord who does not cease to desire, even among woods and in the country, the elegance and refinement of the city. Are you perhaps the lord here?"

"Not I," he answered. "My father is lord here. May God grant him a long life. I can assure you that he is a gentleman who is not wholly inexperienced at court and in the world, for, although he has lived most of his life in the country, he has a brother who has long been

corte di Roma e ch' ivi ancor si dimora, carissimo al buon cardinal Vercelli, del cui valore e della cui auttorità in questi nostri paesi è fatta molta stima. E in qual parte d'Europa e d'Italia è conosciuto, dissi io, il buon cardinale, ove non sia stimato?

Mentre così ragionava, sopragiunse un altro giovinetto di minor età, ma non di men gentile aspetto, il qual della venuta del padre portava aviso, che da veder sue possessioni ritornava. Ed ecco sopragiungere il padre a cavallo, seguito da uno staffiero e da un altro servitore a cavallo: il quale, smontato, incontanente salì le scale. Egli era uomo d'età assai matura e vicina più tosto a' sessanta ch'a' cinquant'anni, d'aspetto piacevole insieme e venerando, nel quale la bianchezza de' capelli e della barba tutta canuta, che più vecchio l'avrian fatto parere, molto accresceva di degnità. Io, fattomi incontra al buon padre di famiglia, il salutai con quella riverenza ch'a gli anni e a' sembianti suoi mi pareva dovuta; ed egli, rivoltosi al maggior figliuolo, con piacevol volto gli disse: Onde viene a noi questo oste, che mai più mi ricordo d'avere in questa o 'n altra parte veduto? A cui rispose il maggior figliuolo: Da Novara viene e a Turino se ne va. Poi, fattosi più presso al padre, gli parlò con bassa voce in modo ch'egli si ristette di volere spiar più oltre di mia condizione, ma disse: Qualunque egli sia, sia il bene arrivato: ch'in luogo è venuto ov' a' forestieri si fa volentieri onore e servizio. E io, della sua cortesia ringraziandolo, dissi: Piaccia a Dio che, come ora volentieri ricevo da voi questo favore dell'albergo, così in altra occasione ricordevole e grato mene possa dimostrare.

Mentre queste cose dicevamo, i famigliari avevan recata l'acqua alle mani; e poi che lavati ci fummo, a

a courtier at Rome. Indeed he still lives there and is much favored by the good Cardinal Vercelli, whose worth and authority are greatly admired in our region."

"In what part of Europe and Italy is the good cardinal known and not admired?" I replied.[6]

While we were talking, another youth, younger but no less noble in appearance, arrived and announced the approach of their father, who was returning from an inspection of his possessions. Almost immediately thereafter the father himself came riding in on horseback, followed by a groom and another servant also on horseback. Having dismounted he came at once up the steps. He was a man of mature age, closer to sixty than to fifty, with a look that was both pleasing and venerable, and his white hair and hoary beard, which made him seem older, added very much to his dignity. I approached the good father of the family and greeted him with the reverence that seemed due to his years and his appearance, whereupon he turned to his elder son and asked pleasantly: "Where has this guest of ours come from? I don't remember having seen him here or anywhere else."

"He has come from Novara," the elder son replied, "and he is going to Turin."

Then the boy went up to his father and explained in a low voice that he should not enquire further into my situation, and the father said, "Whoever he is, let him be welcome, for he has come to a place where honor and service are gladly offered to strangers."

Thanking him for his courtesy, I declared: "I willingly receive this favor of hospitality from you now; may it please God that I have an opportunity on another occasion to demonstrate how mindful and grateful I am."

While we were saying these things, the servants brought in water for our hands, and when we had

tavola ci sedemmo, come piacque al buon vecchio, che volle me come forestiero onorare. E 'ncontinente de melloni fu quasi carica la mensa: e gli altri frutti vidi ch'all'ultimo della cena ad un suo cenno furono riserbati. Ed egli così cominciò a parlare: Quel buon vecchio Coricio, coltivator d'un picciolo orto, del quale mi sovviene d'aver letto in Vergilio,

> Dapibus mensas onerabat inemptis.

E a questa imitazione disse il Petrarca, del suo bifolco ragionando:

> E poi la mensa ingombra
> Di povere vivande,
> Simili a quelle ghiande
> Le quai fuggendo tutto il mondo onora.

Sì che non dovete maravigliarvi s'anch' io ad imitazion loro potrò caricarvi la mensa di vivande non comprate, le quali se tali non saranno quali voi altrove sete solito di gustare, ricordatevi che sete in villa, e a casa di povero oste vi sete abbattuto. Estimo, diss' io, parte di felicità il non esser costretto di mandare alle città per le cose necessarie al ben vivere, non ch'al vivere, delle quali mi pare che qui sia abbondanza.

Non occorre, diss'egli, ch' io per alcuna cosa necessaria o convenevole a vita di povero gentiluomo mandi alla città, perciochè dalle mie terre ogni cosa m' è, la dio mercé, copiosamente somministrata: le quali in quattro parti, o specie che vogliam dirle, ho divise. L'una parte è la maggiore e da me arata e seminata di frumento e d'ogn'altra sorte di legumi; l'altra è lasciata a gli alberi e alle piante, i quali sono necessari o per lo

washed we took seats at the table according to the wishes of the good old man, who sought to honor me since I was a stranger. Swiftly and lavishly the table was loaded with melons, while the other fruits, as I gathered from a sign made by the old man, were reserved for the end of the meal. Then the father of the family began to speak: "That good old Corycius, who cultivated a small plot, and whom I remember reading about in Virgil,

> Loaded the board with unbought food.[7]

And Petrarch imitates the passage when he says of his ploughman:

> And then he weighs the table down
> With humble viands,
> Like those acorns
> That the world honors and yet scorns.[8]

So you ought not to be surprised that I too, in imitation of these characters, can load my table with food that has not been purchased, and if it is not such as you are accustomed to taste, remember that you are in the country and that the host into whose house you happen to have fallen is a poor man."

"I consider it," I said, "part of your happiness that you are not constrained to send to the city for the necessities of a good life (I am not speaking of mere existence). It seems to me that you have an abundance of everything you need right here."

"I do not have to send to the city for anything that is necessary or fitting for the life of a poor gentleman," he replied. "My lands provide all that in abundance, thanks be to God. I have divided them into four parts or, as we like to call them, kinds. The largest is plowed and planted with grain and all kinds of vegetables. Another is reserved for trees and plants that are necessary

fuoco o per l'uso delle fabriche e de gli instrumenti delle case, comech' in quella parte ancora che si semina sian molti ordini d'alberi su' quali le vite secondo l'usanza de' nostri piccioli paesi sono appoggiate; la terza è prateria, nella quale gli armenti e le greggi ch' io ho usano di pascolare; la quarta ho riserbata a l'erbe e a' fiori, ove sono ancora molti alveari d'api: perciò ch'oltre questo giardino nel quale tanti alberi fruttiferi vedete da me piantati e il quale dalle possessioni è alquanto separato, ho un bruolo molto grande, che d'ogni maniera d'erbaggio è copiosissimo molto. Bene avete le vostre terre compartite, dissi io, e ben si pare che di Varrone, non sol di Virgilio, siate studioso. Ma questi melloni, che sono così saporosi, nascono anch'essi su le vostre terre? Nascono, diss'egli, e, se vi piacciono, mangiatene a vostra voglia, né riguardate a me: che se poco n'ho gustati, non l'ho fatto perché ce ne sia carestia, ma perch' io gli giudico assai malsani, come quelli che, se ben sono oltre tutti gli altri di dolcissimo sapore e gratissimi al gusto, nondimeno, non sollevandosi mai di terra né ogni lor parte scoprendo al sole, conviene che molto quasi beano del soverchio umor della terra, il quale il più delle volte non potendo essere né bene né egualmente maturato dalla virtù del sole, che non percuote tutte le parti loro, aviene che pochi melloni buoni si ritrovino e molti di sapore alle zucche e a' cucumeri, ch'anch'essi non s' inalzan dalla terra, sian somiglianti.

Qui egli si tacque; e io, mostrando d'approvare ciò ch'egli diceva, mi taceva, sapendo ch' i vecchi, o quelli che già cominciano ad invecchiare, sogliono esser più vaghi del ragionare che di alcun'altra cosa e che non si può far loro maggiore piacere ch'ascoltarli con attenzione. Ma egli, quasi pur allora aveduto che la moglie vi mancasse, disse: La mia donna, dalla vostra presenza ritenuta, aspetta forse d'essere invitata, onde,

for fuel, for buildings, and for making household implements. In this part too are planted many rows of those trees that we normally use, here in our little villages, to support vines. The third kind of land is pasture, on which my herds and flocks feed. And the fourth I keep for hay and flowers and my beehives. For besides this garden in which you see so many fruit trees that I have planted, and which is some distance from my other lands, I have a very large meadow that supplies me copiously with every variety of fodder."

"You have divided your lands very well," I told him. "It is obvious that you have studied not only Virgil but Varro too.[9] But what about these melons that are so full of flavor? Do they too grow in your gardens?"

"They do," he replied. "If you like them, eat all you want, and pay no attention to me. I have barely tasted them, not because there is any scarcity but because I believe them to be rather bad for the health. Although they are very pleasing to the taste and surpass all other melons in sweetness, nevertheless, because they are never off the ground and do not expose all their sides to the sun they necessarily drink, so to speak, a great deal of the excess dampness of the earth and are not ripened well or evenly by the virtue of the sun. For these reasons there are few good melons and many whose taste resembles that of squash and cucumbers, which also lie on the ground."

Here he ceased speaking, and I too, after indicating agreement with what he had said, was silent, for I knew that old men or those who are approaching old age normally like to talk better than anything else, and that one cannot please them more than by listening to them attentively. But he, as though he had just noticed that his wife was not with us, said: "My wife has stayed away because of your presence, and she may be waiting to be invited in. Therefore, if you agree, I shall

s'a voi pare, la farò chiamare: perché, se ben so ch' i modesti forestieri con alquanto di vergogna e di rispetto maggiore dimorano in presenza delle donne che degli uomini, nondimeno non solo la villa, ma l'uso de' nostri paesi porta seco una certa libertà, alla quale sarà bene che cominciate ad avezzarvi.

Venne la moglie chiamata, e s'assise in capo di tavola in quel luogo che voto era rimaso per lei; e il buon padre di famiglia rincominciò: Omai avete veduto tutte le mie più care cose, perché figliuola femina non m' è stata concessa dal cielo: del ch' io certo molto avrei da ringraziarlo, se non fosse che la mia donna, che da' maschi, com' è costume de' giovani, spesso è abbandonata, della solitudine si lamenta; ond' io penserei di dar moglie al maggiór de questi miei figliuoli, s'egli l'animo molto alieno non ne dimostrasse. Allora io dissi: Io non posso in alcun modo lodar questa usanza di dar così tosto moglie a' giovani, perciochè ragionevolmente non si dovrebbe prima attendere a l'uso della generazione che l'età dell'accrescimento fosse fornita, nella quale vostro figliuolo ancora mi par che sia. Oltre di ciò i padri dovrebbon sempre eccedere i lor figliuoli almeno di ventiotto o di trent'anni, conciosia cosa che, di meno eccedendoli, son anco nel vigor dell'età quando la giovinezza de' figliuoli comincia a fiorire; onde né essi hanno sopite ancora tutte quelle voglie le quali, se non per altro, almeno per essempio de' figliuoli debbon moderare, né lor da' figliuoli è portato a pieno quel rispetto che si dee al padre, ma quasi compagni e fratelli son molte fiate nel conversare, e talora, il ch' è più disdicevole, rivali e competitori nell'amore. Ma se di molto maggiore numero d'anni eccedessero, non potrebbono i padri ammaestrare i figliuoli e sarebbon vicini alla decrepità quando i figliuoli fossero ancor nella infanzia o nella prima fanciulezza, né da lor potrebbono quell'aiuto at-

have her called. For although I know that modest strangers feel more restrained by shame and respect in the company of ladies than when among men, nevertheless, not only the fact that we are in the country but also the customs of this region permit a certain liberty, to which it would be good for you to start to accustom yourself."

His wife came in when she was called and sat at the head of the table, at the place that had remained empty for her. Then the good father of the family began to speak again. "Now you have seen all my dearest things, for heaven has not granted me a daughter. Indeed, I should thank God for that were it not that my wife complains of loneliness because the boys, as young men will, often go off and leave her by herself. Therefore I should be concerned to find a wife for the eldest boy, if he were not so plainly averse to it."

At this I said: "I cannot praise this custom of giving wives to young men so early. It is not reasonable for them to beget children while they themselves are still growing, as I see your son is. Moreover, fathers ought to be at least twenty-eight or thirty years older than their sons; for if they are not that much older, fathers will be still vigorous when youth begins to flower in their sons; they will not have quieted all those desires which, if for no other reason, they ought to restrain for the sake of example to their sons, and their sons will not feel the respect for them that is proper. Instead, fathers and sons will become almost friends and like brothers in their relations, and sometimes—which is even more improper—rivals and competitors in love. If, on the other hand, fathers are too much older than their sons, they are not able to discipline them. Fathers who become nearly decrepit while their sons are still infants and young boys can never expect from them that support and gratitude that nature so desires.

59

tendere e quella gratitudine che tanto dalla natura è desiderata. E in questo proposito mi ricordo che, leggendo Lucrezio, ho considerata quella leggiadra forma di parlare ch'egli usa: *Natis munire senectam*; percioch' i figliuoli sono per natura difesa e fortezza del padre, né tali potrebbon essere s' in età ferma e vigorosa non fossero quando i padri alla vecchiaia sono arrivati; alla quale voi essendo già vicino, mi par che non meno dell'età che delle altre condizioni de' vostri figliuoli debbiate esser sodisfatto e rimaner parimente che 'l vostro maggior figliuolo oltre il piacere, che ragionevole certo è molto, non cerchi di piacervi nel prender moglie, la quale fra dieci o dodici anni assai a tempo prenderà.

Io m'accorgeva, mentre queste cose diceva, che più al figliuolo ch'al padre il mio ragionamento era grato; ed egli, del mio accorgere accorgendosi, con volto ridente disse: Non in tutto indarno sarò oggi uscito fuori alla caccia, poiché non solo ho fatto preda, ma, quel ch'anco non isperai, così buono avocato nella mia causa ho ritrovato. Così dicendo, mi mise su 'l piattello alcune parti più delicate del capriolo, che parte era stato arrostito e parte condito in una maniera di manicaretti assai piacevole al gusto. Venne co 'l capriolo compartito in due piatti alquanto di cinghiaro, concio secondo il costume della mia patria in brodo lardiero, e in due altri due paia di piccioni, l'uno arrosto e l'altro lesso; e il padre di famiglia disse allora: Il cinghiaro è preda d'un gentiluomo nostro amico e vicino, il qual con mio figliuolo suole il più delle volte accomunar le prede, e i piccioni sono stati presi da una colombaia: e in queste poche vivande sarà ristretta la nostra cena, perch' il bue si porta più tosto per un cotal riempimento delle mense che perché da alcuno in questa stagione ancor calda sia gustato. A me basterà, dissi io, se pur non è soverchio,

I remember a graceful phrase on this subject that struck me when I was reading Lucretius: "To defend against old age by means of children."[10] Sons are by nature defenses and fortresses for their fathers, but they cannot be if they have not attained a certain maturity and strength before their fathers reach old age. And since that time of life is nearly upon you, it seems to me that you ought to derive satisfaction no less from the ages of your sons than from all their other qualities, and also from the fact that your eldest son seeks neither to please himself, which would surely be reasonable for him to do, nor to please you, by taking a wife. Ten or twelve years from now will be soon enough for him to marry."

I noticed as I was saying these things that they were more welcome to the son than to the father, and the boy, perceiving that I was conscious of the effect of my words, remarked with a smile: "My hunting today has certainly not been in vain, for I found not only game but something else that I hardly expected—a good advocate for my cause." And with that he served me some of the most delicate portions of the roebuck, some parts of which had been roasted and others prepared in a more refined and very savory manner. With the roebuck came a goodly quantity of boar, served on two platters and cooked in a fatty broth, as is the custom in my part of the country, and on two other platters came two brace of pigeons—one roasted and the other boiled.

Then the father of the family spoke: "This boar comes from a gentleman who is a friend and neighbor and who is in the habit of sharing his game with my son, and the pigeons were taken from a dovecote. Our meal will be restricted to these few dishes, for in this hot season the meat of oxen is brought on more to fill up the table than because anyone wants to eat it."

il mangiar delle due sortie di carni salvatiche, e mi parrà d'essere a cena con gli eroi, al tempo de' quali non si legge che si mangiasse altra carne che di bue, di porco e di cervo o d'altri somiglianti: perciochè i conviti d'Agamennone, come si legge in Omero, tutto che per opinion di Luciano meritasser d'aver Nestore quasi per parasito, non eran d'altre vivande composti; e i compagni d' Ulisse non per cupidità d fagiani o di pernici, ma per mangiare i buoi del sole sopportarono tante sciagure. Vergilio parimente, per non dilungarsi da questo costume, introduce Enea che nell'Africa uccide sette cervi: ove per altro non di cervi, ma d'alcuna sorte d'augelli doveva far preda, perciò che nell'Africa non nascono cervi; ma mentre egli volle aver riguardo alla convenevolezza e al costume degli eroi, si dimenticò, o dimenticar si volle, di quel ch'era proprio di quella provincia. E perché, disse il buon vecchio, è stato finto da' poeti che gli eroi solo di sì fatte carni mangiassero? Perché, risposi, son di gran nutrimento, ed essi, come coloro che molto nelle fatiche s'essercitavano, di gran nutrimento avevan bisogno, il quale non posson dare gli uccelli, che molto agevolmente son digeriti; ma le carni degli animali selvaggi, benché sian di gran nutrimento, sono nondimeno sane molto, perché son molto essercitate, e la lor grassezza è molto più naturale che non è quella de' porci o d'altro animale che studiosamente s'ingrassi, sì che non sì tosto stucca come quella farebbe degli animali domestici. E convenevolmente fu detto da Virgilio:

Implentur veteris Bacchi pinguisque ferinae,

perché ne mangiavano a corpo pieno senza alcuna noiosa sazietà.

Qui mi taceva io; quando il buon padre di famiglia così cominciò: La menzione che voi avete fatta del vino

"For me," I replied, "the two kinds of game will be enough—indeed, more than enough. I shall imagine myself at a feast with the heroes in those days when, as we read, they consumed no meat but that of oxen, swine, stags, and other similar beasts. According to Lucian, the banquets of Agamemnon were fine enough to render Nestor almost a parasite, yet they were composed, Homer tells us, of no other dishes than these, and the companions of Ulysses endured their great trials not out of desire for pheasants or partridges but in order to eat the cattle of the Sun.[11] So as not to depart from tradition, moreover, Virgil has Aeneas kill seven stags in Africa, although he ought to have been hunting birds since there are no stags there. Virgil paid respect to decorum and heroic convention but forgot, or chose to forget, the conditions in that part of the world."[12]

"And why," asked the good old man, "do the poets pretend that the heroes ate only meats of this sort?"

"Because," I replied, "such meats are very nourishing, and heroes, like any men who perform great labors, need very nourishing food; fowl is not sufficient because it is too easily digested. Furthermore, the flesh of wild animals is very healthy in spite of the fact that it is so nourishing, for wild animals are very active, and their fat is much more natural than that of pigs and other animals that are fattened by art. The flesh of wild animals does not surfeit one as quickly as does the flesh of domestic animals, and Virgil speaks fittingly when he says:

They take their fill of old wine and fat game,[13]

for they ate game until they were full without feeling any discomfort."

Here I fell silent, and the good father of the family began to speak: "What you have said about wine and

e de' tempi eroici mi fa sovvenire di quel che da alcuni osservatori d' Omero ho udito, cioè ch'egli sempre, lodando il vino, il chiamava nero e dolce, le quali due condizioni non son molto lodevoli nel vino; e tanto più mi par maraviglioso ch'egli dia sì fatta lode al vino, quanto più mi par d'aver osservato ch' i vini che di Levante a noi sono recati sian di color bianco, come sono le malvagìe e le romanìe e altri sì fatti ch' io in Vinezia ho bevuti: oltre ch' i vini che nel regno di Napoli greci son chiamati, i quali peraventura sortirono questo nome perché le viti di Grecia furono portate, sono bianchi o dorati più tosto di colore, sì come dorato è quel di tutti gli altri de' quali abbiamo ragionato, e bianchi sono più propriamente i vini del Reno, di Germania e gli altri che nascono in paese freddo ove il sole non ha tanto vigore che possa a fatto maturar l'uve inanzi la stagione della vindemmia, se ben forse il modo ancora, co' quali son fatti, di quella bianchezza è cagione. Quivi egli taceva; quando io rìsposi: I vini son da Omero detti dolci con quella maniera di metafora con la quale tutte le cose, o grate a' sensi o care all'animo, dolci sono addomandate, se ben io non negherò ch'egli il vino alquanto dolcetto non potesse amare, il quale a me ancora suol molto piacere, e questa dolcezza sin a certo termine non è spiacevole nel vino; e le malvagìe e i grechi e le romanìe, delle quali abbiam fatta menzione, tutte hanno alquanto del dolce, la qual dolcezza si perde con la vecchiaia: onde si legge: *Ingere mihi calices amariores*, non perch' il poeta desiderasse il vino amaro, ch'alcun non è a cui l'amaritudine nel vino non fosse spiacevole, ma perch' il vin vecchio, perdendo la dolcezza, acquista quella forza piena d'austerità ch'egli chiama amaritudine. Onde vorrei che così intendeste che da Omero sia chiamato il vin dolce come da Catullo è chiamato amaro: negro poi il chiama Omero, avendo forse riguardo ad alcun vin particolare

the days of the heroes reminds me that I have heard from certain students of Homer that he praises wine by describing it as dark and sweet. In fact, however, these qualities are not very praiseworthy in wine, and it seems to me all the more surprising that he praises it in this way because I have observed that the wines that are brought to us from the Levant are white, like the malmsey, the Rumanian wines, and the others that I have drunk in Venice. Moreover, the wines from the Kingdom of Naples that are called Greek—perhaps because the vines were brought from Greece—are white, or rather gold. In fact all the wines that we have been discussing are gold, and white wines, properly speaking, come from the Rhine, from Germany, and from cold countries where the sun lacks the strength to ripen the grapes before the harvest—although perhaps the way in which such wines are made is the real cause of their whiteness."

Then he ceased speaking, and I answered, "Wines are called sweet by Homer metaphorically, just as all things pleasing to the senses or dear to the mind are called sweet. At the same time I will not deny that Homer may have liked his wine a bit sweet. I like it so myself, for within limits sweetness in wine is not unpleasant. The malmseys, the Greek wines, and the Rumanian wines of which we were speaking all possess a certain sweetness that they lose with age. The poet says, "Fill my cups with bitterer wine,"[14] not because he wants his wine to taste literally bitter—no one likes that—but because he wants an old wine that has lost its sweetness and acquired the kind of strength full of austerity that he calls here bitterness, and I should like to persuade you that Homer describes wine as sweet in the same way as Catullus describes it as bitter. Finally, Homer calls it dark perhaps because he is thinking of some particular wine prized at that time like the

ch' in quel tempo fosse in pregio come è ora la lacrima, la quale, tutto che sia premuta da quell'uve stesse dalle quali è espresso il greco, è nondimeno di color vermiglio.

Così diceva io; e avendo la prima volta co' melloni assaggiato d'un vin bianco assai generoso, invitato da lui bevvi un'altra volta d'un claretto molto dilicato, e traponendo tra 'l mangiare alcuna parola, la lieta cena quasi al suo fine conducemmo; per che, levate le carni e i manicaretti di tavola, vi furono posti frutti d'ogni sorte in molta copia, de' quali poi ch'alquanti ebbe il buon vecchio solamente gustati, così a ragionar cominciò: Io ho molte fiate udito questionar della nobiltà delle stagioni e ho due lettere vedute che stampate si leggono, del Muzio l'una e del Tasso l'altra, nelle quali tra 'l verno e la state di nobiltà si contende; ma a me pare che niuna stagione all'autunno possa paragonarsi, percioché la state e 'l verno co 'l soverchio del freddo e del caldo sono altrui tanto noiose che né l'una co' frutti né l'altra co' giuochi e con gli spettacoli può la sua noia temperare: e sono impedimento non solo al nocchiero, che nel verno non ardisce uscir del porto, el al peregrino e al soldato e al cacciatore, ch'or sotto un'ombra, or sotto un tetto d'una chiesa tra' boschi dirupata sono necessitati di ripararsi da gli ardori intolerabili e da' nembi e dalle pioggie e dalle procelle che sopragiungono all'improvviso; ma al padre di famiglia eziandio, che non può senza molto suo discommodo i suoi campi andar visitando. L'una stagion poi è tutta piena di fatica e di sudore, né gode de' frutti ch'ella raccoglie se non in picciola parte; l'altra, pigra e neghittosa, tra l'ozio e la crapula ingiustamente consuma e disperde quel che dalle fatiche altrui l' è stato acquistato. La quale ingiustizia si conosce egualmente nella disegualità delle notti e de' giorni, percioché nel verno il giorno, che per natura è di degnità superiore, cede alla

wine that is called *lacrima* today, which is ruby in spite of the fact that it is pressed from the same grape as Greek wine."

Thus I spoke, and since I had at first, with the melons, tried a rather generous white wine, I now accepted the father's invitation to drink a very delicate claret. As we chatted and continued eating, the pleasant dinner drew toward a close. When the meats and the more refined dishes had been removed, and an abundance of every kind of fruit had been placed before us, the good old man tasted a few fruits and then began to speak: "I have often heard men discuss the nobility of the different seasons, and I have seen two printed letters, one by Muzio and the other by Tasso, which compare the nobility of winter with that of summer.[15] But it seems to me that no season can be compared to autumn. Summer and winter are rendered so unpleasant by excessive heat and cold that neither the fruits of the first nor the games and spectacles of the latter can make them attractive. Summer and winter hinder the pilot, who dares not leave his port in winter, and the pilgrim, the soldier, and the hunter, who must take refuge in some grove or under the roof of some ruined church in the woods from the intolerable heat and from the squalls, the rains, and the tempests that come up unexpectedly. And these seasons hinder a father too, for he cannot go out to visit his fields without great discomfort. Summer is full of labor and sweat and takes only slight pleasure in the fruit it gathers. Winter, on the other hand, is lazy and slothful, and through inactivity and excess unjustly consumes and wastes what has been acquired by others. There is also injustice in the inequality of day and night during these seasons. In winter, day, which is by nature of superior dignity, submits to night—an unreasonable situation—and

notte, dalla quale è irragionevole ch'egli sia superato, e breve e freddo e nubiloso non concede a gli uomini convenevole spazio d'operare o di contemplare, sì che l' operazioni e le contemplazioni sono nella notte riserbate: tempo all'une e all'altre poco opportuno, come quello in cui i sensi, che son ministri dell'intelletto, non possono intieramente il loro ufficio essercitare. Ma nella state il giorno divien vincitore non come giusto signore, ma come tiranno, il qual s'usurpa molto più della parte conveniente, non lassando alla notte pure tanto spazio ch'ella possa a bastanza ristorare i corpi risoluti dal soverchio caldo e afflitti dalle fatiche del giorno; della cui brevità non solo gli amanti, che lunghissime le vorrebbono, soglion lamentarsi, ma la buona madre di famiglia ancora, ch' in quell'ora che nelle braccia del marito vorrebbe di nuovo addormentarsi, è da lui desta e abbandonata.

Così diceva il buon padre, con un cotal sorriso lieto riguardando la sua donna, ch'a quelle parole, tinta alquanto di vergogna, chinò gli occhi; e poi seguitò: Queste sono le noie e gli incommodi, se non m'inganno, del verno e della state, delle quali la primavera e l'autunno son privi, e son pieni di mille diletti: e in loro il sole, giustissimo signore, rende così eguali le notti al giorno che l'uno dell'altro con ragion non può lamentarsi. Ma se vorremo anco della primavera e dell'autunno far paragone, troveremo che tanto la primavera dell'autunno dee esser giudicata inferiore, quanto è ragionevole che cedano le speranze a gli effetti e i fiori a' frutti, de' quali ricchissimo oltre tutte l'altre stagioni è l'autunno, conciosia cosa che tutti quelli che ha prodotti la state durano ancora in lui, e molti ancora egli n' ha, che sono proprissimi della sua stagione: della quale è propria ancor la vindemmia, ch' è la maggior cura e la più nobil che possa avere il padre di famiglia; perciochè, s'egli da' villani è ingannato nelle raccolte

short, cold, misty days do not give man enough time either for work or for contemplation. As a result, both must be pursued at night, which is inconvenient since the senses, which are the ministers of the intellect, cannot perform their offices fully in the dark. And in the summer, day becomes the conqueror not as a just lord but as a tyrant who usurps more than is fitting and does not leave night sufficient time to restore bodies that have been worn down by the excessive heat and weakened by the labors of the day. The night's brevity is lamented not only by lovers, who would like night to last as long as possible, but by the good mother of the family too, who is roused and abandoned just when she would like to fall asleep again in the arms of her husband."

As the good father spoke, he looked at his wife with such a merry smile that she blushed slightly with shame and lowered her eyes. Then he went on: "These, if I am not mistaken, are the annoyances and inconveniences of winter and summer, but spring and fall are free from such drawbacks and full of a thousand delights. In those seasons the sun is a very just lord and makes day and night so equal that neither one can complain of the other. If we should compare spring with fall, however, we should find that spring ought to be judged inferior, just as hopes are reasonably held to be inferior to results and flowers to fruits, for in fruits fall is the richest of all seasons. All the fruits that summer produces last into fall, and fall has many others as well that belong particularly to it. The grape harvest, for example, occurs in the fall and is the greatest and most noble concern that the father of the family can have, for if he is cheated by the peasants who harvest his grain he suf-

de' frumenti, ne sente alcun incommodo e alcun danno solamente, ma s'egli nel fare i vini usa trascuraggine alcuna, non solo danno ne sente, ma vergogna eziandio, quando aviene che nell'occasione d'alcun oste, ch'onori la sua casa, egli non possa onorar la sua cena con buoni vini, senza i quali non sol Venere è fredda, ma insipide son tutte le vivande che potesse condire il più eccelente cuoco ch'abbia il duca. Concludo dunque che l'autunno sia la nobilissima e l'ottima de le stagioni, e quella ch'al buon padre di famiglia più di tutte l'altre suole esser grata: e mi sovviene d'aver udito dir da mio padre, dal quale ancora alcuna delle cose dette udii dire, il qual fu uomo, se 'l vero di lui fu creduto, della naturale e moral filosofia e degli studî dell'eloquenza più che mediocremente intendente, ch' in questa stagione ebbe principio il mondo, s' in alcuna ebbe principio, come per fede certissimamente tener debbiamo ch'avesse.

Cotesta, diss' io allora, è stata opinion d'alcuni dottori ebrei e cristiani di gran grido, della quale, poi ch'ella non è articol di fede, ciascun può credere a suo modo. E io per me son un di coloro che son di contraria opinione; e mi par più verisimile che, se 'l mondo ebbe principio, come si dee supporre, l'avesse la primavera: il che così mi sforzerò di provare. Dovete sapere ch' il cielo è ritondo e ha tutte le sue parti sì uniformi che non si può assignare in lui né principio né fine, né destro né sinistro, né sovra né sotto, né inanzi né dietro, che sono le sei posizioni del luogo, se non forse solo in rispetto del moto, perciochè destra è quella parte dalla quale ha principio il movimento; ma perch' il movimento del sole va contra il movimento del primo mobile, dubitar si potrebbe se queste sei differenze del luogo si debbano principalmente prendere secondo il moto del primo mobile o secondo il moto del sole: nondimeno, perché tutte le cose di questo nostro

fers only inconvenience and damage, but if he is careless in making wine he suffers not only damage but shame besides—especially when some guest honors his house and he is unable to do honor to his table with good wines. Without wine Venus is cold and even the dishes prepared by the duke's best cook remain insipid. Therefore I conclude that fall is the most noble and the best of seasons, and the one that is usually most pleasing to the good father of the family. And I remember hearing from my father—some of whose sayings are still repeated and who, if the truth were known, possessed a more than ordinary understanding of natural and moral philosophy and the study of eloquence— that we ought to believe with most certain faith that the world began in the fall, if it began in any season."

"That was the opinion of some famous Hebrew and Christian men of learning,"[16] I replied, "but since it is not an article of faith, everyone can believe what he wants to. And as for me, I take a contrary view. It seems to me more likely that if the world had a beginning, as it is necessary to suppose, it was in the spring. I shall try to prove the point in the following way. You must know that the heavens are round and that they are uniform in all their parts so that they reveal no beginning or end, no right or left, no above or below, and no before or behind—the six positions of place— except perhaps with regard to motion, for the right is that side from which motion begins.[17] Since the sun moves in the opposite direction from the *primum mobile*, however, one can wonder whether these six different positions of place ought to be determined in relation to the *primum mobile* or the sun. But because everything in this mutable and corruptible world of ours depends

mondo alterabile e corruttibile dipendono dal movimento principalmente, il quale è cagione della generazione e della corruzione e padre degli animali, è ragionevole ch' il moto del sole ditermini le differenze del luogo. Secondo il moto del sole dunque il nostro polo è il superiore, il qual secondo il movimento del primo mobile sarebbe l' inferiore; stante questo fondamento, se noi vorremo investigare da quale stagione è ragionevole che 'l mondo abbia avuto principio, vedremo ch' è molto ragionevole ch'egli l'abbia avuto in quella nella quale il sole, movendosi, non s'allontana da noi, ma a noi s'avvicina e comincia la generazione e non la coruzione: perché secondo l'ordin della natura le cose prima si generano e poi si corrompono. Ma il sole, movendosi dall'Ariete, a noi s'avvicina e alla generazion delle cose dà principio; è ragionevol dunque che, quando il mondo ebbe principio, il sole fosse in Ariete: il che senza alcun dubbio così vedrà essere chi diligentemente considererà le cose che nel *Timeo* di Platone da Iddio padre son dette agli dei minori. Ben è vero che chi volesse prender le posizion del luogo dal movimento del primo mobile, ne seguirebbe ch' il polo antartico fosse il soprano per natura e che 'l mondo dovesse avere avuto principio in quella stagione nella quale il sole, movendosi, s'avvicina a' nostri antipodi e comincia la generazione in quelle parti dell'altro mondo che sono opposte a queste: il che chi concedesse, più ragionevol sarebbe ch' il moto avesse avuto principio nell'equinozio autunnale, quando il sole era in Libra. Tutta volta ne seguirebbe anco ch'egli avuto l'avesse nella primavera, perché questo, ch' è autunno a noi, è primavera a coloro in rispetto de' quali il principio del moto si prenderebbe. Ma la prima opinione, sì come per ragion naturale è più ragionevole, così anco più commodamente dalle persuasioni può esser accompagnata, perciò ch' il nostro mondo fu degnato della pre-

principally upon motion, which is the cause of generation and corruption and the father of living beings, it is reasonable that the motion of the sun should determine relationships of place.[18] Relative to the motion of the sun, then, our pole is the upper one, while it would be the lower one if we took our bearings by the *primum mobile*. Given these fundamental considerations, if we want to investigate the question of which season the world began in, we shall see that it is very reasonable to suppose that it began when the sun was approaching us, not receding from us—when it was initiating the process of generation rather than that of corruption; for according to the order of nature the generation of things precedes their corruption. Now the sun comes toward us out of the Ram and starts the process of generation; therefore it is reasonable to think that the sun was in the Ram at the beginning of the world, and this conclusion cannot be doubted by anyone who carefully considers the things that are said to the lesser gods by God the Father in Plato's *Timaeus*.[19] It is certainly true that anyone who wants to establish positions of place with respect to the motion of the *primum mobile* must conclude that the Antarctic pole is the upper one in nature and that the world began in the season when the sun was approaching our antipodes and causing generation to begin there, and if one grants this point it is more reasonable to suppose that motion began at the autumnal equinox, when the sun was in Libra. Nevertheless it still follows that motion began in the spring, for this season, which is fall here, is spring in those parts with respect to which motion began. But just as the view that I stated first is more reasonable to natural reason, so it can more easily be accompanied by belief, for our part of the world was

senza del vero figliuol d' Iddio, il quale elesse di morire in Gierusalemme, che secondo alcuni è nel mezzo del nostro emisperio: oltre di ciò egli volle morir la primavera per riscuotere l'umana generazione in quel tempo ch'egli prima l'aveva creata.

Qui mi taceva io; quando il buon padre di famiglia, mosso da queste mie parole, con maggiore attenzione cominciò a risguardarmi e disse: A maggior ospite ch' io non credeva conosco d'aver dato ricetto, e voi sete uno peraventura del quale alcun grido è arrivato in queste nostre parti, il quale, per alcuno umano errore caduto in infelicità, è altrettanto degno di perdono per la cagione del suo fallire, quanto per altro di lode e di maraviglia. E io: Quella fama che peraventura non poteva derivar dal mio valore, del qual voi sete troppo cortese lodatore, è derivata dalle mie sciagure; ma, qualunque io mi sia, io mi son uno che parlo anzi per ver dire che per odio o per disprezzo d'altrui o per soverchia animosità d'opinioni. Se voi tal sete, rispose il buon padre di famiglia, poi che non voglio altro per ora investigar de' vostri particolari, non potrete essere se non convenevol giudice d'un ragionamento che 'l mio buon padre, carico d'anni e di senno, mi fece alcuni anni innanzi che morisse, rinunziandomi il governo della casa e la cura famigliare.

Mentr' egli così diceva, i servitori levavano i piatti, ch' in parte eran voti, dalla tavola, e la moglie, accompagnata da' figliuoli, si levò e ritirossi alle sue stanze; i quali poco stante ritornando, dissi io: A me sarà oltre modo grato d'udir ciò ch' in questo proposito da vostro padre vi fu ragionato; ma perché mi sarebbe grave l'ascoltar con disagio degli altri ascoltatori, vi prego che voi commandiate a' vostri figliuoli che seggano. I quali avendo ubbedito al cortese commandamento del padre, egli così cominciò: In quel tempo che Carlo

deemed worthy to receive the true son of God, who chose to die in Jerusalem, which some consider to be the middle of our hemisphere.[20] Moreover, he wanted to die in the spring in order to redeem mankind during the very season in which he had created it."

Here I was silent, and the good father of the family, moved by my words, began to look at me more attentively and said: "I see that I have received a guest of more consequence than I thought. Perhaps you are the man whose fame has to some extent reached these parts —the one who has fallen into unhappiness through human error and whose fault is as worthy of pardon as his virtues are of praise and wonder."

"My fame," I responded, "which you have celebrated too courteously, might never have arisen from my worth alone and derives from my misfortunes. But whatever I am, I am a man who speaks in order to tell the truth rather than out of hatred for others or to disparage them or because of excessive animosity."[21]

"If that is what you are like," answered the good father of the family, "you will be a fitting judge—for I don't want to pry into your private affairs now—of a discourse that my good father, full of years and wisdom, made to me a few years before he died when he turned over to me the rule of the house and the care of the family."

While he was speaking the servants removed the partly empty plates from the table, and the wife rose and withdrew to her rooms, accompanied by her sons. When, after a short time, they had returned, I said: "I should be extremely pleased to hear what your father said on this subject, but since it would be disagreeable to listen while other listeners are uncomfortable, please direct your sons to be seated."

They obeyed his courteous command, and then the father began: "At the time when Charles V gave up the

Quinto depose la monarchia e dall'azioni del mondo alla vita contemplativa, quasi da tempesta in porto, si ritirò, il mio buon padre, ch'era d'età di settanta anni, avendo io passati quelli di trenta, a sé mi chiamò e in questa guisa cominciò a ragionarmi: L'azioni de' grandissimi re che convertono gli occhi a sé di tutte le genti, se ben per la grandezza loro non pare che possano avere alcuna proporzione con quelle di noi altri uomini privati, nondimeno ci muovono talora con l'auttorità dell'essempio ad imitarle in quel modo che noi vediamo che la providenza d' Iddio onnipotente e della natura è imitata non solo dall'uomo, animal ragionevole ch'a gli angioli di dignità s'avicina, ma dalla industria d'alcuni piccioli animaletti eziandio; onde non ti dovrà parere strano se, ora che Carlo Quinto gloriosissimo imperatore ha deposto il peso della monarchia, io penso co 'l suo essempio di sgravarmi di questo della casa, il quale alla mia privata persona non è men grave di quel che sia l' imperio alla sua eroica. Ma prima ch' io a te dia il governo, il quale più a te ch'a tuo fratello non solo per la maggioranza dell'età si conviene, ma per la maggiore inclinazione ancora che dimostri all'agricoltura, cura alla famigliare congiuntissima molto, io voglio così delle cose appertenenti al buon governo ammaestrarti com' io da mio padre fui ammaestrato, il quale, di povero padre nato e di picciolo patrimonio erede, con l'industria e con la parsimonia e con tutte l'arti di lodato padre di famiglia molto l'accrebbe: il qual poi ne le mie mani non è scemato, ma fatto maggiore che da mio padre no 'l ricevei. Perché, se bene con tanta fatica non ho atteso all'agricoltura con quanta egli diede opera, né con tanta parsimonia son vissuto, nondimeno (siami lecito con te, mio figliuol, di gloriarmi) la cognizion ch' io aveva maggior della natura delle cose e de' commerci del mondo è state cagione che con maggiore spesa agevol-

monarchy and withdrew from worldly activity into the contemplative life, as from a tempest into a port,[22] my good father—he was seventy and I had passed thirty—called me to him and began to discourse in the following manner: 'Although the actions of the greatest kings attract the eyes of everyone and seem too great to be compared to the actions of private men, nevertheless great men move us by the authority of their examples to imitate them much as the providence of omnipotent God and nature is imitated by the industry of certain tiny animals, and not only by man, who is a rational animal and close to the angels in dignity. Therefore it ought not to seem strange to you that I, now that the most glorious emperor, Charles V, has put away the burden of the crown, should think of following his example by withdrawing from the task of managing the family, for a family is no less trouble for a private person like me than an empire for an heroic person like him. I intend to turn the governing of the family over to you; it suits you better than it would your brother, not only because you are older but also because you show more inclination for agriculture, a care that is very closely joined to domestic cares.

" 'First, however, I want to teach you about good government, just as my father taught me. He came from a poor family and inherited little, but through hard work and thrift and by employing all the arts of a good father he acquired much, and it has not diminished in my hands, but is now more than when I received it. For while I have not worked as hard as my father did at farming, or lived with as much thrift, nevertheless—permit me, my son, to praise myself when I am with you—my greater knowledge of the nature of things and of the affairs of the world has enabled me, in spite of my greater expenses, to accom-

mente ho fatto quello ch'egli, uomo senza lettere e non esperto del mondo, co 'l risparmio e con la fatica eziandio della persona difficilmente faceva.

Or cominciando, dico che la cura del padre di famiglia a due cose si stende, alle persone e a le facoltà, e che con le persone tre uffici dee essercitare, di marito, di padre e di signore; e nelle facultà due fini si propone, la conservazione e l'accrescimento: e intorno a ciascuno di questi capi partitamente ragionerò, e prima delle persone che delle facultà, perché la cura delle cose ragionevoli è più nobile che quella delle irragionevoli. Dee dunque il buon padre di famiglia principalmente aver cura della moglie con la qual sostiene persona di marito, che con altro nome forse più efficace è detto consorte, conciò sia cosa ch' il marito e la moglie debbon esser consorti d'una medesima fortuna e tutti i beni e tutti mali della vita debbono fra loro esser communi in quel modo che l'anima accomuna i suoi beni e le sue operazioni co 'l corpo e che 'l corpo con l'anima suole accomunarle: e sì come, quando alcuna parte del corpo ci duole, l'animo non può esser lieto e alla mestizia dell'animo suol seguitar l'infermità del corpo, così il marito dee dolersi co' dolori della moglie e la moglie con quei del marito. E la medesima comunanza dee essere in tutti gli affetti e in tutti gli offici e in tutte l'operazioni: e tanto è simile la congiunzione che 'l marito ha con la moglie a quella che 'l corpo ha con l'anima, che non senza ragione così il nome di consorte al marito e alla moglie s'attribuisce, com'a l'anima è stato attribuito; conciosia cosa che, dell'anima ragionando, disse il Petrarca:

L'errante mia consorte,

ad imitazion forse di Dante, che nella canzona della nobiltà aveva detto che l'anima si sposava al corpo, benché per alcun altro rispetto ella più tosto al marito

plish easily what he, an illiterate man and inexperienced in the world, accomplished with difficulty by means of frugality and personal labor.

" 'To begin, then, I say that a father's care extends over two kinds of things: people and property. With people he must exercise three different duties: that of husband, that of father, and that of lord. And in handling property he has two ends: conservation and increase. I shall discuss each of these subjects separately, but I shall start with people rather than with property because caring for rational things is more noble than caring for irrational things. The principal care of a good father, therefore, ought to be for the wife, with whom he plays the role of husband and who might more accurately be called his consort, for husband and wife should be sharers of the same fortune, and all the good things and all the evils in their lives should be held in common, just as the soul shares all its good and its activities with the body and the body likewise shares with the soul. As the soul cannot be joyful when some part of the body suffers, and as infirmity of the body usually follows upon affliction of the soul, so a husband ought to suffer along with the sufferings of his wife and the wife with those of her husband, and in the same way they ought to share all of their affections, their duties, and their activities. So similar is the relationship of a husband and his wife to that of the body and the soul that the name consort has been attributed not without reason to the soul as well as to husbands and wives; thus Petrarch speaks of the soul as

My wandering consort. [23]

In this he may have been imitating Dante, who says in his poem on nobility that the soul is married to the body,[24] but in some other respects the soul ought to

ch'alla moglie debba essere assomigliata. E sì come, poi che s' è disciolto una volta quel nodo che lega l'animo co 'l corpo, non pare che l'anima a niun altro corpo possa congiungersi, perché pazza a fatto fu l'opinion di coloro che volevan che l'anima d'uno in altro corpo trapasasse in quella guisa che 'l peregrino d'uno in altro albergo suol trapassare, così parrebbe convenevole che la donna o l'uomo che per morte sono stati disciolti dal primo nodo di matrimonio, non si legassero al secondo; né senza molta lode e molta maraviglia della sua pudicizia sarebbe Didone continovata nel suo proponimento di non volere il secondo marito: la qual così dice:

Sed mihi vel tellus optem prius ima dehiscat
Vel pater omnipotens adigat me fulmine ad
umbras
Ante, pudor, quam te violem aut tua iura
resolvam.
Ille meos primus qui me sibi iunxit amores
Abstulit; ille habeat secum servetque
sepulchro.

Nondimeno, perché l'usanza e le leggi in ciò dispensano, può così la donna come l'uomo senza biasmo passare alle seconde nozze, massimamente se vi trapassano per desiderio di successione, desiderio naturalissimo in tutte le ragionevoli creature; ma più felici nondimeno sono coloro i quali da un sol nodo di matrimonio nella vita loro sono stati legati. Quanto maggiore e più stretta dunque è la congiunzione del marito con la moglie, tanto più dee ciascun procurar di far convenevole matrimonio. E la convenevolezza del matrimonio in due cose principalmente si considera, nella condizione e nell'età, percioché, sì come due destrieri o duo buoi di grandezza molto diseguali non possono esser ben congiunti sotto un giogo stesso, così

be likened to the husband rather than to the wife. It seems, furthermore, that once the knot that binds a soul to a body is dissolved, that particular soul cannot be joined to any other body—for the opinion of those who thought that a soul passes from one body into another like a traveler from one inn to another was indeed mad,[25] and therefore it also seems fitting that the woman or man whose first marriage knot has been dissolved by death should not form a second. If Dido had held firm in her resolve not to take a second husband, there would have been much praise and much wonder at her nobility. It was Dido who spoke these lines:

> But I would rather the earth engulf me
> Or the omnipotent father strike me with
> > thunder
> Before, Shame, I transgress or loosen your
> > laws.
> The man who first wed me took my love;
> May he keep it and care for it in his tomb.[26]

"'Custom and the laws provide a dispensation in this matter, however, and therefore women, like men, can marry a second time without blame, especially if they do so out of that desire for offspring which is very natural in all rational creatures. Nevertheless, the happiest are still those who have been bound by the marriage knot only once in their lives, and the greater and tighter the bond between husband and wife is to be, the greater the effort that is required from each person to make a proper marriage. Two things must be considered in determining the propriety of a marriage: rank and age. Just as two horses or two oxen of very different size cannot be yoked together effectively, so a lady of high degree cannot well share the yoke of mat-

donna d'alto affare con uomo di picciola condizione o per lo contrario uomo gentile con donna ignobile non ben si posson sotto il giogo del matrimonio accompagnare. Ma quando pure avenga che per qualch'accidente di fortuna l'uomo tolga donna superiore per nobiltà in moglie, dee, non dimenticandosi però d'esser marito, più onorarla che non farebbe una donna d'eguale o di minor condizione, e averla per compagna nell'amore e nella vita, ma per superiore in alcuni atti di publica apparenza, i quali da niuna esistenza sono accompagnati: quali sono quegli onori che per buona creanza si soglion fare altrui; ed ella dee pensare che niuna differenza di nobiltà può esser sì grande che maggior non sia quella che la natura ha posta fra gli uomini e le donne, per le quali naturalmente nascono lor soggette. Ma se l'uomo torrà in moglie donna di condizione inferiore, considerar dee ch' il matrimonio è aguagliator di molte disaguaglianze e ch'egli tolta l' ha non per serva ma per compagna della vita: e tanto sia detto intorno alle condizioni del marito e della moglie.

Or passando all'età, dico ch' il marito dee procurar d'averla anzi giovinetta ch'attempata, non solo perch' in quell'età giovenile la donna è più atta a generare, ma anco perché secondo il testimonio d' Esiodo può meglio ricever e ritener tutte le forme de' costumi ch'al marito piacerà d'imprimerle. E perciò che la vita della donna è circonscritta ordinariamente entro più breve spazio che non è la vita dell'uomo, e più tosto invecchia la donna che l'uomo, come quella in cui il calor naturale non è proporzionato alla soverchia umidità, dovrebbe sempre l'uomo esceder la donna di tant'anni che 'l principio della vecchiaia dell'uno con quel dell'altro non venisse insieme ad accozzarsi e che non prima l'uno che l'altro divenisse inabile alla generazione.

Or, s'averrà che 'l marito con le condizioni già dette tolga la moglie, molto più agevolmente potrà in lui

rimony with a man of lower station, nor can a gentleman with a baseborn woman. When it happens, however, through some accident of fortune that a man marries a woman who is his superior, he ought to honor her—never forgetting that he is her husband—more than he would a woman of his own or an inferior rank. He should treat her as a companion in love and in their daily lives but as a superior in some public acts that are solely for the sake of appearance—in those gestures of honor, for example, that are customarily made to others out of good breeding. For her part, she must think that no difference in rank is as great as the difference in nature between men and women. As a result of that natural difference, women are born to be men's subjects. On the other hand, if a man takes a woman of inferior rank to be his wife, he must consider that marriage is a great equalizer and that he has not taken a wife to be his servant but his life's companion. So much for the question of rank in husbands and wives.

" 'Now, if we turn to the matter of age, I say that a husband should try to find a young wife rather than an old one. Not only are young women more fit for bearing children, but they are also, according to Hesiod, better at receiving and adopting the habits that a husband wants to impart to them.[27] Moreover, since the life of a woman is ordinarily shorter than that of a man, and since women, whose natural heat is not proportionate to their excessive humidity, grow old faster than men, a husband's age ought to exceed that of his wife by enough years so that the beginning of the old age of one of them is not out of step with the old age of the other, and so that one does not become incapable of procreation before the other.

" 'If a man takes his wife under the conditions that I have just described, it will be much easier for him to

essercitar quella superiorità che dalla natura all'uomo è stata concessa, senza la quale alle volte aviene ch'egli così ritrosa e inobediente la ritrovi ch'ove credeva d'aver tolta compagna che l'aiutasse a far più leggiero quel che di grave porta seco la nostra umanità, si trova d'essersi avenuto ad una perpetua nemica, la qual non altramente sempre a lui ripugna di quel che faccia negli animi nostri la cupidità smoderata alla ragione; percioché tale è la donna in rispetto dell'uomo, quale è la cupidità in rispetto dell'intelletto. E sì come la cupidità, ch'è per sé irragionevole, prestando ubbedienza all' intelletto, s'informa di molte belle e leggiadre virtù, così la donna ch'all'uomo ubbedisca, di quelle virtù s'adorna delle quali, s'ella ribella si dimostrasse, non sarebbe adornata.

Virtù dunque della donna è il sapere ubbedire all'uomo non in quel modo che 'l servo al signore e 'l corpo all'animo ubbedisce, ma civilmente in quel modo che nelle città bene ordinate i cittadini ubbediscono alle leggi e a' magistrati, o nell'anima nostra, nella quale, così ordinate le potenze come nelle città gli ordini de' cittadini, la parte affettuosa suole alla ragionevole ubbedire: e in ciò convenevolmente dalla natura è stato adoperato, perciò che, dovendo nella compagnia ch'è fra l'uomo e la donna esser diversi gli uffici e l'operazioni dell'uno da quelli dell'altro, diverse convenivano che fosser le virtù. Virtù propria dell'uomo è la prudenza e la fortezza e la liberalità, della donna la modestia e la pudicizia; con le quali l'uno e l'altro molto ben può far quell'operazioni che son convenienti. Ma benché la pudicizia non sia virtù propria dell'uomo, dee il buon marito offender men che può le leggi maritali, né esser sì incontinente che lontano dalla moglie non possa astenersi da' piaceri della carne; perciò che, se non violerà egli le leggi maritali, molto confermerà la castità della donna, la qual, per natura libidinosa e inclinata a'

exercise the superiority that nature has granted men, and if he cannot make his natural superiority felt he will sometimes find his wife so recalcitrant and disobedient that, in place of the companion whom he expected to help lighten the burden that our humanity brings with it, he will confront a perpetual enemy who is as contrary to him as unbridled desire to reason. Indeed, women are related to men as desire is to the intellect, and just as desire, which is in itself irrational, is informed by many beautiful and comely virtues when it subjects itself to the intellect, so a woman who obeys her husband adorns herself with virtues that she would not possess if she were rebellious.

" 'The virtue of a woman, then, is to know how to obey a man not as a servant obeys a lord or the body the soul but in a civil manner, as the citizens of a well-ordered city obey the laws and the magistrates, or as the passions of the soul—for the soul's faculties are arranged like the ranks of citizens in a city—usually obey reason. And in all this nature has ordered things fittingly, for since the duties and activities of men and women are different, their virtues should be different. The virtues of a man are prudence, courage, and liberality; those of a woman are modesty and chastity. And with these virtues each can do what is fitting. While chastity is not a masculine virtue, however, a good husband ought to offend the laws of marriage as little as possible. He ought not to be so incontinent that he cannot abstain from the pleasures of the flesh when he is away from his wife, because if he refrains from violating the marriage laws he will strengthen the chastity of his wife. Her libidinous nature is as inclined to the

piaceri di Venere non men dell'uomo, solo da vergogna e da amore e da timore suole esser ritenuta a non
romper fede al marito: fra' quali tre affetti anzi di lode
che di biasmo è degno il timore, ove gli altri due son
lodevolissimi molto. E perciò con molta ragione da
Aristotele fu detto che la vergogna, che nell'uomo non
merita lode, è laudevol nella donna; e con molta ragion
disse la figliuola sua che niun più bel colore orna le
guance della donna di quel che da vergogna vi suole
esser dipinto: il qual tanto alle donne accresce di vaghezza, quanto lor peraventura ne tolgono que' colori
artificiali de' quali, quasi maschere o scene, si soglion
colorare. E certo che, sì come giudiciosa donna a niun
modo dovrebbe le bellezze naturali con gli artificiali
imbellettamenti guastare e ricoprire, così il marito non
dovrebbe consentirlo; ma perché l' imperio del marito
conviene che sia moderato, in quelle cose massimamente ch'alle donne come cura feminile appertengono,
le quali, perché dall'usanza son ricevute, in alcun modo
d' impudicizia non possono esser argomento, con
niun'altra maniera potrà meglio il marito far che non s'
imbelletti che co 'l mostrarsi schivo de' belletti e de'
lisci: percioch' essendo tutte le donne vaghe di parer
belle e di piacere altrui, e l'oneste donne particolarmente di piacere al marito desiderose, qualora l'onesta
moglie s'accorgerà di non piacer così lisciata agli occhi
del marito, dal lisciarsi si rimarrà. Molto più facile
nondimeno dee essere il marito in concederle ch'ella
degli ornamenti e delle vaghezze conveniente a sua pari
sia a bastanza fornita, perché, se ben la soverchia pompa par cosa più conveniente a' teatri e alla scena ch'alla
persona d'onesta matrona, nondimeno molto si dee in
questa parte attribuire all'usanza, né si dee così acerba-
mente offender l'animo feminile, che per natura è vago
d'ornare il corpo.

E se ben vediamo che la natura negli animali ha vo-

pleasures of Venus as his, and she is usually prevented from breaking faith with her husband only by shame, love, and fear. Of these passions, fear is worthy of both praise and blame, while the other two deserve only high praise. As for shame, which does not merit praise in a man, Aristotle says very reasonably that it is praiseworthy in a woman, and his daughter very reasonably says that no more beautiful color can grace the cheek of a lady than the color that shame normally paints there—a color that enhances a lady's beauty even more when she does not cover it up with those artificial tints ladies are wont to employ, which resemble masks or painted scenery.[28] Certainly no judicious lady ought to impair or cover up her natural beauties with cosmetics; nor should any husband consent to such practices. At the same time, however, his rule ought to be especially moderate in these feminine concerns, which are accepted by custom and therefore indicate no lack of chastity. There is no better way for a husband to prevent his wife from using cosmetics than by showing that he is unattracted by paints and polishes. All women are eager to seem beautiful and to please others, and honest women are particularly desirous of pleasing their husbands. When, therefore, an honest woman perceives that she is not attractive to her husband after making herself up, she will stop doing so. A husband should be much more easygoing, however, in permitting his wife to be furnished with the ornaments and embellishments appropriate to her position among her peers. Although excessive display seems to befit theaters and the stage more than an honest matron, much must be granted to custom in this matter. One must not act too harshly toward the feminine spirit, which by nature longs to adorn the body.

"'Among the animals, nature has sought to adorn

luto che più adorni siano i corpi de' maschi che delle femine, come quella c' ha adornati i cervi di belle e ramose corna e i leoni di superbe come, le quali alle for femine ha negate, e ha adornata la coda del pavone di molta più vaga varietà di colori che quella delle sue femine, nondimeno vediamo che nella specie dell'uomo ella ha avuto maggior riguardo alla bellezza della femina ch' a quella del maschio, perciò che le carni della donna, sì come son più molli, così per l'ordinario sono ancora più vaghe da riguardare, né hanno il volto ingombrato dalla barba, la qual se ben non si disdice nell'uomo, essendo propria di lui, tuttavolta non si può negare ch' i volti de' giovinetti a' quali non è ancor venuta la barba non sian più belli di quelli degli uomini barbuti; e Amore non barbuto, ma senza barba dalla giudiziosa antichità è stato figurato, e Bacco e Appoline, che fra tutti gli dei furono bellissimi, senza barba furono dipinti, ma con lunghissime chiome: onde i poeti chiamano Febo con aggiunto quasi perpetuo «non tosato» o «comato». Ma le chiome, le quali sono grandissimo ornamento della natura, non crescono mai negli uomini tanto, né sono così molli e sottili come nelle donne, le quali così delle lor chiome si rallegrano come gli alberi delle lor fronde, e ragionevolmente nelle morti de' mariti, quando di tutti gli altri ornamenti sogliono spogliarsi, usano anco in alcune parti d'Italia di troncarsi le chiome: la qual usanza fu usanza degli antichi eziandio, come d' Elena si legge appresso Euripide.

Quanto più dunque la natura ha avuto risguardo alla bellezza delle donne, tanto più è convenevole ch'esse l'abbiano in pregio e che con giudiziosi ornamenti procurino d'accrescerla: onde, se tu prenderai moglie, quale io desidero che tu la prenda, bella e giovinetta e di condizione eguale alla tua e d' ingegno modesto e mansueto, da buona e pudica madre sotto buona disci-

the males more than the females; she has beautified stags with handsome branching antlers, male lions with splendid manes that have been denied to females, and the tail of the male peacock with a much lovelier variety of color than that of the female. With respect to human beings, however, we see that nature has paid more attention to the beauty of women than of men. Woman's flesh is softer and ordinarily more attractive to the eye, and their faces are not encumbered by beards. On men, of course, beards are natural and for that reason not unbecoming, but one cannot deny that the faces of young men whose beards have not yet begun are more beautiful than the faces of bearded men. The figure of Love was represented without a beard by the judicious ancients, and Bacchus and Apollo, who were the most beautiful of all the gods, were portrayed without beards but with long hair. For this reason the poets almost always add the epithet "unshorn" or "long-haired" to Phoebus. Hair is a very great natural ornament, but it never grows as long or as soft or as fine on men as on women. Women rejoice in their long hair as the trees rejoice in their leaves, and therefore it is reasonable that in some parts of Italy when a woman's husband dies and she divests herself of all other ornaments, she also cuts her hair. That this custom obtained among the ancients too we learn from Euripides' account of Helen.[29]

" 'To the extent, then, that nature has been more concerned with the beauty of women, it is more fitting for them to prize it and to strive to increase it by means of judicious ornaments. If you take a wife such as I want you to—young, beautiful, your equal in station, of modest and gentle nature, and raised in good discipline by a good and chaste mother—you should try to

plina allevata, quanto ella a te piacerà, tanto dèi tu procurare non sol di piacere a lei, ma di compiacerla. Di che né di vestimenti né degli altri ornamenti men ornata dèi consentir che vada di quel che vadano l'altre sue pari e di quel che porti l'uso della nostra città; ne sì ristretta tener la dèi ch'ella non possa talora andare alle feste e agli spettacoli publici, ove nobile e onesta brigata di donne suol ragunarsi, né d'altra parte tanto allentarle il freno della licenza ch'ella in tutte le danze, in tutte le comedie, in tutte le solennità sia fra le prime vedute e vagheggiate. Ma dovrai ad alcune sue oneste voglie, le quali la gioventù così suol seco apportare come la primavera reca i fiori e l'altre vaghezze, non far così severo disdetto ch'ella t'odii o ti tema con quel timore co 'l quale i padroni da' servi son temuti; né anco esser così facile a secondarle ch'ella baldanzosa ne divenga e deponga quella vergogna che nelle oneste donne tanto è conveniente, la quale è una specie di timore distinta dal timor servile, che con l'amor così facilmente s'accompagna come il timor servile con l'odio: e di questo timore, che propiamente è vergogna, e della riverenza intese Omero, quando disse:

O da me ognor temuto e paventato
Suocero caro.

E non solo dovrà egli procurar di conservare in lei la vergogna in tutti gli atti e in tutte l'operazioni della vita, ma negli abbracciamenti eziandio, perché non viene a gli abbracciamenti il marito in quel modo stesso che viene l'amante: onde non è maraviglia s'a Catelda parvero più saporiti i baci dell'amante che quei del marito fossero paruti, bench' io crederei più tosto che niuna dolcezza maggiore fosse in amore di quella che dall'onestà del matrimonio è moderata, e assomiglierei gli abbracciamenti del marito e della moglie alle cene degli uomini temperanti, i quali non men gustano

please not only yourself but her as much as she pleases you, and you should not allow her to go about less well-dressed or less ornamented in other ways than her peers or than the customs of our city dictate. Nor should you keep her so restricted that she cannot go now and then to festivals and public spectacles where noble and honest groups of ladies customarily gather. On the other hand, neither should you so loosen the bridle on license that she becomes one of the most looked at and courted at every dance, comedy, and public ceremony. To certain respectable desires, which youth normally brings with it just as spring brings flowers and other charms, you ought not to make such a severe denial that she comes to hate you or to fear you with the kind of fear that servants feel for their masters, but you must also avoid encouraging her desires so much that she becomes bold and discards that shame that is so fitting in a decent woman. Shame is a different kind of fear from servile fear. Shame accompanies love as easily as servile fear goes with hatred, and it was of the fear that is really shame, and of reverence, that Homer spoke when he said,

> O dear father-in-law, whom I ever fear
> And dread.[30]

A husband should strive to preserve his wife's sense of shame not only in all the other acts and occupations of life but also when embracing her: husbands do not embrace their wives as lovers. No wonder, then, that her lover's kisses seemed sweeter than her husband's to Catelda[31]—although I should sooner believe that there is no sweetness in love greater than that which is tempered by the decency of marriage, and I should compare the embraces of husband and wife to the dinners of temperate men. They enjoy their food no less than incontinent men, and may even enjoy it more, because

delle vivande di quel che gli incontinenti soglian gustarne, anzi peraventura tanto più quanto il senso moderato dalla ragione è più dritto giudice degli oggetti. Né voglio in questo proposito tacere che, quando Omero finge che Giunone, togliendo il cinto di Venere, va a ritrovare il marito su 'l monte Ida e, allettatolo nel suo amore, con lui si corca nell'erba, ricoperta da una nuvola maravigliosa, altro non significa se non ch'ella, vestitasi la persona d'amante e spogliatasi quella di moglie, va a ritrovar Giove; perché le lusinghe e i vezzi e i molli susurri ch'ella da Venere aveva presi insieme co 'l cinto, sono cosa anzi d'amante che da moglie: onde convenevol fu che, vergognandosi ella di se medesima, le fosse concessa una nuvola che la ricoprisse. Ben è vero che, dicendogli Giove che non aveva avuto egual disiderio di lei da quel dì che prima la prese per moglie, par che ci dia a divedere ch'a gli sposi di sostener per alcun breve tempo la persona d'amante non si disdica; la qual nondimeno molto tosto si dee deporre, percioch' è inconvenientissima a coloro che come padre o madre di famiglia voglion con onestà e con amor maritale regger la casa. Né altro mi soviene che dire del vicendevole amore che dee esser tra 'l marito e la moglie e delle leggi del matrimonio; perciò che il considerare se 'l marito dee ucciber la moglie impudica o 'n altro modo secondo le leggi punirla, è considerazione che peraventura può più opportunamente in altro proposito esser avuta. E se tu tale la prenderai qual figurata l'abbiamo, non dèi temer che mai ti venga occasione per la quale d'esser da me stato intorno a ciò consigliato debba desiderare.

Or passando a' figliuoli, dee la cura loro così tra il padre e la madre esser compartita ch'alla madre tocchi il nutrirli e al padre l'ammaestrarli: ché non dee la madre, se da infermità non è impedita, negare il latte a' propi figliuoli, conciò sia cosa che quella prima età,

when the senses are moderated by reason they are better judges of things. While I am on this subject, moreover, I don't want to pass over in silence that passage in which Homer imagines that Juno, taking the girdle of Venus, goes to find her husband on Mount Ida, ensnares him in love, and lies with him in the grass, covered by a wonderful cloud.[32] The significance of this is simply that Juno abandons her role as a wife and seeks Jove disguised as a lover; the allurements, the charms, and the soft whispers that she took from Venus along with her girdle befit a lover rather than a wife, and it was appropriate because of her shame that a cloud was granted to her for covering. It is true, of course, that Jove's remark that he had not desired her so much since the day he took her as his wife seems to give us to understand that it is not unfitting for husband and wife to adopt the roles of lovers for a short time, but they must quickly cast them off, because such roles are very inappropriate for those who, as fathers and mothers of the family, wish to rule their households with decency and marital love. Nothing further occurs to me to say about the mutual love that should obtain between husband and wife, and about the laws of matrimony, for to consider whether a husband ought to kill an unchaste wife or punish her in some other way according to the laws can perhaps be treated more fittingly elsewhere, and if you take the kind of wife that I have described, you need not fear that you will ever have occasion to wish that you had been counseled by me on this matter.

" 'To move on now to children: their care should be divided between the father and the mother, so that the mother feeds them and the father instructs them. Unless she is prevented by infirmity, the mother ought not to deny her milk to her own children. In their first

tenera e molle e atta ad informarsi di tutte le forme, agevolmente suol ber co 'l latte alcuna volta i costumi delle nutrici; e s' il nutrimento non potesse molto alterare i corpi e in conseguenza i costumi de' bambini, non sarebbe alle nutrici interdetto l'uso soverchio del vino; ma essendo le nutrici per l'ordinario vili feminelle, è convenevole che quel primo nudrimento che da lor prendono i bambini non sia così gentile e delicato come quel delle madri sarebbe. Oltreché chi niega il nutrimento par ch' in un certo modo nieghi d'esser madre, percioché la madre si conosce principalmente per lo nutrimento. Ma passata quella prima età che di latte è nudrita e che di cibi più sodi può esser pasciuta, rimangono anco i bambini sotto la custodia delle madri, le quali sogliono esser così tenere de' figliuoli ch'agevolmente potrebbono in soverchia dilicatura allevarli; onde conviene ch' il padre proveda ch'essi non siano troppo mollemente nudriti: e percioché quella prima età abonda di calor naturale, non è inconveniente l'assuefarli a sopportrare il freddo, conciosiacosa che, tanto più restringendosi dentro il caldo naturale e facendo quella ch'antiparistasi è detta da' filosofi, la complession de' fanciulli ne diventa gagliarda e robusta. Ed era costume d'alcune antiche nazioni, e de' Celti particolarmente, come leggiamo appresso Aristotele, di lavare i bambini nel fiume per indurarli contra il freddo: la qual usanza è da Virgilio attribuita a' Latini, come si legge in que' versi:

> Durum a stirpe genus, natos ad flumina primum
> Deferimus saevoque gelu duramus et undis:
> Venatu invigilant pueri silvasque fatigant
> Flectere ludus equos et spicula tendere cornu.

years children are tender, malleable, and apt to receive every influence, and it can easily happen that they imbibe the habits of a nurse along with her milk—for if food had little effect on the bodies and consequently on the habits of children, nurses would not be forbidden to drink too much wine. Since nurses are usually from the lower classes, it is not surprising that the first nourishment children get from them is not as noble and delicate as the milk of their mothers. Besides, a mother who denies her milk seems in a certain way to deny that she is a mother, because a mother can be recognized principally by the food she supplies. But when the first age, which is nourished on milk but can also be fed with more solid foods, has passed, children still remain in the custody of their mothers, who are usually too tender with them and may well raise them too softly. Therefore it is fitting that the father take care that the children are not fed with too much delicacy. Because the first age abounds in natural heat, moreover, it is not inappropriate to accustom children to endure cold; the more the natural heat is forced within and causes what the philosophers call *antiperistasis*,[33] the more vigorous and robust the constitution of children becomes. Among some ancient nations—especially the Celts, as we read in Aristotle—it was a custom to wash children in the river in order to toughen them against the cold,[34] and from the following lines we can see that Virgil attributes this habit to the Latins:

> A tough race, we bring our young sons
> To the river to harden them in the cold and
> the waves.
> Our youths attend to hunting; their play
> Is to guide horses and send shafts from the
> bow.[35]

E bench' io quel costume non vitupero, mi pare
nondimeno d'ammonirti che, se piacerà al cielo di darti
figliuoli, tu non debba educarli sotto sì molle disciplina
che riescan simili a que' Frigi, de' quali dal medesimo
poeta si fa menzione:

> Vobis picta croco et fulgenti murice vestis,
> Et tunicae manicas et habent redimicula
> > mitrae.
> O vere Phrigiae (neque enim Phriges), ite per
> > alta
> Dindima, ubi assuetis biforem dat tibia
> > cantum.
> Tympana vos buxusque vocat
> > Berecyntia matris
> Ideae: sinite arma viris et cedite ferro;

simili a' quali mi pare ch'oggi siano quelli d'alcuna
città di Lombardia, percioché, s'alcuno n'esce valo-
roso, molti ancora tra' Frigi erano valorosi. Ma non
vorrei anco che sì severamente gli allevassi come i Lacedemoni erano allevati o pur come Achille da Chirone
fu nudrito: non vorrei, dico, che sì fattamente gli allevassi, perché quella educazione rende gli uomini fieri,
come de' Lacedemoni fu giudicato; e quando ella pur
fosse conveniente a gli eroi, benché tale non fu Achille
ne' costumi ch'alcun eroe se 'l debba proporre per essempio, la tua privata condizione ricerca che tu pensi
d'allevare in modo i tuoi figliuoli ch'essi possan riuscir
buon cittadini della tua città e buon servitori del tuo
principe, il quale de' soggetti ne' negozî, nelle lettere e
nella guerra è usato di servirsi: alle quali professioni
tutte i tuoi figliuoli riesceranno non inabili, se tu cer-
cherai che divengano di complessione non atletica né
feminile, ma virile e robusta, e che s'essercitino negli
essercizî del corpo e dello intelletto parimente. Ma per-

" 'And while I do not speak ill of that custom, nevertheless I would warn you that if it pleases Heaven to grant you sons, you ought not to bring them up under such soft discipline that they turn out like those Phrygians the same poet mentions:

> Your clothes are dyed with saffron and bright
> purple;
> Your tunics have long sleeves, your turbans
> ribbons.
> O Phrygian women—not men—go up
> On high Dindymus where the double flute
> Sings to the initiate. Drums and the
> Berecynthian
> Flute of the great mother of Ida call you:
> Leave arms to men, and yield the sword.[36]

Today, it seems to me, these Phrygians might be compared to the inhabitants of some city in Lombardy; a brave man occasionally comes from that region, but then there were many brave men among the Phrygians too. On the other hand, I should not want you to raise your sons as severely as the Lacedaemonians were raised, or as Achilles was brought up by Chiron. I say this because such an education makes men proud and fierce, as the Lacedaemonians were held to be. Such an upbringing may have been appropriate for heroes—although the habits of Achilles were not the kind that any hero ought to take for an example—but your private circumstances require that you think of raising your sons to be good citizens in your city and good servants of your prince, who usually employs his subjects in the fields of business, letters, and war. Your sons will not lack proficiency in any of these professions if you encourage them to become neither wholly athletic nor effeminate but rather manly and robust, and if you try to make them exercise their bodies and

cioché tutta questa parte dell'educazion de' figliuoli è cura in guisa del padre in famiglia ch'ella insieme è del politico, il quale dovrebbe prescrivere a' padri il modo co 'l quale dovessero i figliuoli allevare accioché la disciplina della città riuscisse uniforme, voglio questo ragionamento lasciar da parte o almeno da quel della cura famigliare separarlo: e mi basterà solo di consigliarti che tu gli allevi nel timor d' Iddio e nella ubbedienza paterna, egualmente nell'arti lodevoli dell'animo e del corpo essercitati.

Abbiam già parlato, quanto è stato convenevole, di quel che tu dovrai far come marito e come padre: or rimane che vegnamo alla considerazione della terza persona, a quella di padrone, dico, o di signore che vogliam chiamarla, il quale al servo è relativo. E se noi vogliam prestar fede a gli antichi che del governo famigliare hanno scritto, con l'opera, co 'l cibo e co 'l castigo il signore dee tener sodisfatti ed essercitati i servitori in ubbedienza; ma perciò ch'anticamente i servi erano schiavi presi nella guerra, i quali furono detti servi *a servando* perché da morte erano conservati, e oggi sono per lo più uomini liberi, mi pare che tutta questa parte del castigo si debba lasciare a dietro come poco convenevole a' nostri tempi e alle nostre usanze, se non forse in quelle sole parti ove degli schiavi si servono, e in vece del castigo debba dal padrone essere usata l'ammonizione, la qual tal non dee essere qual dal padre co 'l figliuolo è usata, ma piena di maggiore austerità e di più severo imperio: e se questa anco non gioverà, dee il padrone dar licenza al servitore inobbediente e inutile e provedersi d'altro che maggiormente gli sodisfaccia.

Una cosa anco dagli antichi è stata lasciata a dietro, la qual con gli schiavi non era convenevole, ma co' liberi uomini è non sol convenevole ma necessaria: e questa è la mercede; con la mercede dunque, co 'l cibo, con

their minds equally. This part of the education of sons, however, concerns not only the father of the family but also the political man, who must prescribe to fathers the manner of educating their sons so that instruction in the city will be uniform. Therefore I want to set this discussion aside, or at least separate it from the discussion of strictly family cares. It is enough for me to advise you to raise your sons in the fear of God, in obedience to you, and trained in the praiseworthy arts of soul and body.

" 'We have now said as much as is fitting about what you ought to do as a husband and father; what remains is to consider your third role: that of master, as I call it, or lord, if you will—the role that you adopt with servants. If we believe the ancients who have written on governing a family, the lord ought to keep his servants satisfied and practiced in obedience by means of work, food, and punishment.[37] In ancient times, however, servants were slaves taken in war and were called servants *a servando*, because they had been saved from death, while today most servants are free men.[38] For this reason it seems to me that punishment ought to be abandoned as inappropriate for our times and customs, except perhaps in those places where slaves are still used. Instead of punishing his servants the master ought to admonish them, not as he would a son but with greater strictness and severer authority. If this method does not work, the master should dismiss the disobedient and useless servant and find another who will give him more satisfaction.

" 'In addition, the ancients neglected one thing which is inappropriate for slaves but both appropriate and necessary for free men: wages. With wages, then, as

l'opera e con l'ammonizione il padre di famiglia governerà in modo ch'essi resteranno contenti di lui ed egli dell'opera loro rimarrà sodisfatto. Ma percioché, se ben le leggi e l'usanze degli uomini sono variabili, come vediamo in questo particolar de' servi, i quali oggi son per lo più uomini di libertà, le leggi nondimeno e le differenze della natura non si mutano per varietà di tempi e d'usanze, tu hai da sapere che questa differenza di servo e di signore è fondata sovra la natura, percioch'alcuni ci nascono naturalmente a commandare, altri ad ubbedire; e colui che per ubbedire è nato, se ben fosse di schiatta di re, veramente è servo, nondimeno tale non è giudicato percioch' il popolo, che guarda solamente alle cose esteriori, giudica delle condizioni degli uomini non altramente che'egli faccia nelle tragedie, nelle quali re è chiamato chi, vestito di porpora e risplendente d'oro e di gemme, sostiene la persona d'Agamennone o d'Atreo o d'Eteocle: e s'aviene ch'egli non ben rappresenti la persona della quale s'è vestita, non perciò altro che re è chiamato, ma si dirà ch' il re non bene ha fatta la sua parte. Similmente chi non ben sostiene la persona di principe o di gentiluomo ch' in questa vita, ch' è quasi teatro del mondo, dalla fortuna l' è stata imposta, non sarà però dagli uomini chiamato se non principe o gentiluomo, tuttoch'a Davo o a Siro o a Geta sia somigliante. Ma quando aviene che si ritrovi alcuno non sol di condizione e di fortuna ma d' ingegno e d'animo servile, costui è propissimamente servo, e di lui e de' simili a lui il buon padre di famiglia, che vuol per servitori persone alle quali egli ragionevolmente possa commandare, compone la sua famiglia, né desidera in loro se non tanto di virtù solamente quanto gli renda capaci ad intendere i suoi commandamenti e a esseguirli; i quali da' cavalli e dall'altre bestie che la natura ha formate docili e atte ad essere ammaestrate dall'uomo, in tanto son differenti,

well as with food, work, and admonition, the father of
the family will govern his servants so that they are
happy with him and he is satisfied with them. From
the case of servants, who are mostly free men today,
we see that the laws and customs of men vary, but the
laws and distinctions of nature do not change with
times and customs, and you must understand that the
distinction between servant and lord is founded on nature. Some are by nature born to command and others
to obey, and he who is born to obey—although he
may be of royal stock—is truly a servant. Of course
this is not the common judgment, for the people consider only outward things, and in judging men's conditions respond just as they do at a tragedy, when whoever is dressed in purple and shines with gold and
gems and takes the role of Agamemnon or Eteocles is
called king. And if it happens that he is ineffective in
the part for which he is dressed, he is not for that reason called anything but king; all that will be said is that
the king did not do his part well. Similarly, whoever
fails to perform well the role of prince or gentleman
that fortune has imposed on him in this life, in this
theater of the world, will still be called prince or gentleman by the people, even if he resembles Davus, Syrus, or Geta.[39] When it happens, however, that someone is servile not only in station and fortune but also in
mind and soul, he should be a servant, and from men
like him the good father, who wants servants he can
rule reasonably, composes his family.[40] He desires them
to have only enough virtue to make them able to understand and follow his orders, and to make them different from horses and other beasts that nature has

che, lontani ancora dalla presenza del padrone, riten-
gono a memoria le cose a lor commandate e possono
esseguirle: il che delle bestie non aviene. È dunque il
servo animal ragionevole per participazione in quel
modo che la luna e le stelle per participazion del sole
son luminose, o che l'appetito per participazione del
lume dell' intelletto ragionevole diventa; percioché, sì
come l'appetito ritiene in sé le forme delle virtù che
dalla ragione in lui sono state impresse, così il servo
ritiene le forme delle virtù impressegli nell'animo dagli
ammaestramenti del padrone: e si può di loro e de' padroni dire alcuna fiata quel che, di sé e di madonna
Laura ragionando, disse il Petrarca:

.... Sì che son fatto uom ligio
Di lei, ch'alto vestigio
M' impresse al core e fece 'l suo simile.

E perché non t' inganni l'auttorità d' Esiodo, antichissimo poeta, il quale, annoverando le parti della
casa, pose il bue in vece del servo, voglio che tu intenda più propriamente che 'l modo co 'l quale sono
ammaestrati i servi da quel co 'l quale sono ammaestrate le bestie è molto differente, conciosia cosa che la
docilità delle bestie non è disciplina e non è altro ch'una
assuefazione scompagnata da ragione, simile a quella
con la qual la man destra adopra meglio la spada che la
sinistra, benché non più di ragione abbia in sé che la
sinistra. Ma la docilità de' servi è con ragione, e può
divenir disciplina come quella de' fanciulli eziandio:
onde irragionevolmente parlano coloro che spogliano i
servi dell'uso della ragione, conciosia cosa che lor si
conviene non meno ch'a' fanciulli, anzi più peraventura, e in loro è ricercato tanto di temperanza e di fortezza quanto lor basti per non abbandonare l'opere
commandate da' padroni o per ubbriachezza o per altro

made docile and receptive to training by man—unlike
beasts, servants must be able to remember their orders
and to follow them. Thus the servant is a rational animal by participation, just as the moon and the stars are
luminous by participation in the light of the sun or as
the appetite becomes rational by participation in the
light of the intellect. The appetite retains the forms of
the virtues impressed on it by reason, and the servant
retains the forms of the virtues impressed on him by
the training of his master. One might say of servants
and masters what Petrarch says at one point when he is
discussing himself and madonna Laura:

> . . . so I became vassal
> To you, who left a deep mark
> On my heart, and whom I now resemble.[41]

" 'And so that you will not be deceived by the authority of the very ancient poet Hesiod, who in enumerating
the parts of the household puts the ox in the servant's
place,[42] I want you to understand more exactly that the
manner in which servants are trained differs very much
from that in which beasts are trained. The docility of
beasts results not from education but from a process of
habituation that is unconnected with reason, but resembles the process by which the right hand comes to
wield a sword better than the left in spite of the fact
that the right hand possesses no more reason than the
left. The docility of servants, on the other hand, is accompanied by reason and is educable, like the docility
of young people. Therefore, those who deny that servants have reason speak unreasonably, for reason is as
fitting in servants as in children, and perhaps even
more so. One wants enough temperance and courage
in servants so that they will not neglect—either because of drunkenness or some other pleasure—the
tasks that their master has appointed, or abandon their

piacere, o pure i padroni medesimi ne' pericoli delle brighe civili e negli altri che possono avenire. E però convenevolmente fu detto dal poeta toscano:

Ch' innanzi a buon signor fa servo forte.

E convenevolmente i servi di Milone da Cicerone nella sua difesa furon lodati, e tutti quegli altri de' quali si leggono in Valerio Massimo alcuni memorabili essempi; benché, s' io volessi addurre tutti gli essempi memorabili de' servi, mi dimenticherei di quel che pur ora dissi, che servi propriamente son coloro che son nati per ubbidire, i quali agli uffici della cittadinanza sono inabili per difetto di virtù, della quale tanto hanno, e non più, quanto gli rende atti ad ubbedire. E se tu hai letto nell'istorie ch' i Romani ebbero una guerra pericolosa assai, la quale addimandaro guerra servile perché da servi fu concitata, e se parimente hai letto ch'a' nostri tempi gli esserciti de' Soldani eran formati di schiavi e oggi per lo più quell'osti formidabili ch' il gran Turco suol ragunare di schiavi son formate, riduci alla memoria la nostra distinzione, la qual da te ogni dubbio discaccerà: e questa è che molti son servi per fortuna, che tali non son per natura, e da questi alcuna maraviglia non è ch'alcuna pericolosa guerra sia concitata. Tuttavolta grand'argomento della viltà che la fortuna servile suol negli animi generare, è l'essempio degli Sciti, i quali, avendo assemblata un'oste contra i servi loro che s'eran ribellati, non potendo altramente debellarli, presero per consiglio di portare in guerra le sferze, le quali rinovellando ne' servi la memoria delle battiture che sotto il giogo della servitù avevan ricevute, gli posero in fuga.

Ma ritornando a' servi de' quali dee esser composta la famiglia, questi non loderei che fossero né d'animo né di corpo atti alla guerra, ma sì bene di complession

master himself amidst the dangers of a civil or any other kind of upheaval. The Tuscan poet put it fittingly when he said,

> In the presence of a good lord, a servant acts
>   bravely.[43]

Fitting, too, was Cicero's praise of the servants of Milo, and the praises of all those other servants whose memorable examples can be found in Valerius Maximus.[44] If I tried to mention them all now, however, I should be forgetting what I just said: that proper servants are born to obey and are not qualified to fulfill the duties of a citizen because their virtue is defective— they possess just enough virtue to make them able to obey, but no more. You may have read in history books that the Romans had a very dangerous war which they called the servile war because it was stirred up by slaves, and you may also have read that in our times the armies of the sultan were formed of slaves, as are today those formidable hosts that the Grand Turk assembles. If you remember our distinction, it should dispel any doubts you may have on this score: many are servants by fortune who are not such by nature, and it is not surprising that a dangerous war can be stirred up by such men. At the same time, an important proof that a servile lot often generates baseness in the soul is furnished by the example of the Scythians, who assembled a host to fight their rebellious slaves but managed to subdue them only after accepting advice to carry whips into battle. By reminding the slaves of the beatings they had received under the yoke of servitude, the whips put them to flight.[45]

" 'To return to the servants who ought to make up the family, however, I should not praise such as are suitable either in mind or body for war, but rather such as are constitutionally robust and capable of the neces-

robusta, atta alle fatiche e a gli essercizî nella casa e nella villa necessarî. Questi in due specie distinguerei, l'una all'altra sottordinata: l'una di soprastanti o di sopraintendenti, o di mastri che vogliam chiamarla; l'altra d'operarî. Nella prima sarà il mastro di casa, a cui dal padrone la cura di tutta la casa è raccomandata, e quel che della stalla ha particolar cura, come nelle case grandi suole avenire, e il fattore, c'ha la sopraintendenza sovra le cose di villa tutte; nell'altra saranno coloro ch' a' primi ubbediscono. Ma percioché la nostra fortuna non ha a noi data tanta facoltà che tu possa così distinti e così moltiplicati aver gli uffici della famiglia, basterà che d'uomo ti provegga il quale di mastro di casa e di stalla e di fattore faccia l'ufficio: e commanderai a gli altri tutti ch'a lui ubbediscono, dando il salario a ciascuno maggiore e minore secondo il merito e la fatica loro, e ordinando che 'l cibo sia lor dato sì che più tosto soverchi che manchi. Ma dèi nondimeno nutrir la famiglia di cibi differenti da quelli che verranno su la tua mensa, su la quale non ti sdegnare che vengano ancora le carni più grosse che secondo le stagioni saran comprate per li servitori, acciò ch'essi, vedendo che tu ti degni di gustarne talora, le mangino più volentieri. Fra' quali quelle reliquie delle carni e delle vivande più nobili che dalla tua mensa saran levate, debbon esser compartite in modo che s'abbia riguardo alla condizione e al merito di ciascuno.

Ma perché la famiglia ben nutrita e ben pagata nell'ozio diverrebbe pestilente e produrrebbe malvagi pensieri e triste operazioni in quel modo che gli stagni e l'acque che non si muovon soglion marcire e generar pesci poco sani, sarà tua cura principale, e anco del tuo mastro di casa, di tener ciascumo essercitato nel suo ufficio e tutti in quelli che sono indivisi, percioché non ogni cosa nella casa necessaria può esser fatta da una persona ch'abbia una cura particolare. Onde, quando

sary fatigues and exertions at home and in town. Such servants I should divide into two kinds, one subordinate to the other: the first consists of supervisors or superintendents or master workmen, whatever we choose to call them; the second, of laborers. In the first rank are the chief steward, to whom the master entrusts the management of the house; the stablemaster, whose special care is the stable; and the foreman, who superintends the business of the whole estate. In the second rank are those who obey the first rank. But because our fortune will not permit you to have so many different overseers to perform these various duties for the family, it will suffice if you find a single man who will fulfill the duties of chief steward, stablemaster, and foreman. Order all the others to obey him; pay them more or less according to their merit and labor; and arrange for their food, providing rather too much than too little. You ought to feed the servants different food from your own, but you also should not disdain to allow the coarser meats that are purchased in season for the servants to appear on your own table. The servants will eat such meats more willingly when it is seen that you deem them worthy of eating. In addition, the remains of the nobler meats and dishes from your table should be distributed to the servants in a manner that befits the station and merit of each.

" 'The family that is well-fed and well-paid in idleness, however, becomes mischievous and full of wicked thoughts and deeds, just as ponds and other bodies of water that do not move go bad and produce unhealthy fish. Your principal care and that of your chief steward, therefore, will be to keep each servant busy about his own special duties as well as about matters of common concern—for not every task in the household can be assigned to a single servant for his particular atten-

lo spenditore avrà compro da mangiare e 'l cameriero avrà fatto il letto e nettate le vesti e 'l famiglio di stalla stregghiati i cavalli e ciascun altro avrà fatto quello che di fare è tenuto, dee il sollecito mastro di casa imporre or a l'uno, or a l'altro alcuna di quelle opere che sono indivise, e sovra tutto aver dee cura che niuna bruttura si veda nella casa o nel cortile o nelle travole o nelle casse, ma che le mura, il pavimento, il solaro e tutti gli arnesi e instrumenti della casa sian politi e, per così dire, risplendano a guisa di specchi: perché la politezza non solo è piacevole a risguardare, ma giunge anco nobiltà e dignità alle cose vili e sordide per natura, sì com'all' incontra la lordura le toglie alle nobili e alle degne; oltre ch'altrettanto giova alla sanità la politezza quanto nuoce la sordidezza. E ciascun servitore dee così particolarmente aver cura che gli instrumenti i quali egli adopera nel suo ufficio sian politi, come il soldato l' ha della politezza dell'armè: ché tali sono a ciascuno gli instrumenti ch'egli adopera, quali sono l'arme al soldato; onde, de gli instrumenti del zappatore parlando, il Petrarca disse:

L'avaro zappator l'arme riprende,

ad imitazion di Vergilio, il quale prima aveva chiamate armi quegli instrumenti ch'adoperano i contadini:

Dicendum et quae sint duris agrestibus arma,

e arme eziandio gli instrumenti da fare il pane:

Tum Cererem corruptam undis cerealiaque
arma
Expediunt fessi rerum.

Ma percioch'alle volte aviene ch'alcun sia di soverchio occupato nel suo ufficio e alcun altro avanzi sempre molto più del giorno che dell'opera, dee così l'uno l'altro conservo aiutare come veggiamo che nel corpo,

tion. Thus when the buyer has bought the food, the housekeeper has made the beds and cleaned the clothes, the stableman has groomed the horses, and each of the others has done what he was supposed to, the diligent chief steward should order each to undertake one of the tasks that belong to everyone. Above all he should take care that no dirt be seen in the house or courtyard or on the tables or the cupboards; the walls, floors, ceilings, and all the utensils and implements of the house should be cleaned and, so to speak, shining like mirrors. Cleanliness is not only pleasant to look at but also confers nobility and dignity on things that are base and mean by nature, just as, in contrast, filth takes away natural nobility and dignity. Besides, cleanliness is as conducive to health as filth is detrimental. Each servant should take as much care to ensure that his tools are clean as a soldier takes with his arms, for tools are to the servant what arms are to the soldier, and hence Petrarch says of the ploughman's tools,

> The avid ploughman takes again his arms.[46]

Here, moreover, Petrarch is imitating Virgil, who was the first to refer to the tools of peasants as arms:

> Now we must speak of rude peasants' arms.[47]

And Virgil also used the term to describe implements for making bread:

> Then, wearily, they prepare the sodden grain
> And the arms for making bread.[48]

" 'Because it sometimes happens, however, that a certain servant is overburdened by his duties while another has more day than work, servants ought to help one another just as the parts of the body cooperate.

quando l'una gamba è stanca, su l'altra si suol riposare, e come l'una mano affaticata chiama l'altra per aiutatrice delle sue operazioni. E quando amore e cortesia vicendevole a ciò fare non gli inviti, dee il mastro di casa o 'l padrone stesso commandare al neghitoso e allo scioperato ch'al faticoso e affacendato porga aiuto. Ma sovratutto la carità del padrone e de' conservi nelle infermità dee dimostrarsi, nelle quali gli infermi in letti più morbidi e agiati debbono esser posti a giacere e di più dilicate vivande esser nutricati; né 'l padrone dee della sua visita esser loro superbo o discortese, perché, se gli animali bruti si rallegrano delle carezze de' padroni, come veggiamo ne' cani, quanto più creder debbiamo che se ne rellegrino gli uomini, animali ragionevoli: onde i buoni servitori, diventando affezionati a' padroni, non altramente intendono i padroni a cenno e ubbediscono ad un picciol movimento del ciglio o della fronte loro di quel che que cani soglion fare, che barboni sono addomandati. Anzi più tosto non come il cane al padrone, ma come la destra si muove ad ubbedire a' commandamenti dell'animo, il servo ad ubbedire a' commandamenti del padrone si mostra pronto: conciò sia cosa che, sì come la mano è detta instrumento degli instrumenti, essendo quella che s'adopera in nutrire, in vestire, in pulire tutte l'altre membra, ch'instrumenti pur son detti, così il servo è addomandato instrumento degli instrumenti, percioch'egli adopera tutti gli instrumenti che nella casa sono stati ritrovati affine non sol di vivere, ma di ben vivere: differente dagli altri instrumenti, perch'ove gli altri sono inanimati, il servo è animato. È differente dalla mano, perché la mano è congiunta al corpo, ed egli è separato dal signore; è differente ancora dagli artefici, perché gli artefici sono instrumenti di quelle che propriamente si dicon fattura, e 'l servo è instrumento dell'azione, la qual dalla fattura è distinta.

When one leg is exhausted we rest on the other, and a tired hand calls upon the other hand for help; and when love and mutual courtesy do not move servants to help each other, the chief steward, or even the master himself, should order the indolent and lazy ones to aid those who are hard-working and busy. Above all, the charity of the master and fellow servants should become evident when sickness occurs. Servants who fall sick ought to be laid in softer and more comfortable beds and fed with more delicate food, and the master should not act proudly or discourteously when he visits them. For if brute beasts, such as dogs, are cheered by their master's caresses, we must suppose that the effect on men, who are rational animals, will be even greater. Good servants will respond with affection to such attention from their masters. Like those dogs called poodles, they will come to understand their masters at a glance and learn to obey even slight movements of an eyelash or brow. In demonstrating his readiness to obey orders, however, the servant does not resemble a dog with his master so much as the right hand obeying the commands of the mind. Just as the hand is called the instrument of instruments because it labors to feed, clothe, and clean the other limbs, which are properly called instruments, so the servant can be called the instrument of instruments because he uses all the instruments of the house that have been invented not simply in order to live but in order to live well. He is different from other instruments because they are inanimate and he is animate, and he differs from the hand because the hand is joined to the body while he is separate from his lord. The servant differs from the craftsman, moreover, because the craftsman is an instrument of what is called, properly speaking, production, but the servant is an instrument of action, and action is distinct from production.

È dunque il servo, se tu vuoi aver di lui perfetta cognizione, instrumento dell'azioni, animato e separato. Ma perché dell'azioni alcune si fermano nella cura famigliare e ne' bisogni della casa, alcune escono fuori e si distendono a' negozî civili, tengon talvolta gli agiati gentiluomini, fra' quali desidero che tu sii, alcun giovane che nelle opportunità cittadinesche possa servirli, a' quali dando l'ufficio di scrivere e di trattare alcune lor bisogne, sogliono anco dare il nome di cancelliero: ma questi dagli altri sono molto diversi, consciosia cosa che per lo più sono e debbono essere d'ingegno non punto servile o materiale e atto alle azioni e alle contemplazioni, e tra loro e i padroni non è propriamente servitù o signoria, ma più tosto quella sorte d'amicizia che da Aristotele è detta in eccelenza; se ben ne' buoni secoli della romana republica questi ancora erano tolti dal numero degli altri servi. E tale fu Terenzio, scrittore delle comedie, il quale di Lelio e di Scipione fu così famigliare che fu creduto ch'essi nell'opere sue avessero alcuna parte; tale anco fu Tirone, al quale sono scritte molte lettere di Marco Tullio: il quale, eruditissimo grammatico, era diligente osservatore d'alcune cosette delle quali Cicerone fu più tosto sprezzatore ch'ignorante. Ma percioché tutta quella usanza di servitù, come detto abbiamo, è affatto mancata, oggi tra' padroni e questi sì fatti le leggi dell'amicizia in superiorità debbon essere osservate; e sovra questi particolarmente fu scritto dal signor Giovanni della Casa quel trattato degli uffici minori il qual da te, che molto sei vago di legger l'opere sue, so che molte fiate dee esser letto e riletto: sì ch'altro di loro non dirò di quello ch'ivi n'è scritto. Ma perché della cura della persona a bastanza s'è ragionato, se non forse quanto

"'Therefore, the servant—if you wish a perfect knowledge of him—is an instrument of action, animate and separate. But since some kinds of action pertain only to family cares and domestic necessities while others extend beyond and involve public affairs, gentlemen of wealth, among whom I want you to take your place, sometimes retain a young man to look out for their business in the city. They give him the duty of handling written business and certain other necessities, and usually call him their chancellor. Such servants, however, are very different from the others and ought not to be in any way servile or coarse in mind. They ought to be capable of both action and contemplation, and the relationship between them and their masters should not be one of slavery and lordship but should rather reflect that kind of friendship praised by Aristotle,[49] although in the good periods of the Roman Republic, these too were taken from the lists of the other servants. Terence, the author of comedies, was from this class; he was so close to Laelius and Scipio that it was thought that they had some part in writing his works.[50] From this class too came Tiro, to whom many of Cicero's letters are addressed. He was a most learned grammarian and attended diligently to certain of Cicero's minor affairs—matters that Cicero himself understood but that he felt to be beneath him.[51] As we pointed out, the use of slavery has entirely disappeared, and therefore the laws of friendship between unequals ought to be observed today between masters and servants like these. It was particularly about such servants that Lord Giovanni della Casa wrote his treatise on the minor duties.[52] I know that you, who are so fond of reading his works, must have read and reread this one many times, and therefore I shall say nothing on the matter beyond what is written there. About the care of persons, however, enough has been said, although per-

tu potessi desiderare che così delle fantesche si parlasse come de' servitori s' è favellato, e perché niuna cosa è stata da me lasciata a dietro, ch'a buon marito o a buon padre o a buon signore appertenga, mi pare che debbiamo venire a quella che fu da noi posta per seconda parte del nostro ragionamento: alla cura, dico, della facoltà, nella quale dell'ufficio della madre di famiglia e delle donne con buon proposito faremo menzione.

La cura della facoltà, come dicemmo, s'impiega nella conservazione e nell'accrescimento ed è divisa tra 'l padre e la madre di famiglia, percioché par così proprio del padre di famiglia l'accrescere come della madre il conservare; nondimeno a chi minutamente considera, la cura dell'accrescimento è propria del padre di famiglia e l'altra è commune, che che gli antichi in questo proposito s'abbiano detto. Ma perché niuna cosa può essere accresciuta se prima o 'nsieme non è conservata, dee il padre di famiglia, che la sua facoltà desidera di conservare, saper minutamente la quantità e la qualità dell'entrate sue e anco delle spese ch'egli per sostener onorevolmente la sua famiglia è costretto di fare, e, aguagliando le ragioni delle rendite con quella delle spese, fare in modo che sempre la spesa sia minore e abbia quella proporzion con l'entrata c' ha il quattro con l'otto o almeno co 'l sei: percioché, s'egli tanto volesse spendere quanto raccoglie dalle sue possessioni, non potrebbe poi ristorare i danni che sogliono avenire per caso o per fortuna, se pur avenissero, quali sono gli incendî e le tempeste e l' innondazioni, né supplire a' bisogni d'alcune spese che non possono esser provedute. E per chiarirsi delle sue facoltà e della valuta loro, conviene ch'egli stesso abbia vedute e misurate le sue possessioni con quelle misure le quali diedero principio alla geometria in Egitto, le quali se ben

haps you would like to hear as much about maid-servants as you have heard about menservants. I have left out nothing that pertains to a good husband or a good father or a good lord, and it seems to me, there-fore, that we ought to proceed to the subject that was established for the second part of our discussion: that is, the care of property. During this part it will be ap-propriate for us to speak about the duty of the mother of the family and of women.

"'The care of property, as we said, aims at conserva-tion and increase, and is divided between the father and the mother of the family. It appears that increase is the proper task of the father of the family and that conser-vation is the proper task of the mother, but whoever considers the matter precisely finds that increase is the father of the family's proper care and that the other care is proper to both the father and the mother, as in fact the ancients pointed out.[53] Nothing can be in-creased unless it is first or simultaneously conserved, however, and the father of the family who wants to conserve his property must know exactly the quantity and quality of his revenues and of the expenses that he is constrained to incur in order to support his family honorably. Then, comparing the computation of his income with that of his expenses, he must see to it that his expenses are less than his revenues and that the for-mer are related proportionally to the latter as four is to eight, or at the most, as six is to eight. If he should spend as much as he makes he would be unable to repair the damages that normally occur as the result of chance or fortune—the damages caused by fires, storms, and floods, for example—or to meet those ex-penses that cannot be foreseen. To know his property and its value clearly, he ought to have seen it and mea-sured it personally with those measurements that gave rise to geometry in Egypt, for although methods of

varie sono secondo la varietà de' paesi, la varietà nondimeno non è cagione di differenza sostanziale: e conviene che sappia com' il raccolto risponde alla semenza
e con quale proporzione la terra gratissima suol resti-
tuir le cose ricevute. E la medesima notizia conviene
ch'egli abbia dell'altre cose appertenenti all'agricoltura
o a gli armenti; né minore averla dee de' prezzi ch'alle
cose sono imposti o da publici magistrati o dal con-
senso degli uomini, né meno essere informato come le
cose si vendano o si comprino in Turino, in Milano, in
Leone o 'n Vinezia che come nella sua patria sian vendute o comprate: della quale cognizione s'egli sarà bene
instrutto, non potrà da' fattori o da altri nella raccolta o
nella vendita delle sue entrate esser ingannato. Ma percioch' io ho detto ch'egli dee essere instrutto della
quantità e della qualità delle sue facoltà, chiamo quantità non sol quella che dalle misure di geometria è misurata, come sono i campi e le vigne e i prati e i boschi,
o quella ch' è misurata da' numeri aritmetici, come il
numero delle greggi e degli armenti, ma quell'anco che
dal danaro è misurata; perciocché nell'agguagliare della
entrata e della spesa niuna quantità viene in maggior
considerazione che quella del danaro che dalle rendite
si può raccorre, la quale è molto incerta e molto varia-
bile, conciosia cosa che le terre non sono sempre nel
medesimo pregio e molto meno i frutti loro, e 'l danaro, non ch'altro, suole or crescere, or calare: nella
quale incertitudine e varietà di cose il giudizio e la esperienza e la diligenza del buon padre di famiglia tanto
suol giovare quanto basta non sol per conservare, ma
per accrescer le facoltà, le quali in mano de' trascurati
padri di famiglia soglion molto diminuire.

Qualità chiamo poi delle facoltà ch'elle siano o artificiali o naturali, o animate o inanimate. Artificiali
sono i mobili della casa e forse la casa stessa e i danari, i

measurement vary according to the variations of the country, their essential validity remains unaffected.[54] He must also know the relationship between what is harvested and what is sowed, and the increase with which the grateful earth can be expected to render what it receives. He should have an equal grasp of the other things related to the cultivation of his fields or to his herds. He should be no less informed about the prices of goods established by the public magistrates or general agreement, and he should know as much about the way things are sold and bought in Turin, Milan, Lyons, or Venice as he does about buying and selling in his own region. If he is well instructed in these matters he cannot be cheated out of his revenues at the time of harvest and market. Now, I said that he must be instructed in the quantity and the quality of his property. By quantity I mean not only what is measured by geometry—such as fields, vineyards, meadows, and woods—or by arithmetic—such as the size of flocks and herds—but also what is measured by money. In comparing income with expense no quantity is more important than the quantity of money that can be obtained from one's resources. That quantity, however, is very uncertain and variable, for pieces of land are not always equally valuable, the prices for produce are even less consistent, and money too now increases, now diminishes in worth. Amid this uncertainty and variety of circumstances, the judgment, experience, and diligence of the good father of the family normally suffices not only to conserve but also to increase property. In the hands of negligent fathers of the family, however, property usually diminishes considerably.

" 'As for what I call the quality of property, it can be either artificial or natural, and either animate or inanimate. Artificial property includes the furniture of the house, perhaps the house itself, and money, which was

quali per instituzion degli uomini sono stati ritrovati, potendosi viver senza, come si viveva negli antichissimi secoli ne' quali la permutazion delle cose si faceva senza il danaro. Fu poi trovato il danaro per legge degli uomini: onde *numus* fu detto, quasi *nomos*, ch' in lingua greca significa «legge»; il qual, commodamente agguagliando tutte le disaguaglianze delle cose cambiate, ha renduto il commerzio facile e anco più giusto che non era ne' tempi che s'usava solo la permutazione.

Artificiali ricchezze potranno esser chiamate ancora tutte quelle cose nelle quali più tosto l'artificio del maestro che la materia è venduta o estimata. Naturali son poi le cose dalla natura prodotte, delle quali alcune sono inanimate, come son le possessioni, le vigne e i prati e metalli; altre sono animate, come le greggi e gli armenti: dalle quali cose tutte il buon padre di famiglia suol raccorre entrata. Nella considerazione ancora della qualità viene se le possessioni siano vicine o lontane dalla città; s'abbiano vicino stagno o palude ch'esali maligni vapori onde l'aria ne divenga cattiva, o rivo o fiume che per lungo corso acquisti virtù di purgar l'aria; se siano ristrette da' colli o 'n parte percossa e signoreggiata da' venti; s' in ripa ad alcuna acqua navigabile o 'n paese piano per lo quale l'entrade su' carri agevolmente alla città posson esser trasportate; o pur in erto e malagevole e faticoso ne' quali l'opera de' somari sia necessaria; se vicine a strade correnti per le quali i peregrini e i mercanti d'Italia in Germania o 'n Francia soglion trapassare, o lontane dalla frequenza de' viandanti e de' commerci; s' in colle che signoreggi e che goda di bella veduta, o 'n valle umile che ne sia priva: le quali condizioni tutte, sì come molto accrescono o diminuiscon di valore e di prezzo alle cose possedute, così possono esser cagione di risparmiar le spese e di conservare e accrescer l'entrate, se ben saranno dal padre di famiglia considerate.

invented through human convention and which it is possible to live without, as men did in the most ancient times when things were bartered. Money was invented by human law and therefore was called *numus*—a word that is close to the Greek word *nomos*, which means law.[55] By making it possible to equalize all the inequalities in things exchanged, money has facilitated commerce and made it more just than it was in the days of barter.

" 'All those things in which it is rather the skill of the maker than the material itself that is sold or valued can also be called artificial riches, while natural riches are the things produced by nature, some of which are inanimate, like land, vineyards, meadows, and metals, and some of which are animate, like flocks and herds. From all of these the good father usually derives income. In determining the quality of property, moreover, one must consider whether it is close to or distant from the city; whether it lies near ponds or swamps that poison the air with unhealthy vapors, or near streams and rivers whose long course enables them to clear the air; whether it is constricted by hills or partly beaten and dominated by winds; whether it is on the bank of some navigable body of water, in flat country through which goods can be transported easily to the city, or in rough and difficult terrain that necessitates the use of donkeys; whether it is near highways by which travelers and merchants are accustomed to pass from Italy into Germany or France, or located far from all traffic; whether it is among hills that enjoy beautiful views or in low valleys that are viewless. All of these conditions can increase or diminish the value and price of property, and therefore, when well considered by the father of the family, can also be the causes of decreased expenses or of savings and increases of revenues.

Ma per venire alquanto più a' particolari della cura che da lui si ricerca, egli dee far che dalla villa alla città sia portato tutto ciò che per l'uso della casa è necessario o convenevole, e lasciare anco la casa di villa fornita di quel che basti a nudrir lui e la sua famiglia in que' tempi che suole venirvi, il rimanente vendere a' tempi che più caro si vende, e co' danari che ne trae comprare quelle cose che dalle sue possessioni non raccoglie e che nell'uso di gentiluomo son necessarie, a' tempi ne' quali con minor prezzo son comprate: il ch'agevolmente potrà fare, quando co 'l risparmio della spesa che prima avrà fatto si troverà avere avanzata alcuna somma di danari. E potrà anche trattener alcuna volta l'entrate secondo i pronostichi e i giudìci che si fanno della carestia e dell'abbondanza degli anni e delle stagioni, e ricordarsi dell'essempio di Talete, che per la cognizione delle cose naturali ch'egli aveva facilmente arricchì con la compra dell'oglio ch'egli fece. Questa sarà cura del padre di famiglia. Ma le cose che nella casa saranno dalla villa o da' mercati portate, tutte alla cura della madre di famiglia debbono esser raccomandate, la quale dee riserbarle in luoghi separati secondo la natura loro; perch'alcune amano l'umidità e il freddo, altre i luoghi asciutti, altre vogliono talora al sole e al vento esser dimostrate, e alcune si possono lungamente conservare, altre breve tempo. Le quali considerazioni avendo la buona madre di famiglia, dee procurar che più tosto sian mangiate quelle che si corrompono più facilmente e far conserva dell'altre che più lungamente si difendono dalla corruzione, se ben quelle ancora che son corruttibili posson ricever molti aiuti, co' quali si conservano lungamente: percioch' il sale e l'aceto difendono dalla corruzione non solo le carni, che son di più lunga durata, ma i pesci e i piccioni eziandio, che son corruttibilissimi molto; e i frutti, che facilmente son soggetti alla putrefazione,

" 'Now let us examine in more detail the care that the father of the family is expected to exercise. He must see to it that everything necessary or fitting for the house is brought into the city from the farm, and he must also leave the country house furnished with whatever is necessary to feed him and his family when they are normally there. The rest he must sell when prices are high, and with the proceeds he should purchase— when prices are low—whatever a gentleman needs that cannot be supplied from his own land. He will be able to do this easily when he has put aside a sum of money out of the savings on expenses that he has made earlier. Sometimes he can also hold back his produce in response to predictions and judgments concerning the scarcity and abundance of the year and the season, and he should remember the example of Thales, who through his knowledge of natural things easily made himself rich selling the oil he made.[56] The father of the family must take care of all this. As for the things that are brought into the house from the market, however, they should be entrusted to the care of the mother of the family, and she should store them in different places according to their natures. Some things love damp, cold places, others dry places; still others want to be exposed now and then to the sun and wind, and some can be kept a long time, others only briefly. The good mother of the family must take all this into consideration and make sure that whatever corrupts most easily is eaten first, while the things that are most resistant to decay are kept for later. Of course, even goods that tend to spoil easily can be treated in many ways to preserve them. Salt and oil prevent decay not only in meat, which usually lasts a long time anyway, but also in fish and pigeons, which go bad very quickly. Fruits, too, which spoil readily, usually last a long time in oil if they have been picked while still rather green.

s'acerbetti son colti anzi che no, lunga stagione nell'aceto sogliono mantenersi, e il fumo e il forno, traendo dalle carni e da' pesci e dall'uve e da' fichi e da altri frutti la soverchia umidità, la quale è cagion della corruzione, fan ch'essi si mantengano lunga stagione. Sono alcune cose all'incontra le quali aride diverrebbono e dure e non buone da mangiare, se non fossero con alcuna sorte di liquore conservate; delle quali cose tutte avendo fatta copiosa conserva la buona madre di famiglia, qualora averrà che per alcuno impedimento non sian portate vivande di piazza a bastanza per la tavola o per la famiglia, o qualora da qualche forestiero saran sopragiunti, potrà in un punto arricchire la mensa in modo che non lassi desiderar la copia delle vivande comprate. Deve ella ancora aver cura che tutti i frumenti ch' in casa sono si macinino e se ne faccia il pane, il qual con debita misura a' servitori e alle fanti sia distribuito: fra le quali così ella avrà una principale come ha il padrone fra' servitori, e fra questi due saran comuni le chiavi, accioch' in difetto del mastro di casa, il qual molte fiate fuor della casa e della città si ritrova, sia chi comparta le cose necessarie e chi ancora, s'arriva un forestiero, possa dargli bere; ché strana usanza è certo quella d'alcune case nelle quali il canevaro o 'l dispensiero sene porta con le chiavi ogni facoltà ancora di sovvenir a' bisogni della famiglia o agli appetiti de' padroni e degli amici loro. Dee nondimeno la buona madre di famiglia procurar che tutte le cose, s'occasione di forestieri altramente non ricercasse, sian compartite parcamente, perché la parsimonia è virtù così propria di lei come dell'uomo la liberalità, e dee ella stessa andar rivedendo molto spesso le cose conservate e misurando le misurabili e le numerabili numerando. Né solo la cura sua si dee stendere nelle dispense e nell'altre cose già dette, ma sovra i vini ancora, i quali, potendo lunga stagione conservarsi, sogliono anco

Furthermore, smoke and heat draw out the excess humidity that causes rot in meat, fish, grapes, figs, and other fruits, and thus make them keep longer. Some things, on the other hand, become hard and inedible when dried unless they are preserved in spirits of some kind. The good mother of the family should lay in an ample supply of these preserved foods so that whenever, because of some difficulty, not enough food has been brought from the marketplace or the family is surprised by a visit from a stranger, she will be able to embellish the table in an instant and in a manner that will leave no desire for food from the market. She must also take care to see that all the grain in the house is ground and made into bread to be distributed in the proper measure to both menservants and maidservants. Moreover, just as the master has a principal servant among the men, the mistress should have a principal servant among the maids, and these two principal servants should hold the keys of the house in common. In the absence of the master, who will often be out of the house and the city, they can dispense necessities, and if a stranger arrives, they can also give him something to drink. It is a strange custom, albeit followed in some houses, to allow the butler or pantryman to carry away with the keys every means of supplying either the needs of the family or the appetites of the master and his friends. In any case, unless the presence of guests demands something different, the good mother of the family should see to it that everything is dispensed frugally, for parsimony is her proper virtue, just as liberality is a man's, and she ought to inspect her stores frequently, measuring the things that are measurable and counting those that can be counted. Her care should extend not only to the pantry and the other things already mentioned but also to the wines that can be kept for a long time and that tend to improve with

tanto esser migliori quanto più invecchiano: parlo de' vini generosi, i quali acquistan forza con l'età, perché i piccioli e di poco spirito, che facilmente la perdono, debbono i primi esser bevuti o venduti, se soverchiano.

Ma principalissima cura sua dee esser quella de' lini e delle tele e delle sete, con le quali ella potrà non solamente provedere a' bisogni e alla orrevolezza della casa, ma fare anco alcuno onesto guadagno, il qual così è a lei convenevole com'all'uomo par che sia quel che dalle altre cose vendute o comprate o cambiate si raccoglie. Né dee la buona madre di famiglia sdegnarsi di porre anco talvolta le sue mani in opera, non nella cucina o 'n altre cose sordide che posson bruttare il corpo, perché le sì fatte da nobil matrona non debbon esser maneggiate, ma in quelle solamente che senza lordura e senza viltà possono esser trattate: e tali sono particolarmente le tele e l'altre opere dell'arte del tessere con le quali la buona madre di famiglia può fare alla figliuola ricco e orrevol corredo. Né senza ragione quest'arte a Minerva, dea della sapienza, fu attribuita, sì che da lei prese il nome, come si comprende in quei versi di Vergilio:

Inde, ubi prima quies medio iam noctis abactae
Curriculo expulerat somnum, cum foemina
                     primum,
Cui tolerare colo vitam tenuique Minerva,
Impositum cinerem et sopitos suscitat ignes,
Noctem addens operi castum ut servare cubile
Coniugis et possit parvos educere natos.

Ne' quali versi si comprende ch'egli parla non delle vili feminelle ma dalla madre di famiglia, la qual da molte serve suol esser servita; e tanto di nobiltà par che questa arte abbia recata seco che non solo alle private madri di famiglia, ma anco alle donne di reale condizione è stata attribuita, come di Penelope si legge:

age. I am speaking of noble wines, which grow stronger with age, for small wines with little spirit, which easily lose their strength, ought to be drunk first or sold if there is too much of them.

" 'The mother of the family's principal care, however, must be her linens, cloths, and silks; with these she can not only provide for the needs and dignity of the house but also make some honest profit, and for her to do so is just as fitting as it seems to be for a man to make money by selling, buying, or exchanging other things. The good mother ought not to disdain to set her hands to work now and then—not in the kitchen or at any other mean labor that coarsens the body, for such work should not be touched by a noblewoman, but at tasks that do not involve filth or baseness. Especially appropriate are the making of cloth and the various arts of weaving by which the good mother of the family can provide a rich and honorable trousseau for her daughter. Not unreasonably was this art attributed to Minerva, goddess of wisdom, who gave it its name, as these lines from Virgil make clear:

> Then, when early rest had expelled sleep—
> The night only half gone—at the hour when
> A wife, who supports life with her distaff
> And Minerva's subtle art, stirs the fire,
> Laboring by night to preserve the chaste bed
> Of her husband and to bring up her
>   children.[57]

" 'It is clear that in these lines Virgil is speaking not of base women but of the mother of the family who is accustomed to being served by many servants, and the art that he mentions seems to possess so much nobility that it has been attributed not only to mothers of the family who occupy a private station but also to royal ladies like Penelope:

Come la Greca ch'a le tele sue
Scemò la notte quanto il giorno accrebbe;

e Virgilio di Circe, che non solo era donna
ma dea, cantò:

Arguto tenueis percurrens pectine telas,

nel quale essempio seguì Omero, che non solo Penelope e Circe introduce a tessere, ma anche Nausicaa,
figliuola del re Alcinoo, pone in ischiera fra le lavatrici.
E se ben i Greci non osservano tanto il decoro quanto
par convenevole, i Romani nondimeno, che ne furono
maggiori osservatori, tutto ch' il cucinare e altre simili
operazioni alla madre di famiglia proibessero, gli con-
cedevano il tessere non senza molta laude della tessi-
trice: e in questa operazione fu ritrovata Lucrezia da
Collaltino, da Bruto e da Tarquinio, quando se n' ina-
morò. Ma ritornando alla nostra madre di famiglia la
qual, quando che sia, madre sia fortunata de' suoi figliuoli, quanto ella più sarà lontana dalla condizione
reale, tanto meno dovrà sdegnarsi d'adoprarsi in opere
ancora che portan seco men di dignità e d'artificio che
non porta la testura: e in questa parte par ch'ella in un
certo modo s'avanzi e che co 'l marito possa venire in
paragone, perciochè non solo con l'opere di tali arti
conserva, ma acquista eziandio; tuttavolta, perché gli
acquisti sono assai piccioli, assolutamente parlando,
diremo che della moglie è proprio il conservare e del
marito l'acquistare.

Ma perché le cose conservate molto meglio si possono porre in opera se sono ordinate, d'ordine diligente dee sovra ogn'altra cosa esser vaga la buona
madre di famiglia, perciochè, se non riserverà le cose
confuse, ma separate secondo la natura e l'opportunità
degli usi loro, l'avrà sempre preste ad ogni sua voglia e
sempre saprà quel ch'ella abbia e quel che non abbia. E

> Like the Greek lady whose loom's play
> Diminished night and lengthened day.[58]

And Virgil sang of Circe, who was not only a lady but also a goddess,

> Running the sharp comb through the fine
> cloth.[59]

In this, moreover, he followed the example of Homer, who introduces Penelope and Circe at their weaving and even places Nausicaa among a band of ladies doing the laundry.[60] Although the Greeks were not as observant of decorum as seems proper, the Romans were more careful and would not permit ladies to cook or engage in similar activities, but nevertheless allowed weaving and granted great praise to ladies who worked at the loom. Collatine, Brutus, and Tarquin found Lucrece at this work when Tarquin became enamored of her.[61] To return, however, to the mother of the family—when she is a mother, may she be blessed in her offspring—the further she is from royalty the less she ought to disdain work, even those kinds that are less dignified and involve less skill than weaving. It seems that in a way a woman raises herself through work and can be compared to her husband, for by her arts she not only conserves property but acquires it. Nevertheless, her acquisitions are rather small, and we shall speak precisely if we say that conservation is the wife's proper business and acquisition the husband's.

" 'Because things that have been conserved can be much better used when they are ordered, the good mother of the family must desire a careful order in everything. If she avoids confusion and arranges things according to the nature and the occasion of their uses, she will always have them ready for any purpose and will always know what she has and does not have. And

se niun paragone si può addurre in questo proposito degno di considerazione, degnissimo è quel dell'umana memoria, la qual, facendo conserva in se medesima di tutte le imagini e di tutte le forme delle cose visibili e intelligibili, non potrebbe in tempo opportuno trarle fuori e alla lingua e alla penna dispensarle, s'ella non le ordinasse, e molte fiate cose in sé conterrebbe ch'ella medesima quasi non saprebbe di contenere; di tanta virtù è l'ordine quanta detta abbiamo, ma è di non minor bellezza. Il che di leggiero potrà comprendere chi leggerà i poeti, i quali con niuno altro artificio aggiungono più di vaghezza a' versi loro che con ordinare le parole in guisa che l'una con l'altra o come simile o come pari s'accordi o come contraria risponda: artificio che parimente dagli oratori è stato usato, il quale, comeché sia di molto ornamento, agevola ancora molto la fatica di coloro ch'imparano le prose e i versi a mente. E se vero è quel che dicono alcuni filosofi, che la forma dell'universo altro non sia che l'ordine, le cose picciole alle grandi paragonando, diremo che la forma d'una casa sia l'ordine e che 'l riformare la casa o la famiglia altro non sia che riordinarla. Né voglio tacere in questo proposito cosa la qual, se ben per se stessa non pare che possa portare alcuna dignità, tutta volta tanto acquista per l'ordine e per la politezza che, sì come non solo senza schifo, ma con maraviglia fu da me veduta, così, se non con maraviglia, senza indegnità almeno potrà esser raccontata.

Io ritornava da Parigi e, passando per Beona, entrai nello spedale, nel quale, comech'ogni stanza ch' io vidi mi paresse degna di lode, la cucina nondimeno mi parve maravigliosa, la quale (ben è vero che non era quella che di continuo era adoperata) così polita ritrovai come sogliono esser le camere delle novelle spose: e vidi in lei tanta moltitudine d'instrumenti necessarî non sol per uso proprio ma della mensa eziandio, e con

while there is no analogy truly capable of illuminating this subject, the best is with human memory, which preserves all the images and forms of visible and intelligible things but would not be able to draw them forth in time and dispense them to the tongue and pen, and would even lose track of what it possessed, if it were not orderly. We have been describing the virtue of orderliness; the beauty of it, however, is no less considerable. This point should be easily understood by anyone who reads the poets; nothing increases the charm of their verses more than the art with which they arrange their words so that they harmonize through similarity or sameness, or answer each other as opposites. The orators, too, employ this art, and even when it involves much elaboration, it greatly facilitates the labor of memorizing either prose or verse. If certain philosophers speak truly when they claim that the form of the universe is nothing but order,[62] I should say, comparing small things to great, that the form of a household is also order and that reforming a household or a family is nothing but reordering it. While on this subject, moreover, I don't want to fail to mention something which in itself seems without dignity but which acquired so much from its order and cleanliness that I looked upon it not only without disgust but with wonder; as a result I feel confident that I can describe it, if not so as to excite wonder, at least without loss of dignity.

"'I was returning from Paris, and as I was passing through Beaune, I visited the hospital.[63] Every room that I saw seemed to me worthy of praise, but the kitchen seemed to me wonderful, for—although it is true that it is not the one that they use all the time—I found it as clean as marriage chambers usually are. In it, I saw a great multitude of implements not only for the kitchen but for the table as well, and they were

sì discreto ordine compartiti e con tanta proporzione l'une dopo l'altro acconcio o contra l'altro collocato, e così il ferro netto dalla rugine risplendeva al sole, che per alcune fenestre di bellissimo vetro purissimo v'entrava, che mi parve di poter rassomigliarla a l'armeria de' Viniziani o degli altri principi, ch'a' forestieri sogliono esser dimostrate. E se Gnatone, ch'ordinò la famiglia del suo glorioso capitano in guisa d'uno essercito, questa avesse veduto, son sicuro che con più alto paragone che con quello dell'armeria l'avrebbe inalzata.

Ma passando omai dalla conservazione all'acquisto, si può dubitare se questa arte dell'acquistare sia la stessa che la famigliare, o pur parte d'essa o vero ministra; e se ministra, perché ministri gli instrumenti come il fabbro dell'armi dà la corazza e l'elmetto a' soldati, o perché ministri il soggetto, o la materia che vogliam chiamarla, come colui che fa le navi riceve il legno da colui che taglia le selve. E cominciando a risolvere i dubbi, chiara cosa è che non sia un'arte istessa la famigliare e quella dell'acquisto, percioch'all'una conviene apparecchiar le cose, all'altra porre in opra le apparecchiate: or resta che si consideri se l'arte dell'acquisto sia una specie o una parte della famigliare, o pur se sia a fatto estranea e diversa da lei. La facoltà dell'acquisto può esser naturale e non naturale: naturale chiamo quella ch'acquista il vitto da quelle cose che dalla natura sono state prodotte per servigio dell'uomo; e perciò che niuna cosa è più naturale che 'l nutrimento che la madre porge al figliuolo, pare oltre tutti gli altri acquisti naturale quello che si trae da' frutti della terra, conciosia cosa che la terra è madre naturale di ciascuno. Naturali sono ancora gli alimenti che si traggono dalle bestie e dagli acquisti che si fanno d'essi, i quali si distinguono secondo la distinzion delle bestie, perché delle bestie altre sono muntuose e congregabili, altre

neatly arranged one on top of another or side by side. The ironware, free from rust, was shining in the sun that came in through very beautiful and very clear glass, and the effect reminded me of the armory of the Venetians or of other princely armories that are often shown to foreigners. If Gnatho, who ordered the family of his glorious captain in the manner of an army, had seen this kitchen, I am sure he would have extolled it by comparing it with something even nobler than an armory.[64]

" 'But let us proceed now from conservation to acquisition. One can wonder whether the art of acquiring is identical to the domestic art, or rather a part of it or ministerial to it. And if the art of acquiring is ministerial, does it provide instruments, as the armorer provides breastplate and helmet to the soldier, or does it provide the matter—the material, if you will—as the shipbuilder receives wood from the woodcutter? Let us begin to resolve these questions. It is clear that the domestic and the acquisitive arts are not identical, because one provides and the other makes use of what is provided. What remains, then, is to determine whether the acquisitive art is a kind or part of the domestic art, or whether the two arts are wholly foreign and different from each other. The acquisitive faculty can be natural or unnatural. I call that faculty natural which acquires nourishment from the things that have been produced by nature for the service of men, and since nothing is more natural than the nourishment that mothers offer to their sons, and since the earth is the natural mother of each man, the acquisition that seems natural above all others is that of the fruits of the earth. Natural, too, are the foods that come from animals and from their maintenance. These differ according to the differences among animals: some can be milked and are gregarious, while others are solitary and wander-

solitarie ed erranti: di quelle si formano le greggi e gli armenti e altre congregazioni, dalle quali tutte non picciola utilità si suol raccorre; di queste si fanno prede, con le quali molti soglion sostentar la vita.

Pare ancora che la natura abbia generato non solo i bruti a servigio de gli uomini, ma gli uomini che sono atti ad ubbedire a servigio di coloro che sono atti a commandare, sì che par naturale l'acquisto eziandio che si fa nelle prede della guerra, quando la guerra sia giusta; né voglio tacere quel che da Tucidide nel proemio della sua istoria è osservato, cioè che negli antichissimi secoli l'arte del predare non era vergognosa: onde si legge ne' poeti che l'uno addomanda a l'altro s'egli è corsaro, quasi niuna ingiuria gli faccia con sì fatta dimanda. Alla quale usanza, o più tosto ragione, avendo riguardo Vergilio, introduce Numano così a vantarsi:

> Caniciem galea premimus semperque recentes
> Coniectare iuvat praedas et vivere rapto;

e oggi acquisto naturale e giusto si può chiamar quello ch' i cavalieri di Malta e gli altri fanno delle prede de' Barberi. Tutte quest'arti dunque dell'acquisto naturale par che convengano al padre di famiglia, e l'agricultura principalmente; e chi tutte le mescolasse e le cose che da questi acquisti raccoglie cambiasse, non farebbe arte peraventura al padre di famiglia disdicevole. La qual arte quella è che mercantia oggi si chiama comunemente, la quale è di molte sorti; ma giustissima è quella la quale, prendendo le cose soverchie di là ove soverchiano, le porta ove n' è difetto, e in quella vece ivi altre ne porta delle quali v' è carestia: e di questa ragionando, disse negli *Uffici* M. Tullio che la mercantia, s'era picciola, era sordida, ma se grande, non era molto da vituperare.

ing. The former make up the flocks, herds, and other groupings that are normally so useful, and the latter are the prey on which many men ordinarily live.

" 'It seems, moreover, that nature has not only created animals for men's service but has also made some men fit to obey for the service of those men who are fit to rule. Consequently, the acquisitions made by preying upon an enemy in war are also just, provided the war is just, and I do not want to omit Thucydides' observation, in the preface to his history, that in the most ancient times the art of preying was not shameful.[65] We see in reading the poets that asking a man whether he is a pirate is hardly an insult, and Virgil reflects this custom or way of speaking when he puts the following boast in the mouth of Numanus:

> We crush grey hair with a helmet and rejoice
> To gather fresh prey and live by plunder.[66]

Today, the booty that the Knights of Malta and others have taken from the people of Barbary can be called a natural and just acquisition. Thus it seems that all these arts of natural acquisition, and especially agriculture, are suitable for the father of the family, and if he were to blend all these arts and market all the things he gets by them, he might perhaps practice an art that would not be unseemly for a father. This art is now commonly called trade, and there are many kinds of it. Most just is the kind that transports the surplus goods from one region to another where they are needed and returns with things from the second region that are lacking in the first. Discussing this subject in the *Offices*, Cicero says that trade is sordid when conducted on a small scale, but when carried out on a grand scale is not to be blamed overmuch.[67]

Ma le sue parole debbono esser prese in quel luogo come dette da filosofo stoico, il qual troppo severamente parla di queste materie; percioch' in altri luoghi, ov'egli come cittadino ne ragiona, loda e difende i mercanti e le lor ragioni, e chiama onestissimo l'ordine de' publicani, il quale aveva in mano l'entrate della republica e da' quali la mercantia era essercitata. Ma sì come giusta è quella mercantia la qual porta le cose ove mancano e ne trae utilità, così assai ingiusta è quella la qual, comprando le cose native d'un paese, le rivende nel medesimo luogo, aspettando l'opportunità del tempo con molto vantaggio; se ben ch'altri aspetti l'opportunità nel vender le sue proprie entrate e le cose che raccoglie dalle sue possessioni e dagli armenti suoi, non pare che sia in alcun modo disconveniente al buon padre di famiglia. E tanto sia detto dell'acquisto naturale ch'al padre di famiglia è conveniente, nel quale egli molto s'avanzerà se sarà a pieno instrutto non sol della natura e della bontà e del valor di tutte le cose che si cambiano o che da luogo a luogo si trasportano, ma anco in qual provinzia nascano le migliori, in qual le peggiori, e in quale in maggiore abbondanza, in quale in minore, ove con maggior prezzo, ove con minor sian vendute: e dee essere parimente informato de' modi e delle facilità e delle difficultà del trasportarle, e de' tempi e delle stagioni nelle quali ciò più commodamente si può fare, e delle corrispondenze c' hanno le città con le città e le provinzie con la provinzie, e de' tempi ne' quali si raccogliono quei mercati che comunemente fiere sono addomandate.

Dee nondimeno trattare il padre di famiglia quest'arti come padre di famiglia e non come mercante: percioch'ove il mercante si propone per principal fine l'accrescimento della facoltà, che si fa con la trasmutazione, e per questo molte volte si dimentica della casa e de' figliuoli e della moglie e va in paesi lontanissimi,

" 'In that passage, however, his words are to be taken as those of a Stoic philosopher who judges the matter too severely; elsewhere, when he is speaking as a citizen, he praises and defends the merchants and their rights, and describes as extremely honest the class of tax collectors that controlled the finances of the republic and carried on its trade.[68] But while that form of trade that transports goods where they are needed and makes them useful is just, so that which buys things up in one area and then waits for an advantageous time to sell them back in the same place is very unjust. On the other hand, to wait for the right moment to sell his own goods and the produce of his own lands and herds does not seem in any way improper for the good father of the family. Let this much be said about the natural acquisition that befits the father of the family. He will do very well if he knows thoroughly not only the nature, excellence, and value of everything that is traded or transported from place to place, but also which province produces the best quality and which the worst, which greater amounts and which smaller, which more expensively and which more cheaply. He must be equally well informed about the means and ease of transporting goods, the times and seasons in which transportation is most convenient, the relations between cities and between provinces, and the times at which those markets commonly called fairs are held.

" 'In exercising these arts, however, the father of the family must continue to act as the head of the family and not as a merchant. The merchant aims principally at increasing his property through trade and therefore often forgets his house, children, and wife, and travels to distant lands, leaving domestic affairs to his agents

lasciandone la cura a' fattori e a' servitori, il padre di famiglia ha l'acquisto della trasmutazione per obietto secondo e dirizzato al governo della casa, e tanto solo egli vi spende o dell'opera o del tempo, quanto la prima e principal sua cura non ne può essere impedita. Oltre di ciò, sì come ciascun'arte vuole i suoi fini in infinito, percioch' il medico vuol sanar quanto può e l'architetto vuol l'eccelenza della fabrica in soprana perfezione, così il mercante par che desideri il guadagno in infinito; ma il padre di famiglia ha i desideri delle ricchezze terminati. Percioché le ricchezze altro non sono che multitudine d' instrumenti appertenenti alla cura famigliare e publica; ma gli instrumenti in alcun'arte non sono infiniti né di numero né di grandezza: che s' infiniti fossero di numero, non potrebbe l'artefice aver di loro cognizione, conciosia cosa che l' infinito, in quanto infinito, non è compreso dal nostro intelletto; se di grandezza, non potrebbono esser maneggiati; oltreché non si concede corpo d' infinita grandezza. E sì com' in ciascun'arte gli instrumenti debbono esser proporzionati non meno a colui che gli adopera ch'alla cosa intorno alla quale sono adoperati, ché nella nave il timone non dee esser minore di quel che basti a dirizzare il suo corso, né sì grande che non possa esser trattato dal nocchiero, e nella scoltura lo scarpello non dee esser sì grave che non possa esser sostenuto dallo scultore, né sì leggiero che con fatica rompa le scheggie del marmo, così parimente le ricchezze debbono esser proporzionate al padre di famiglia e alla famiglia ch'egli sostiene e che di quelle dee essere erede: e tante, e non più, quanto bastino non solo per vivere, ma per ben vivere secondo la condizion sua e 'l costume de' tempi e della città nella quale egli vive. E se Crasso diceva che non era ricco colui che non poteva nutrire un essercito, aveva peraventura risguardo alla ricchezza ch'era convenevole ad

and servants, but the father considers acquisition through trade only secondary and subordinates it to running the house. To trade he devotes only as much labor and time as does not interfere with his first and principal care. Furthermore, although each art desires its own ends infinitely—the doctor seeks to cure as much as he can, the architect wants the highest perfection in a building, and similarly the merchant seems to want infinite profit—the father of the family has only a limited love of riches. Riches are nothing but a multitude of instruments to serve the family and the public, and the instruments of an art are never infinite in number or size. If they were infinite in number, the craftsman would not be able to understand them, for the infinite as such cannot be known by our minds. And if they were infinite in size, they would be unusable, not to mention the fact that a body of infinite size is considered an impossibility. In each art the instruments must be proportioned not only to the person who uses them but also to the thing on which they are used. Thus, the rudder of a ship must not be smaller than it needs to be for steering the ship nor too large to be handled by the pilot, and the sculptor's chisel must not be too heavy for him to hold nor too light to chip away marble effectively. Thus, too, riches must be proportioned to the father of the family, his family, and his heirs. He needs enough not only to live but to live well in accord with his station and the customs of his time and city, but he does not need more. When Crassus said that no one is rich who cannot feed an army, he may have been thinking of the wealth befitting a prin-

un principe cittadin di Roma, la quale ad un di Preneste o di Nola sarebbe stata smoderata, e fors'anco in uomo romano era soverchia: percioch' il poter assoldar gli esserciti si conviene a' re e a' tiranni e a gli altri prinprocipi assoluti, non al cittadino della città libera, il qual non dee esceder gli altri tanto in alcuna condizione che guasti quella porzione ch' è ricercata in una ragunanza d'uomini liberi, conciò sia cosa che, come in un corpo il naso, crescendo oltre il convenevole, tanto potrebbe crescere che non sarebbe più naso, così nella città un cittadino che tanto s'avanzi non è più cittadino. Comunque sia, perché le ricchezze si consideran sempre in rispetto di colui che le possede, non si può prescriver quante debbian essere, ma solo si può dire ch'elle debbon esser proporzionate al posseditore, il quale tanto e non più dee procurar d'accrescerle, quanto poi possano, compartite tra' figliuoli, bastar al ben vivere cittadinesco.

Né più mi riman che dire intorno all'acquisto naturale, conveniente al padre di famiglia, il qual propriamente si trae dalle terre e da gli armenti, comeché possa esser fatto ancor con la mercantia e con la caccia e con la milizia: percioché ricordar ci debbiamo che molti Romani dall'aratro eran chiamati a' magistrati e, deposta la porpora, ritornavano all'aratro. Ma percioch'il padre di famiglia dee aver cura della sanità non come medico, ma come padre di famiglia, dee più volentieri ancora attendere a quella maniera d'acquisto che maggiormente conserva la sanità; onde volentieri esserciterà se medesimo e vedrà esscercitare i suoi in quell'operazioni del corpo le quali, non bruttandolo né rendendolo sordido, giovano alla sanità, alla quale l'ozio e la soverchia quiete suole esser contraria: amerà dunque la caccia e più stimerà quelle prede le quali con la fatica e co 'l sudore s'acquistano, che quelle che con l' inganno, scompagnato da ogni fatica, sono acqui-

cipal citizen of Rome.[69] Such wealth would have been immoderate in a man from Praeneste or Nola, however, and was perhaps excessive even in a Roman. The power of raising armies belongs to kings, tyrants, and other absolute princes, but not to a citizen of a free city. A citizen ought not to exceed his fellows in any way that violates the relationships that are proper in a group of free men. Just as a nose might become so large that it would no longer be considered a nose in relation to the human body, so a citizen who becomes too great in a city is no longer a citizen. Nevertheless, riches must always be considered in relation to their possessor, and therefore one cannot prescribe their limit but must say simply that they should be appropriate, and that one ought not to try to increase them beyond what is necessary to provide each of one's children with the opportunity to lead the good life of a citizen.

" 'Nothing remains to be said about the natural acquisition befitting the father of the family. His wealth comes properly from his lands and his herds, although he may also derive it from trade, hunting, and war. We ought to remember that many Romans were called to high office from the plow and returned to it again upon laying aside the purple. Since the father of a family's care for health is not the same as that of a doctor, however, the father ought to devote himself even more willingly to the kind of acquisition that best preserves health. He ought to take exercise willingly himself, and also see to it that his family exercises in ways that help to make the body healthy without degrading or demeaning it. Leisure and excessive ease are normally injurious to health, and therefore he will love hunting and will esteem the prey that must be captured by an expense of labor and sweat more highly than the prey that is taken by trickery and without any labor. But

state. Ma poiché abbiam ragionato di quella maniera d'acquisti ch' è naturale, non è disconveniente che facciamo menzion dell'altra che naturale non è, tutto ch'ella al padre di famiglia non appertenga. Questa in due specie si divide, l'una detta cambio, l'altra usura: e non è naturale, perch'è pervertimento dell'uso proprio, conciò sia cosa ch' il danaro fu ritrovato per agguagliare le disaguaglianze delle cose cambiate e per misurare i prezzi, non perch'egli dovesse cambiarsi; percioché del danaro, in quanto metallo, non ci è alcun bisogno, né se ne riceve alcun commodo nella vita privata o civile, ma in quanto aguagliator della disugualità delle cose e misurator del valor di ciascuna, è necessario e commodo. Quando dunque il danaro si cambia, in quanto danaro non dirizzato ad altro uso, è usato oltre l'uso suo proprio: non s' imita poi la natura nel cambio, perché, così il cambio come l'usura potendo multiplicare i guadagni suoi in infinito, si può dire ch'egli non abbia alcun fine determinato; ma la natura opera sempre a fine determinato, e a fine determinato operano tutte quell'arti che della natura sono imitatrici. Ho detto ch' il cambio può multiplicare i guadagni in infinito, perch' il numero, in quanto numero non applicato alle cose materiali, cresce in infinito e nel cambio il danaro non si considera applicato ad alcun'altra cosa. Ma accioché tu meglio intenda quel che si ragiona, tu hai a sapere ch' il numero o si considera secondo l'essere suo formale o secondo il materiale: numero formale è una ragunanza d'unità non applicata alle cose numerate, numero materiale è la ragunanza delle cose numerate. Il numero formale può crescere in infinito, ma 'l materiale non può multiplicare in infinito: perché, se ben per rispetto della sezione, o della division che vogliam dirla, par ch' in infinito possa multiplicare, nondimeno, poiché nel nostro proposito non ha luogo divisione, diremo ch'egli non possa cre-

since we have discussed the natural means of acquisition it is not inappropriate to mention the unnatural, in spite of the fact that it is not fitting for the father of the family. There are two kinds of unnatural acquisition: one is called money-changing and the other usury.[70] Both are unnatural because they pervert money from its proper uses. Money was invented to make up for the inequalities in goods that are exchanged and to provide a measure by which prices can be established, not for the sake of being exchanged itself. If money were only metal it would offer no advantage to our private and public lives, and there would be no need of it; it is necessary and advantageous because it makes up for the inequalities in things and measures their values. When, then, money is changed and not directed to any further use, it is perverted. Money-changing is not natural because, like usury, it can multiply profits infinitely and therefore can be said to have no fixed end, but nature always has a fixed end, and all the arts that imitate nature aim at fixed ends too. I asserted that money-changing can multiply profits infinitely because number can be infinite when it is not applied to material things, and the money involved in money-changing is not thought to be applied to anything except the process of making money itself. To understand this matter better, you must realize that number can be considered with regard to either its formal being or its material being. A formal number is a group of units that have no reference to things; a material number is a group of things that have been enumerated. Formal numbers can increase infinitely, but material numbers cannot. Although it seems that through sectioning or, as we say, division, material numbers too can multiply infinitely, division is irrelevant to our subject, and we shall say that material numbers cannot

scere in infinito perché gli individui in ciascuna specie sono di numero finito.

Stante questa divisione, molto più può multiplicare la ricchezza che consiste nel danaro, in quanto danaro, che quella che consiste nelle cose misurate e numerate dal danaro: perché, se ben il numero del danaro non è formale, come quello ch' è applicato all'oro e all'argento, più facilmente si può raccogliere gran multitudine de danari che d'altre cose; e par che co 'l desiderio s'aspiri all' infinito. Fra 'l cambio nondimeno e l'usura è qualche differenza, e 'l cambio può essere ricevuto non solo per l'usanza, che l' ha accettato in molte nobilissime città, ma per la ragione eziandio, percioch' il cambio è in vece del trasportamento del danaro di luogo in luogo; il quale non potendosi far senza discommodo e senza pericolo di fortuna, è ragione ch'al trasmutatore sia proposto alcun convenevole guadagno. Oltrech'essendo il valor de' danari vario e alterabile così per legge e instituzion degli uomini come per la diversa finezza delle leghe dell'oro e dell'argento, si possono i cambi reali del danaro ridurre in alcun modo ad industria naturale, alla quale l'usura non si può ridurre, come quella ch' è scompagnata da ogni pericolo e che niuna di queste cose considera: la qual non sol fu dannata da Aristotele, ma proibita ancora nella nuova legge e nella vecchia; e di lei ragionando, Dante disse:

> E se tu ben la tua fisica note,
> Tu troverai dopo non molte carte
> Che l'arte vostra quella, quanto pote,
> Segue, com' il maestro fa il discente,
> Sì che vostr'arte a Dio quasi è nipote.
> Da queste due, se tu ti rechi a mente
> Lo Genesì dal principio, convene
> Prender sua vita ed avanzar la gente.

increase infinitely because the individuals of each kind are themselves finite in number.[71]

"'Because of this difference, wealth in the form of money can be increased far more than wealth in the form of goods that are measured and evaluated by money. The numbers applied to money are not formal, for they refer to gold and silver, but it is easier to accumulate money than other goods, and it seems that money, like desire, aspires to the infinite. Between money-changing and usury, however, there is some difference. Money-changing can be permitted not only because of the customs that have made it acceptable in many noble cities but also because it obviates the necessity of transporting money from place to place, and since this cannot be accomplished without difficulty and risk, it is reasonable that the money-changer be rewarded with some suitable profit. Since, moreover, the value of money varies and is alterable both because of human laws and institutions and because of the different qualities of gold and silver, real money-changing[72] can be made to some extent a natural industry. Usury, on the other hand, cannot, for it is devoid of any risk and takes no account of any of the things just mentioned. Usury was not only condemned by Aristotle but also prohibited by both the new and the old laws,[73] and Dante has this to say about it:

> And if you pay attention to your *Physics*
> You'll find, soon after you begin to read,
> That your art follows her, when possible,
> As students follow masters. Thus, to God
> Your art's a kind of grandchild. Now recall
> The book of *Genesis*, in the beginning,
> Which says that by these two it's suitable
> For man to aid the race and earn a living.

E perché l'usuriere altra via tiene,
    Per sé natura e per la sua seguace
    Dispregia, poi ch' in altro pon la spene.

Co' quai versi mi par che non solo possa aver fine il nostro ragionamento dell'acquisto naturale e non naturale, ma quel tutto ch' intorno alla cura famigliare proponemmo di fare; la qual già hai veduto come si volga alla moglie e com'a' figliuoli e come'a' servi e com'alla conservazione e all'acquisto delle facoltà: che furon le cinque parti delle quali partitamente dicemmo di voler trattare. Ma perch' io desidero che le cose delle quali ora ho ragionato ti si fermin nella mente in modo ch' in alcun tempo non tene debba dimenticare, io le ti darò scritte; perché, spesso rileggendole, possa non solo appararle, ma porle in opera eziandio, percioch' il fine degli ammaestramenti ch'appertengono alla vita dell'uomo è l'operazione.

Questo fu il ragionamento di mio padre, il qual fu da lui raccolto in picciol libretto, letto da me e riletto tante volte che non vi dee parer maraviglia se così bene ciò che da lui mi fu detto ho saputo narrarvi. Or rimarrebbe solo, accioché questo mio lungo ragionare non fosse stato indarno, che, s'alcuna cosa da lui detta vi paresse che potesse ricever miglioramento, non vi fosse grave di darglielo. Per quel ch'a me ne paia, dissi io, ogni cosa non solo da lui bene e dottamente vi fu insegnata, ma da voi bene e diligentemente è stata posta in opera: solo si potrebbe forse desiderare ch'alcuna cosa alle cose da lui dette s'aggiungesse, e questa particolarmente, s'una sia la cura e 'l governo famigliare o se più, e se, più essendo, son cognizione e operazione d'un solo o di più. Vero dite, egli rispose, ch' in ciò il ragionamento di mio padre fu manchevole, percioch'altro è il governo famigliare delle case private e altro quello delle case de' principi; ma io direi ch'egli

Another way attracts the usurer.
> Elsewhere he puts his hope, despising nature
> In herself and in her follower.[74]

" 'With these verses it seems to me that we can bring to a close not only our discourse about natural and un-natural acquisition but everything that we proposed to say about caring for a family. You see that we have already discussed wives, children, servants, and the preservation and acquisition of property, and these are the five subjects that we said we would treat separately. But I want the things that I have said to fix themselves in your mind so that you will not forget them, and therefore I shall put them in writing for you. By frequently reading them over you will be able not only to learn them but to put them into practice too, for the end of all teaching about life is action.'

"This was my father's discourse. He set it down in a little book, and I have read and reread it so many times that you should not be amazed at my ability to tell you so exactly what he said. Now only this remains to be said, so that my long speech will not have been made in vain: if anything in my remarks seems to you capable of being improved, it would not be out of place for you to tell us how."

"As far as I can see," I replied, "everything was well and learnedly taught by him and has been well and diligently applied in practice by you. All that one could ask is that more had been said, and especially on this question: whether the care and governance of a family are one thing or more than one, and whether, if they are more than one, they are the knowledge and practice of a single thing or of more."

"You are right," he said. "On this question my father's discourse was deficient, for governing a private household is different from governing a princely house-

non ne ragionasse perché la cura delle case de' principi ad uomo privato non s'appartiene. Molto più veloce intenditore siete stato voi, diss' io, ch' io non avrei creduto; ma poi che trovato abbiamo che più siano i governi famigliari, resta che consideriamo se l'uno dall'altro per grandezza solamente o ancora per ispezie sia differente, conciosiacosa che, se per grandezza solo sarà diverso, sì com'al medesimo architetto appertiene il considerar la forma del gran palagio e della picciola casa, così del medesimo curatore sarà propria la cura della gran casa e della picciola. Così diss' io; ed egli: Se veloce intenditore sono stato, non sarò pronto ritrovatore o giudizioso giudice delle cose trovate; ma pur direi che, s'a me darebbe il cuore di governare qual si voglia gran casa privata, ma non peraventura la famiglia d'un picciol principe, posso creder che la casa del privato da quella del principe per altro che per la grandezza sola sia differente. Ben avete estimato, diss' io, perché, sì come il principe dal privato per ispezie è distinto e sì come distinti sono i modi del lor commandare, così anco distinti sono i governi delle case de' principi e de' privati; perch' in parità di numero eziandio, quando pur avenisse che la famiglia d'un povero principe fosse sì picciola come quella d'un ricchissimo privato, diversamente debbono esser governate.

Tutta volta, se vero è quel che nel *Convito* di Platone da Socrate ad Aristofane è provato, ch'ad un medesimo artefice appertenga il comporre la comedia e la tragedia, se ben la comedia e la tragedia sono non sol diverse di spezie ma quasi contrarie, vero dee esser in conseguenza ch' il buono economico non meno sappia governar la famiglia d'un principe che la privata, e ch'alla medesima facoltà appertenga trattar parimente di tutti i governi: e io ho veduto in un libretto, ch'ad

hold. But I should say that he did not discuss the latter because it is not the business of a private man."

"You understand much more quickly than I expected," I remarked. "Now that we have discovered that there is more than one variety of family rule, we must consider whether one differs from the other in kind or simply because because of the different sizes of the households involved. If they differ simply because of size, just as the same architect must understand the plans of a great palace and a small house, the same guardian should know how to care for both large and small households."

Thus I spoke, and he replied: "I may be quick to understand, but I am not quick to discover new ideas on my own, nor am I a good judge of them when they are discovered. I will say, however, that since I should dare to govern any large private house but perhaps not that of even a small prince, I think that private households differ from those of princes in other ways besides size."

"You judge well," I remarked, "for just as a prince and his method of commanding differ in kind from a private man and his, so too the methods of governing princely and private households differ. And this holds true even when there is no difference of size. If the household of a poor prince were no larger than that of a very rich private man, the two households would nevertheless need to be governed differently."

"Yet if it is true, as Socrates proves to Aristophanes in Plato's *Symposium*, that the same artist should be able to compose both tragedies and comedies in spite of the fact that comedy and tragedy are not only different in kind but almost contrary to each other,[75] it ought to follow that the good household manager knows how to govern princely as well as private households, and that the same faculty properly deals with all

Aristotele è attribuito, che quattro sono i governi, o le dispensazioni della casa che vogliam chiamarle, la regia, la satrapica, la civile e la privata. La qual distinzion io non riprovo, perché, se bene i tempi nostri sono dagli antichi in molte cose differenti, veggo ch' i governi delle case del viceré di Napoli e di Sicilia e del governator di Milano così per proporzione corrispondo a quello delle case reali com'anticamente quello de' satrapi; la qual proporzione ancora si può ritrovare fra le case de i duchi di Savoia, di Ferrara e di Mantova e quelle de' governatori d'Asti, di Vercelli, di Modona e di Reggio e di Monferrato. Ma non veggio già come sia diverso il governo civile della casa dal privato, se forse civile egli non chiama quello dell'uomo ch'attende a gli onori della republica, e privato quel di colui che, separato dalla republica, tutto s' impiega nella cura famigliare: e che ciò così stia, si può raccorre da quelle parole ch'egli dice, che 'l governo privato è minimo e trae utilità eziandio dalle cose che dagli altri son disprezzate; ove per altri dee intender gli uomini civili ch'occupati in cose d'alto affare, molte cose disprezzano che da' privati non son disprezzate. Ma percioch'esser potrebbe ch'alcun de' vostri figliuoli, seguendo gli essempi del zio, ne' servigi delle corti volesse adoperarsi, vorrei ch'alcuna cosa ancora della cura della famiglia reale si ragionasse; ma già l'ora è sì tarda che no 'l concede, tuttoché poche cose oltre le dette si possono addurre, le quali egli parte da' libri d'Aristotele e parte dall'esperienza delle corti potrà facilmente apparare.

Così diss' io; ed egli, mostrando di rimanere alle mie parole sodisfatto, levandosi, in quella camera mi condusse che per me era stata apparecchiata, ov' io in un agiatissimo letto diedi le membra affaticate dal viaggio al riposo e alla quiete.

kinds of government. In a little book by Aristotle I have read that there are four ways of governing a household—four household dispensations, so to speak: the royal, the satrapic, the civic, and the private.[76] I have no disagreement with these distinctions, for while our times are in many ways different from antiquity, I see that the household governments of the viceroy of Naples and Sicily and of the governor of Milan are related to royal houses today in the same way as satrapic households were related to royal households in ancient times. And the same relationship exists between the households of the dukes of Savoy, Ferrara, and Mantua, on the one hand, and those of the governors of Asti, Vercelli, Modena, Reggio, and Monferrato, on the other.[77] I do not quite understand, however, how the civic way of governing a household differs from the private, unless perhaps he means by civic the government of a man who seeks the honors of a republic and by private the government of one who withdraws from public life and devotes himself wholly to family affairs. That this might be the case can be gathered from the passage in which he says that the private way of governing a household is the lowest way and makes use of things that are disdained by the other ways.[78] Since some of your sons may want to follow the example of their uncle and serve at court, however, I should like some further discussion of the care of a royal family, but the hour is already late and prevents it. In any case, there is little to add to what has been said, and this he can easily learn in part from the books of Aristotle and in part from experience with courts."

Thus I spoke. The father expressed his satisfaction with what I had said and, rising, led me to the chamber that had been prepared. There, in a most comfortable bed, I surrendered my travel-wearied limbs to rest and quiet.

Malpiglio,
or On the Court

Malpiglio, or On the Court offers a witty
examination of the political and social
institution that dominated much of Tasso's
life. The young Giovanlorenzo Malpiglio
wants to become a courtier; his father,
Vincenzo, wishes Giovanlorenzo were less
attracted to the court and more attentive to
his studies; the Neapolitan Stranger, who
functions as Tasso's spokesman, presents a
cautiously balanced view, stressing the
court's potential virtues but also hinting at
its dangers.

Il Malpiglio
overo de la corte

Interlocutori:
VINCENZO E GIOVANLORENZO MALPIGLIO,
FORESTIERO NAPOLITANO

v.m.   Noi siamo a buona ora avisati de la vostra venuta.

f.n.   E da chi sì tosto l'avete inteso?

v.m.   Da mio figliuolo, il quale è stato il primo a saperlo, perché desiderava di venir con esso noi a diporto.

f.n.   Non volete condurlo e compiacerlo in questo?

v.m.   Non possiamo oggi andarvi perché non abbiamo il cocchio, se forse con qualche barchetta non volessimo passar a San Giorgio. Ma 'l desiderio di mio figliuolo non era tanto di vedere il monistero, ov' è stato molte volte, quanto d'udirvi ragionare in qualche materia, e particolarmente de la corte: e forse per riverenza non ve l' ha palesato; ma spesso meco e con la madre s' è doluto di non avere occasione.

f.n.   Poco da me ne potete udire, perch' in questa corte sono anzi nuovo e inesperto che no, e ne l'altre ho sì rade volte usato che molto m'avanza che ricercarne.

v.m.   Ove manca peraventura l'esperienza, abonda l' ingegno, il sapere e la dottrina, sì ch'a niun altro egli si potrebbe avvenire, da cui più credesse d'intenderne.

f.n.   S'egli non cerca i prattici cortigiani, ma coloro che ne parlano o scrivono per alcuna scienza, molti potrà ritrovarne, a' quali io sono tanto inferior di sapere

Malpiglio,
or On the Court[1]

Interlocutors:
VINCENZO MALPIGLIO,
GIOVANLORENZO MALPIGLIO,
NEAPOLITAN STRANGER[2]

V.M.　We learned of your arrival early this morning.

N.S.　From whom did you learn so soon?

V.M.　From my son. He was the first to know, because he has been eager to come with us on this excursion.

N.S.　Do you not want to bring him along and humor his eagerness?

V.M.　We cannot go today because we do not have the coach—unless you want to take a small boat over to San Giorgio. But my son was not as eager to see the monastery, which he has visited many times, as he was to hear you talk, particularly about the court. Out of respect he may never have revealed this desire to you, but to me and to his mother he has often complained that he has never had a chance to listen to you.

N.S.　You cannot learn much from me on this subject. I am rather new and inexperienced in this court, and I have been around the others so little that it would do me a lot of good to find out about them myself.

V.M.　It sometimes happens that wit, knowledge, and learning abound where experience is lacking. There is no one from whom he could expect to learn more.

N.S.　If he is not looking for actual courtiers but rather for men who speak or write about them knowl-

quanto minor d'età; ma fratanto può leggere i libri di coloro c' hanno formata l' idea del cortigiano.

v.m.   Egli ha letto il *Cortigiano* del Castiglione e lo ha quasi a mente, e forse meglio che l' *Epistole* di Cicerone o le *Comedie* di Terenzio; ma desidera d' intender cose nuove, avendo udito dal nostro Sanminiato che le corti si mutano a' tempi.

f.n.   Chi forma l' idea non figura alcuna imagine che si muti con la mutazione fatta de gli anni, ma, isguardando in cosa stabile e ferma, la ci reca ne' suoi scritti quale nel pensiero l' ha formata. Né stimo già che 'l Castiglione volesse scrivere a gli uomini de' suoi tempi solamente, tuttoch'egli alcuna volta faccia per gioco menzione di que' più vecchi cortigiani i quali al tempo di Borso portarono lo sparaviero in pugno per una leggiadra usanza: perché la bellezza de' suoi scritti merita che da tutte l'età sia letta e da tutte lodata; e mentre dureranno le corti, mentre i principi, le donne e i cavalieri insieme si raccoglieranno, mentre valore e cortesia avranno albergo ne gli animi nostri, sarà in pregio il nome del Castiglione. Ma s'alcuna cosa è forse la qual si cambi e si vari co' secoli e con l'occasioni, non è di quelle che son principali nel cortigiano: laonde io non posso se non lodar vostro figliuolo ch'abbia più tosto voluto per suo famigliare il formator de le corti che lo scrittor de le comedie.

v.m.   Se per l'adietro egli volentieri leggeva il *Cortigiano*, per l'avvenire no 'l lascerà giamai, poiché da voi tanto è commendato, al quale non soglion piacere tutte le cose che piacciono a gli altri.

f.n.   Molte sono le cagioni per le quali onoro la memoria del Castiglione, e mi riserbo di parlarne con maggiore opportunità.

v.m.   Ma pur in questo libro alcune particelle furono già da voi notate, le quali mio figliuolo non vorrebbe udire da alcun altro che da voi: perché la verità de le

edgeably, he will be able to find many who surpass me as much in knowledge as in age. And in the meantime he can read the books of those who have described the ideal courtier.

v.m.   He has read Castiglione's *Courtier* and has almost memorized it. He may know it better than Cicero's *Epistles* or Terence's *Comedies*. But he wants to learn about new developments, for he has heard from our Sanminiato that courts change with the times.[3]

n.s.   The man who creates an image of the ideal does not base it on anything mutable; he gazes on what is stable and fixed and re-creates it in his writing as he has formed it in his thought. I certainly do not think that Castiglione wanted to write only for the men of his time. Although sometimes he jokes about those old-fashioned courtiers who, in Borso's day, used to carry a sparrow hawk on their wrists as a mark of elegance,[4] the beauty of Castiglione's writing should make it read and praised in every age; while courts last, while princes, ladies, and knights assemble, and while courage and courtesy dwell in our souls, his name will be prized. And if, by chance, there is something in courtiers which alters and varies with time and occasion, it is not essential. I can only praise your son, therefore, for having taken to heart the creator of courts rather than the writer of comedies.

v.m.   If he was eager to read *The Courtier* before, now that it has been so highly commended by you he will never put it down, for you are seldom pleased by all those things that please others.

n.s.   I honor the memory of Castiglione for many reasons, and I shall speak of them when I have more opportunity.

v.m.   You have commented on some parts of his book before this, however, and my son would like to hear those comments from you personally rather than

cose le quali passano di lingua in lingua, molte volte si perde, come l'altre che sono trasportate di luogo in luogo.

F.N.   La mia è balba, com'udite, ma pur assai vera e fedel interprete de l'animo: laonde ciò che dentro l'intelletto scrive o dipinge, ella si sforza di mandar fuori con parole assai popolari, a le quali ne son mescolate alcune raccolte da' libri non per istudio posto da me nel parlare, ma per usanza ch'io ho di leggere o di scrivere: e per questa cagione non ragiono se non famigliarmente con gli amici co' quali ho ragionato altre volte in questo soggetto. Ma le cose richiamate in dubbio furono assai poche in comperazione di quelle ch'io lodai, le quali son molte: e di quelle poche non ben mi ricordo, perché la mia indebolita memoria è simile ad una pittura ne la qual, se pur v'è alcuna imagine formata, i colori ne son caduti e bisogna rinovarli: e percioch'avviene assai spesso che non solo il simile ci riduce in mente il simile, ma il contrario il contrario, molte volte l'opinioni de gli altri mi fanno ricordar le mie, de le quali mi dimentico agevolmente. Non è dunque maraviglia ch'io ne divenga sollecito investigatore.

V.M.   Mio figliuolo vorrebbe esser oggi participe di que' medesimi ragionamenti domestici i quali solete far con gli amici: perché, se maggior cosa volgete ne l'animo, ora non ardirebbe di pregarvi che la manifestiate.

F.N.   La materia propostami è così ampia che non si può tutta ristringere in un breve discorso; e 'l fare elezione de le cose più importanti è difficile altrettanto quanto il narrarle tutte partitamente. Ma di quali egli vorrebbe che particolarmente si ragionasse?

V.M.   Questo a lui medesimo richiedete; che se vergogna no 'l ritiene, certo per averne picciol desiderio non si ramarrà di rispondervi.

from someone else. Like merchandise transported from place to place, truth passed from tongue to tongue is often lost.

N.S.   My tongue falters, as you hear,[5] yet it represents my mind truly and faithfully enough. Whatever my mind writes or describes within itself, my tongue strives to bring forth in popular terms mixed with some fruits of my reading. These appear not because of any deliberate effort on my part but simply as a result of my habitual reading and writing. Because of my manner of speaking, I usually do not discuss things except in familiar terms and with my friends. It was among friends that I formerly talked about this subject, but the things that I criticized were few in comparison with the many that I praised. Moreover, I do not remember those few very clearly, for my weakened memory is like a painting in which some form remains but which has lost its color and which needs retouching. And as it frequently happens that not only similar things but also contraries bring each other to mind, so the opinions of others often make me recall what I so easily forget. It is no wonder, then, that I examine other men's opinions so carefully.

V.M.   My son wants to take part in one of those intimate discussions which you usually have with your friends. If you have something more important on your mind, he would not presume to ask you to reveal it now.

N.S.   The subject you propose cannot be treated briefly as a whole, and to choose its more important part is as hard as to discuss each part separately. But what is he most interested to hear about?

V.M.   Ask him, not me. Unless he is ashamed he will not hesitate to answer. He certainly will not be held back by lack of desire.

F.N.   Piacciavi dunque, signor Lorenzo, ch' io sappia la vostra intenzione.

G.M.   Io vorrei spezialmente sapere come s'acquisti la grazia de' principi e come si schivi l' invidia e la malivoglienza de' cortigiani.

F.N.   Non è mica picciola dimanda, perché ne la grazia del principe e ne la benevoglienza de i cortigiani tutte l'altre cose paiono esser contenute. Ma questo a che fine, di ragionarne solamente o pur d'operare?

G.M.   D'operar più tosto.

F.N.   Dunque volete esser cortigiano? Voi non rispondete?

V.M.   Vorrebbe, e si vergogna di palesarlo perché teme ch' io non me ne sodisfaccia, al qual piacerebbe più tosto ch'egli attendesse a lo studio.

G.M.   In vero non mi spiacerebbe l'esser cortigiano, perch' io sono allevato in questa città, ne la quale il valor de gli uomini risplende più chiaramente ne le corti ch' in altro luogo; ma nondimeno mi sarebbe grave di tralasciare gli studî, perché mi pare che ne le corti simili a questa accrescano molto d'ornamento a' cavalieri.

V.M.   E de la cavalleria s' è invaghito parimente.

G.M.   In questo proposito avrei caro particolarmente intendere quali sono l'operazioni del cavaliero.

F.N.   Le operazion di cavaliero chiamate, se non m'inganno, il cavalcare, il correre a la quintana e a l'anello, il giostrare, il combattere a la sbarra e nel torneamento.

G.M.   Queste.

F.N.   Ma non vi paiono ancora operazioni di cavaliero quelle che fa il liberale donando, e 'l magnifico albergando ed edificando, e 'l forte esponendosi a' pericoli de la guerra?

N.S.   If you please, then, Signor Lorenzo, let me know what you want.

G.M.   I should especially like to know how to win grace from princes and avoid the envy and ill will of courtiers.

N.S.   That is no small demand, for in the grace of princes and the goodwill of courtiers every other part of the subject seems to be contained. But why do you ask this—for the sake of argument only or for some practical end?

G.M.   More for a practical end.

N.S.   Then you want to be a courtier? Why do you not answer?

V.M.   He wants to be one, and he is ashamed to answer because he is afraid that I shall be angry. It would please me more if he would attend to his studies.

G.M.   In fact it would not displease me to be a courtier, for I have been brought up in this city where a man's worth shines out more clearly in courts than anywhere else. I am reluctant to abandon my studies altogether, however, because it seems to me that they confer great luster on gentlemen in courts such as ours.

V.M.   He is in love with chivalry too.

G.M.   As for chivalry, I am especially eager to hear about what gentlemen do.

N.S.   Unless I am mistaken, the activities considered proper for a gentleman are riding, tilting at the quintain and at the ring, jousting, and fighting in the lists and at tournaments.

G.M.   Those are the ones.

N.S.   But do you not also find it proper for a gentleman to make gifts like a liberal man, to provide hospitality and to engage in building like a magnificent man, and to expose himself to the dangers of war like a brave man?

G.M. Oltre tutte l'altre mi paiono azioni di cavaliero: e questa ho creduta sempre che fosse la cagione per la quale alcuni cortegiani non solamente hanno seguito il principe ne le guerre, ma con sua licenza, mentre egli in pace governava il suo stato, sono andati ricercandole.

F.N. Dunque gli essercizî del corpo e 'l valor de l'animo e le virtù de' costumi saranno quelle, o signor Giovanlorenzo, che faranno il cortigiano assai grato al suo principe.

G.M. Saranno.

F.N. Ma ne le corti si stimano le virtù egualmente, o l'una più de l'altra?

G.M. Io stimo che sian più stimate la fortezza e la liberalità, perch'elle più giovano a ciascuno.

F.N. E peraventura le più stimate son quelle che prendono l'animo del signore, perch' è ragionevole ch'egli ami più coloro de' quali si fa maggiore stima.

G.M. Assai mi pare ciò ragionevole.

F.N. Or vorrem noi che s'esserciti il corpo solamente del cortigiano, o quella parte de l'animo la qual è soggetta a le passioni, o l'intelletto ancora?

G.M. L'intelletto parimente.

F.N. Dunque si debbono apprender le matematiche scienze e la filosofia de' costumi e la naturale e la divina, e aver buona cognizione de gli istorici e de' poeti e de gli oratori e de l'arti più nobili, come sono quella de lo scolpire e del pingere e l'architettura: e di tutte queste cose il cortigiano dee tanto sapere che non possa alcuno riprenderlo d' ignoranza, perch' in tal guisa egli sarà molto onorato dal principe, e la benevolenza seguirà l'onore.

G.M. Niuna altra cosa mi pare così vera: perché l'amar quel che non si stima non par che proceda mai da giudizio, ma sempre da passione.

G.M.   More than all the others, in fact, these seem to me to be a gentleman's proper activities. And I have always believed this to be the reason that some courtiers have not only followed their own prince to war but have even, with his permission, gone out to seek other wars when he was governing in peace.

N.S.   Then physical training, a good mind, and moral virtue, Signor Giovanlorenzo, are what make a courtier pleasing to his prince.

G.M.   So they are.

N.S.   But are the virtues all esteemed equally in courts, or one more than another?

G.M.   I suppose that courage and liberality are the most esteemed, because they are the most useful to everyone.

N.S.   And perhaps the virtues which are most esteemed are also the ones which most impress the lord of the court. It is reasonable for him to prefer those which are valued most highly.

G.M.   It seems reasonable enough to me.

N.S.   Well now, do we want the courtier to exercise only his body? Or only that part of his soul which is subject to the passions? Or his intellect too?

G.M.   His intellect too.

N.S.   Then he ought to learn mathematics and moral philosophy as well as natural science and theology, and he ought to be well acquainted with the historians, the poets, the orators, and with the noble arts, such as sculpture, painting, and architecture. He ought to know enough about all of these subjects so that no one can accuse him of ignorance. Such knowledge will win high honor from his prince, and goodwill will follow honor.

G.M.   In my opinion nothing is truer. Love for what is not esteemed never seems to result from judgment but always from passion.

F.N.   Ma l'eccelenza di tutte queste arti e di tutte quelle virtù è degna d'alcuna invidia?

G.M.   Anzi di molta.

F.N.   Quelle cose medesime dunque le quali acquistan la benevoglienza de' principi, generan l' invidia cortigiana: laonde, non si potendo l'una e l'altra conseguire, non ci debbiamo curar d'esser invidiati da la corte, o non conviene con tanto studio ricercar la grazia de' signori.

G.M.   Gran difficoltà è questa; ma senza l'uno e l'altro non istimo che 'l cortigiano possa giamai esser felice.

F.N.   Dunque per altre vie che per queste di tante virtù, di tante scienze e di tante cose apparenti e risguardevoli dee procedere il cortigiano a due fini così disgiunti, se pur le cose disgiunte si possono congiungere per artificio.

G.M.   Questo era quello a punto ch'aspettava d'intendere.

F.N.   Io, come ho detto, sono quasi smemorato, però non mi sovvengono tutte le cose da me pensate altre volte; ma, ricercandole, soglio richiamarle ne la memoria: e se vi piace, mi potreste aiutare in questa investigazione, altramente se ne potrebbe smarrire alcuna. Or cominciamo da questo lato: non vi pare che la corte sia un'adunanza overo una compagnia?

G.M.   Certo.

F.N.   E de l'adunanze alcune son fatte per diletto, come quelle del carnevale, ne le quali ciascun porta la sua parte de la cena e si sforza di superar ciascuno ne la bontà de le vivande e de' vini preziosi; altre sono raccolte insieme per utilità, come le compagnie di mercanti; ma questa de la corte, quantunque ad alcuni sia molto utile, a molti piacevole, nondimeno non è congregata per utile o per diletto simplicemente, ma per altra cagione.

N.S.   But is excellence in all these arts and virtues worthy of any envy?

G.M.   Of a great deal, in fact.

N.S.   Then those very things that win goodwill from princes cause envy in courtiers, and since it is impossible to attain both of the goals you mentioned earlier, we must either cease to care about being envied by the court or refrain from seeking the grace of princes with so much eagerness.

G.M.   This is a great difficulty, for without both the prince's grace and the goodwill of other courtiers I do not see how the courtier can ever be happy.

N.S.   If there is any way to achieve two such disparate goals, then, it will not be through great virtue or knowledge or other such qualities which call attention to themselves but through some other art.

G.M.   This is exactly what I have been waiting to hear about.

N.S.   As I said, my memory is almost gone, and my former ideas do not help me much any more. When I make an effort, however, I often recall them. And you can help me too, if you will, to keep this inquiry from going astray. Now, let us begin in this way. Would you not say that the court is a gathering or a company?

G.M.   Of course.

N.S.   And some gatherings are for pleasure—carnival parties, for example, when everyone brings part of the feast and tries to outdo everyone else by providing better food and more precious wines. Other gatherings are utilitarian, like the merchant companies. But the gathering which constitutes a court, albeit useful to some and pleasurable to many, has a completely different purpose.

G.M.   Così stimo.

F.N.   Ma qual altra può essere che l'onore?

G.M.   Niun'altra a mio parere.

F.N.   Ma chi dicesse che fosse il servizio del principe?

G.M.   Direbbe quasi il medesimo, perch'altri serve i principi per onore.

F.N.   La corte dunque è congregazion d'uomini raccolti per onore.

G.M.   È veramente.

F.N.   Ma lo onore s'acquista ne le republiche ancora, ne le quali il padre vostro e gli avoli con la giustizia e co 'l valore e con l'altre virtù cittadine conseguirono i principali magistrati e furono più volte ne' supremi gradi de la civil dignità.

G.M.   Io sono così amico a la buona fama de' nostri maggiori ch'assai volentieri confermo quel che voi dite non senza verità, ma con molta cortesia.

F.N.   L'onor dunque si ricerca ne la republica e ne la corte.

G.M.   Ne l'una e ne l'altra.

F.N.   Ma se la republica e la corte sono l'istessa adunanza, l'onore il quale si propone per fine dovrebbe esser il medesimo: e se le compagnie son diverse, diverso parimente sarà l'onore.

G.M.   Pare assai ragionevole.

F.N.   Dunque, concedendo quello che si conosce chiaramente, la republica non esser corte, mi concederete che non sia l'istesso onore quel che ne l'una e ne l'altra è ricercato: e voi l'onore de la republica, anzi gli onori non desiderate, ma bramate que' de la corte; e se questo è vero, non vorrei che nel vederli fosser da noi presi gli uni per gli altri.

G.M.   I agree.

N.S.   What end could it have but honor?

G.M.   None whatsoever, in my opinion.

N.S.   But what if someone should say that courts exist for the service of princes?

G.M.   He would be saying almost the same thing, because it is honor that makes men serve princes.

N.S.   The court, then, is a gathering for the sake of honor.

G.M.   It is indeed.

N.S.   But honor can be acquired in republics too. Your father and grandfathers lived in a republic, and with their justice, their courage, and the other virtues of citizens they obeyed the principal magistrates and often reached the highest ranks of civil dignity themselves.

G.M.   I love the reputation of my ancestors so much that I shall agree willingly with what you have said. Your words are not untrue, and they are also very courteous.

N.S.   Honor, then, is sought both in republics and in courts.

G.M.   In both.

N.S.   But if republics and courts are the same kind of gathering, each ought to be seeking the same kind of honor, and if they are different, they will seek different kinds of honor.

G.M.   That seems reasonable enough.

N.S.   It is obvious, however, as I am sure you will agree, that republics and courts are not the same and that the same kind of honor is not sought in both. You do not desire republican honor or, I should say, honors; you long for the honors of a court. And if this is the case, I do not want our discussion to mistake one kind of honor for the other.

G.M.   È facil cosa che io gli prenda per iscambio, come avviene de' simili.

F.N.   È convenevol dunque che procuriamo di separarli in guisa che la somiglianza non c' inganni e la dissimilitudine ancora non vi spaventi dal vostro nobile proponimento. Ditemi dunque: non credete ch' i cittadini desiderino gli onori de la republica?

G.M.   Sogliono molti e quasi tutti desiderarli.

F.N.   E quali son più desiderati, i minori o pure i maggiori e i supremi?

G.M.   I maggiori e i supremi.

F.N.   Ma coloro ch'ottengono gli onori e le dignità supreme commandano a gli altri?

G.M.   Così avviene.

F.N.   Dunque il desiderar sovrano onore ne la republica altro non è che desiderio di commandare.

G.M.   È desiderio di commandare secondo le buone leggi e come si conviene a gli uomini che son cresciuti in libertà: perché, s'alcuno in altra guisa tentasse di commandare, avrebbe spesso in vece d'onore l' infamia che soglion dare le republiche a' tiranni e a gli altri usurpatori.

F.N.   Né io altramente intendo, quantunque molte volte le republiche mutino forma in meglio, e si conceda per utilità publica autorità sovrana a principi prudentissimi, come fu . . . , ; la quale autorità molti hanno cercata, molti non rifiutata, adoprandola per beneficio di coloro a' quali si commanda.

G.M.   Così in molte republiche molte volte è succeduto.

F.N.   Ma 'l desiderio d'onore il qual sospinge il cortigiano a la grazia del signore è desiderio di commandare o di servir più tosto?

G.M.   Anzi di servire che di commandare.

F.N.   Il signor Lorenzo Malpiglio dunque, figliuolo di tanti illustri cittadini, i quali han commandato a gli

G.M.   I confuse them easily, as often happens when things are similar.

N.S.   Then we must manage to keep them distinct so that the similarity does not deceive us and also so that the difference does not frighten you away from your noble purpose. Tell me, now, do you not think that citizens desire republican honors?

G.M.   Many do. Usually almost all of them do.

N.S.   And which honors are the most desired: the lesser or the greater and highest?

G.M.   The greater and highest.

N.S.   But do not those who obtain the highest honors and dignity rule the others?

G.M.   That is the way it turns out.

N.S.   In a republic, then, the desire for supreme honor is nothing less than the desire to rule.

G.M.   It is a desire to rule in accord with good laws and in a way suitable to men raised in freedom, for anyone who tries to rule differently often wins instead of honor the infamy that republics usually confer upon tyrants and other usurpers.

N.S.   I meant nothing else. Republics often change for the better, however, and for the sake of the public good, they surrender their sovereign authority to princes of the highest prudence. Such a prince was. . . .[6] Many have sought such authority, and many who have been offered it have accepted for the good of those they ruled.

G.M.   That is the way it has happened in many republics.

N.S.   But what about the love of honor that drives the courtier to seek grace from his prince? Is it a desire to rule or to serve?

G.M.   To serve, not to rule.

N.S.   Am I to conclude that Signor Lorenzo Malpiglio, descended from so many illustrious citizens,

altri leggitimamente, non ha il medesimo desiderio di onore, ma desidera di servire? Essend'egli d'animo generoso, non è verisimile che, lasciato l'onor del commandare, seguisse questo che si ritrova ne la servitù, se lo splendor d'alcuna rara virtù non l'abbagliasse, o più tosto non l' illustrasse: perciochè questi medesimi i quali servono a' principi commandano assai volte ad uomini eccelenti e a signori con maggiore e più libera autorità di quella che ne le republiche è conceduta.

G.M.   Ne le republiche si serve e si commanda parimente: perciochè coloro che sono ne l' infimo ordine seguono i commandamenti del primo, e alcuna volta quelli che inanzi commandorono ubbediscono dapoi, e quelli che prima ubbedirono al fine commandano a gli eguali: anzi quelli stessi ch'ascendono a' magistrati supremi sono come servi de le leggi.

F.N.   Ma la servitù è diversa: l'una chiameran più tosto libertà, benché abbia qualche simiglianza di servitù; l'altra servitù, quantunque in molte azioni dimostri la grandezza del principato.

G.M.   Assai mi pare ch' i nomi a le cose abbiate compartiti.

F.N.   Ma l'onor ch' è in queste maniere di vite nasce da virtù.

G.M.   Nasce senza fallo.

F.N.   Ma se fosse diversa la virtù de l'una e de l'altra, come si dubita, noi debbiam cercar quella del cortigiano.

G.M.   Quella, pare, e non altro.

F.N.   E forse meglio la conosceremo, se con l'altra, ch' è del cittadino, faremo di lei paragone. Or quale stimate voi che sia la virtù che si ricerca principalmente al buon cittadino?

G.M.   Alcuni han creduto la fortezza e la liberalità, le quali son tanto onorate, come testimoniano le statue

from men who have exercised legitimate rule over others, does not have the same desire for honor as his ancestors but prefers to serve? With his generous spirit he would hardly abandon the honor of ruling for the honor of serving if the splendor of some rare quality had not dazzled him, or rather illuminated him. The servants of princes often rule worthy men and lords with a greater and more independent authority than republics ever give.

G.M.   In republics, a man both serves and rules. Men in the lower ranks obey their leaders, but sometimes the positions are reversed. Then those who used to rule their equals obey, and those who once obeyed rule. And even those who have reached the highest offices are like servants of the laws.

N.S.   But there are different kinds of servitude. In spite of appearances, we prefer to call this one freedom, and we call what I was describing servitude, although in many ways it reveals the greatness of princely rule.

G.M.   It seems to me that you have very nicely given things their proper names.

N.S.   In courts and in republics alike, however, honor springs from virtue.

G.M.   Without fail.

N.S.   And if the virtues of the courtier and of the citizen differ, as we may suspect, we must try to discover the courtier's.

G.M.   His, it seems, and no other.

N.S.   Perhaps we shall be able to recognize his virtue more readily, however, if we compare it with the other, the virtue of the citizen. Which virtue do you think is most sought after by good citizens?

G.M.   Some say courage and liberality, for the statues, funeral orations, verses, and other memorials,

dirizzate a' valorosi, l'orazioni funebri e i versi e gli altri segni d'onore publici e privati.

F.N.   E la virtù suprema del cortigiano pare a voi la fortezza o pur alcuna altra?

G.M.   La fortezza parimente, la qual è propria virtù del cavaliero: e quella è cui più si conviene il saper adoperar l'armi per onor proprio e per servigio del suo principe.

F.N.   Nondimeno la fortezza così civile come cortigiana per difetto di prudenza è precipitata molte volte in casi molti pericolosi, come a' tempi antichi (ché mi giova tacer de' nostri) quella di Flaminio e di Minuzio e di Paulo o pur di Regolo istesso.

G.M.   Così avvenne.

F.N.   Ha dunque bisogno di guida e di freno e di chi la regga e l' indrizzi: e questa è la prudenza, senza cui la fortezza è cieca e temeraria, o più tosto non è vera fortezza.

G.M.   La fortezza a me par simile a' destrieri generosi, che quanto sono più feroci, tanto hanno maggior bisogno di morso.

F.N.   Tutta volta chi pare a voi più nobile, il cavallo o 'l cavaliero, il guidato o la guida, lo sfrenato o chi pone il freno?

G.M.   Non si può negar che non sia maggior nobiltà in coloro che governano ch' in quelli che son governati.

F.N.   La prudenza dunque, ch' è scorta de la fortezza, è più nobil virtù: e questa nel cittadino è civile e nel cortigiano peraventura è cortigiana prudenza.

G.M.   Facilmente mi persuadono le vostre ragioni.

F.N.   E la differenza ch' è fra l'una e l'altra è quella che si piglia dal fine: perciòch' il cortigiano ha per fine la riputazione e l'onor del principe, dal qual si deriva il proprio come rivo da fonte; e 'l cittadino la conservazione de la libertà.

G.M.   Assai questa differenza distingue l'una da l'al-

both public and private, dedicated to courageous men, testify to the honor in which these virtues are held.

N.S.   And does courage seem to you to be the highest virtue of the courtier, or is it some other?

G.M.   Courage is also the courtier's highest virtue. And to exercise it he must know how to use his arms for his own honor and for the service of his prince.

N.S.   All the same, both the courageous citizen and the courageous courtier often fall into grave danger through lack of prudence. I prefer not to mention our own times, but consider Flaminius, Minucius, Paullus, or even Regulus.[7]

G.M.   This happens.

N.S.   Courage, then, needs guidance and restraint and something to rule and direct it. This something is prudence; without prudence, courage is blind and rash. Indeed, it is not really courage at all.

G.M.   Courage seems to me like a generous war horse; the more spirited it is, the more it needs the bit.

N.S.   Which seems to you more noble, however, the horse or the rider, the thing guided or he who guides, the thing restrained or he who does the restraining?

G.M.   It cannot be denied that the ruler is more noble than the ruled.

N.S.   Therefore prudence, which guides courage, is the nobler virtue, and the citizen's prudence is civil while that of the courtier is courtly.

G.M.   Your arguments persuade me easily.

N.S.   And the difference between the two kinds of prudence derives from their ends, for the courtier's end is the reputation and honor of his prince, from which his own reputation and honor flow as a stream from a spring, while the citizen's end is the preservation of freedom.

G.M.   This nicely distinguishes the two kinds of pru-

tra, e ce le fa conoscere in quella maniera che le monete d'oro e d'argento sono conosciute per la diversità de l'imagine impressa.

F.N. Ma oltre questa prudenza èccene alcun'altra, o pur l'una basta ne la città e l'altra ne la corte? E accioch' io meglio mi dichiari, io vi chiedo s'a la prudenza del cittadino s'appartiene il far sue leggi e 'l riformale, e a quella del cortigiano il segnar le suppliche e 'l conceder le grazie non altramente ch'egli fosse il signore.

G.M. Questa sarebbe ne l'uno e ne l'altro impru-denza odiosa.

F.N. Dunque oltre questo è necessaria la prudenza del principe, la quale in comparazione de l'altre virtù è quasi architetto per rispetto de gli operari.

G.M. Necessaria senza dubbio.

F.N. La prudenza dunque del cortigiano consisterà ne l'essercitare i commandamenti del principe.

G.M. Così mi pare.

F.N. Ma l'essecutore e 'l ministro, in quanto egli è tale, è sempre inferiore a colui che gli commanda. Dunque dee il cortigiano in guisa operare ciò che gli è imposto che dimostri prudenza inferiore non sol di persona inferiore: e molte volte è disdicevole ch'egli spii le cagioni di quel che gli è commandato, o che voglia più saper di quel che gli conviene; ma con la sua piacevolezza e con la destrezza modera la severità de le commissioni, e come i venti prendon qualità da' luoghi onde passano, divenendo tepidi per camino, così le se-vere commissioni per l'accortezza del cortigiano so-gliono parer men dure e spiacevoli il più de le volte.

G.M. Assai per mio parere sarà lodato il cortigiano ch' in questo modo saprà ubbedire: e già veggio come

dence and makes it possible to tell them apart just as the different images on gold and silver coins make it possible to tell them apart.

N.S.   In addition to these kinds of prudence, however, is there another? Or is one of these adequate for the city and the other for the court? To speak more clearly, let me ask you whether the citizen's prudence extends to the making and reforming of his laws and whether that of the courtier includes the granting of petitions and the bestowing of grace as though he were the lord.

G.M.   In doing such things both citizens and courtiers would be acting with odious imprudence.

N.S.   In addition to the courtier's prudence, then, there must be the prince's. And the relationship of the prince's prudence to the other virtues is rather like the relationship of an architect to his workers.

G.M.   No doubt the prince's prudence is also necessary.

N.S.   The courtier's prudence, then, consists in carrying out the prince's orders.

G.M.   So it seems to me.

N.S.   But an executor and minister is, as such, inferior to a ruler. The fact that the courtier must obey orders shows that he is inferior not only in position but in prudence. It is often improper for him to inquire into the reasons behind the orders he receives; he must not want to know too much. With his charm and cleverness, however, he can soften the harshness of the prince's commands, and just as winds are modified by the lands through which they pass and become warm as they go along, so severity usually comes to seem less rigorous and wounding as a result of the courtier's skill.

G.M.   I think that the courtier who knows how to obey his prince in this manner will be highly praised.

insieme si possa acquistar la grazia del principe e la benevoglienza de' servitori, la qual da principio mi pareva
assai malagevole da conseguire.

F.N. L'inferiorità dunque manifestata ne la pronta
ubidienza e ne l'umiltà di non contradire è quella che fa
grato al principe il cortigiano.

G.M. Così stimo.

F.N. Ma perché colui che di prudenza è superiore,
per niun'altra cagione par che debba esser riputato inferiore, essendo l' intelletto quello al quale da la natura
è conceduto il principato, ogni maggioranza d'ingegno
suole essere odiosa al principe: laonde, quando ella sia
nel cortigiano, come aviene alcuna volta, dee più tosto
esser coperta con modestia che dimostrata con superba
apparenza. Dunque appari il cortigiano più tosto d'oc-
cultare che di apparere.

G.M. A me pare così difficile l'apparere quel ch' io
non sono, come il celar quel ch' io sono; nondimeno,
perché celando celerò molte imperfezioni e discoprendo
non discoprirei alcuna mia perfezione, prenderò partito
più volentieri di nascondermi che manifestarmi.

F.N. Questo nascondersi nondimeno si può fare
con alcuno avvedimento, per lo quale la picciola parte
che si dimostri generi desiderio di quella che si ricopre,
e una certa stima e opinion de gli uomini e del principe
medesimo, che dentro si nasconda un non so che di
raro e di singolare e di perfetto: il che par che più si
convenga a gli amatori del principato ch' a quelli del
principe, perché debbono mantener la sua riputazione
accioch' i consigli abbiano autorità; gli altri fanno
il principal fondamento sovra l'amore e sovra la
benevolenza.

G.M. Io amerei meglio essere un giorno simile ad
Efestione che molti anni eguale a Parmenione: laonde
niun mio difetto mi curerei di celare al principe, sì veramente ch'egli insieme conoscesse la fede.

Now I see how the prince's grace and the courtiers' goodwill can be acquired together—an accomplishment which at first seemed to me very difficult.

N.S.   Then a courtier who expresses his inferiority by obeying promptly and agreeing humbly will please his prince.

G.M.   I agree.

N.S.   But since the intellect is meant by nature to rule, it seems that the man who possesses superior prudence ought not to be considered inferior for any reason. And this is why princes usually hate any greatness of mind. When a courtier has great intelligence, which sometimes happens, he ought to cover it up modestly, not show it off with pride. Concealment becomes the courtier more than showing off.

G.M.   I think that it will be very difficult for me to seem to be what I am not and to hide what I am. Because I am imperfect in so many ways and perfect in none, however, I shall be more easily persuaded to hide than to show off.

N.S.   But this concealment can be shrewdly managed. The little part of oneself that is revealed can create a desire to know what is covered up; it can cause men generally and even the prince to believe that something rare, singular, and perfect is being hidden. But such shrewdness seems more appropriate in lovers of the principality than in lovers of the prince himself. For the former must maintain their reputations so that their counsels will have authority, but the latter build principally on love and goodwill rather than on authority.

G.M.   I should rather resemble Hephaestion for a single day than Parmenion for many years.[8] Therefore I should not try to hide any of my defects if my prince were also truly aware of my faithfulness.

F.N. Questi sono due modi e, per così dire, due strade per le quali si perviene quasi egualmente a la grazia del principe: ma l'una è propria de i consiglieri e de' secretari, l'altra di compagni e di quelli che servono a la persona; e se questi per quella o quelli per questa caminassero, non ci giungerebbono così agevolmente. Ciascun dunque deve elegger quella via che più gli si conviene, avendo risguardo a la nobiltà, a la ricchezza, a l' industria, al valore e a l'altre condizioni datele da la natura e da la fortuna.

G.M. Conoscitor di se stesso dunque dee essere il cortigiano.

F.N. La cognizion di se stesso dee preceder tutte l'altre; ma chi se medesimo conosce e conosce il principe, non può in modo alcuno ingannarsi, tuttoché al principe non si manifesti.

G.M. Il nascondersi al principe non è argomento di benevolenza.

F.N. È nondimeno segno di riverenza, perch' il discoprir tutte le passioni de l'animo si fa con molta domestichezza, la quale a le persone più gravi, come sono consiglieri e secretari, par meno conveniente: e s'alcun ve n' è mai, il quale con la cognizione e con la benevolenza, serrando e disserrando, soavemente s'apra l'animo del principe in modo che tolga tutti gli altri da i secreti, facilmente è sottoposto a l' invidia.

G.M. Questa vorrei sapere come si potesse schivare.

F.N. L'invidia è del principe verso i cortigiani o del cortigiano verso il principe o pur del cortigiano verso il cortigiano.

G.M. Io credo che 'l cortigiano non soglia mai invidiare il principe o 'l principe il cortigiano, ma che solamente porti invidia l'uno a l'altro cortigiano.

F.N. Nondimeno, o sia fastidio o riverenza, quella mestizia che genera l'apparente eccelenza, per la qual Pompeo pareva constristarsi a la presenza di Catone,

N.S.   There are two methods, two roads, so to
speak, by which to win a prince's grace; one is for counselors and secretaries and the other for those who serve
the prince's person. And if the latter group travels by
the former road or the former group by the latter road,
neither will arrive very easily. Everyone must consider
his rank, his wealth, his industriousness, his courage,
and the other qualities given him by nature and fortune; then he must choose the road that suits him.

G.M.   Then the courtier must know himself.

N.S.   Self-knowledge must precede all other knowledge. The courtier who knows himself as well as his
prince will never deceive himself in any way—
although he may not be open with his prince.

G.M.   Concealing oneself from one's prince is no argument of goodwill.

N.S.   But it is a sign of respect. Revealing all one's
passions smacks of too much familiarity in dignified
men such as counselors and secretaries. And any coun-
selor or secretary who exploits his knowledge and
favor, who manipulates the prince so as to gain access
to his soul and exclude others from his secrets, will be
subject to envy.

G.M.   That is what I want to know how to avoid.

N.S.   A prince can envy a courtier, a courtier can
envy a prince, or courtiers can envy each other.

G.M.   In my opinion a courtier is hardly likely to
envy a prince or a prince a courtier. Courtiers envy
only each other.

N.S.   All the same, there is a melancholy created in
some men by obvious excellence in others. Pompey
used to feel sad in the presence of Cato,[9] and, whether

dee schivarsi dal cortigiano non solamente quando egli ragiona con gli altri, ma quando è inanzi al principe istesso; né si può meglio fuggire che ricoprendo o, come dice alcuno, tacendo.

G.M.   Io niun altro migliore ne saprei ritrovare.

F.N.   Dunque occultando il cortigiano shiva la noia del principe, e occultando ancora par ch'egli possa celarsi da l'invidia cortigiana.

G.M.   Con l'arti medesime.

F.N.   Né solamente la dimostrata cognizione de le scienze divine e umane e quella de l' istoria e de la poesia e de l'arte oratoria, ma l'opinion del valore, ricercata armeggiando ambiziosamente, e la soverchia pompa e l' importuna liberalità e la magnificenza, che non prende, ma cerca l'occasioni, sogliono spesso generare invidia.

G.M.   Infelice dunque in questo è la vita de' cortigiani.

F.N.   E s'alcuno è fra' cortigiani il quale sia più dotto che ne la corte non par necessario, non deve amar le contese e le quistioni in quel modo che si fa ne le scuole de' filosofanti; perch'anzi buon loico che buon cortigiano si dimostrerebbe.

G.M.   Così mi pare.

F.N.   Dunque la prudenza è quella virtù che supera ne le corti tutte le difficultà, o la cognizione de le cose naturali; ma questa è propria del filosofo, quella del cavaliero: i quali, se pur son cortigiani, non debbon molto ricercar a gli altri ne le lettere o ne l' armi, perché, facendosi eguali in queste cose, superano con la prudenza, ch' è la principal virtù de le corti.

G.M.   In questo modo voi ristringete in una le molte virtù del cortigiano, e l'altre non ci avranno luogo.

out of politeness or respect, the courtier ought to avoid causing such melancholy when he is conversing with others and even when he is with the prince. The best way to accomplish this, moreover, is by concealment or, as some say, by keeping quiet.

G.M. I know of no better way.

N.S. By concealment, then, the courtier can avoid his prince's displeasure and also, it seems, protect himself from the envy of courtiers.

G.M. The same arts accomplish both ends.

N.S. Showing off one's knowledge of divine and human studies, of history, poetry, and oratory, however, is not the only way to cause envy. A reputation for courage, if it seems to have been won too ambitiously, excessive pomp, and that kind of liberality and magnificence which actually goes around looking for opportunities for display often have the same effect.

G.M. For this reason too, the courtier's life is unhappy.

N.S. Moreover, if some courtier is more learned than necessary, he ought not to love disputes and debates as they do in the schools of philosophy, or he will prove that he is a better logician than courtier.

G.M. So it seems.

N.S. Prudence, then, is the virtue that overcomes all difficulties at court—prudence or, perhaps, knowledge of nature. Properly speaking, however, the latter is the philosopher's virtue, while the former belongs to the knight. And when either a philosopher or a knight is also a courtier, he should not try to outdo others in letters or arms. For by making himself seem equal to the other courtiers in these activities he will conquer and show his superiority in prudence, which is the principal virtue in courts.

F.N.   La virtù del cortigiano è tutta la virtù, ma fra le particolari virtù maggiore è la prudenza: e questa non è disgiunta da l'altre; ma come il capitano conduce seco la sua schiera, così la prudenza è seguita da le virtù de i costumi, de le quali è lume e guida e quasi imperatrice.

G.M.   Ma forse non si mostreranno, quantunque siano sempre dove è la prudenza.

F.N.   Non tutte egualmente né sempre si manifestano, ma sì come ne le pitture con l'ombre s'accennano alcune parti lontane, altre sono da' colori più vivamente espresse, così avverrà parimente de le virtù che sono con la prudenza: perciochè la fortezza e la magnanimità e alcun'altre si veggono adombrate e paiono quasi di lontano discoprirsi; ma la magnificenza, la liberalità e quella che si chiama cortesia con proprio nome e la modestia è dipinta con più fini colori ch'abbia l'artificio del cortigiano, anzi viva più tosto: parimente le virtù del conversare, io dico la verità, l'affabilità e la piacevolezza.

G.M.   Io veggio non solo il disegno, ma l'imagine del cortigiano e 'l ritratto già colorito. E se l'altro del Castiglione fu per quella età ne la qual fu scritto, assai caro dovrà essere il vostro in questi tempi, in cui l'infinger è una de le maggior virtù.

F.N.   Ma può egli infingere il verace?

G.M.   Veggaselo Socrate e Giotto, a' quali niuna falsa accusa, niuna calunnia, niuna frode può torre il nome di verace, ma solamente soverchia modestia.

F.N.   Or credete voi ch'alcuna mediocrità sia mai soverchia?

G.M.   Veggio quel che volete conchiudere, che, s'ella è soverchia, non è mediocrità né virtù.

G.M.   By this argument you reduce the courtier's many virtues to one: the others have been left out.

N.S.   Courtly virtue includes all virtue, but the most important single virtue is prudence. It is not unconnected with the other virtues but rather leads them as a captain leads his company; it is their light, their guide, almost their empress.

G.M.   Perhaps they are not visible in spite of the fact that they are to be found wherever prudence is.

N.S.   Not all the virtues are always equally visible. Just as some parts of the background of a painting are hinted at with shadows while others are represented in a more lively way with colors, so it is with the virtues that accompany prudence. For courage, magnanimity, and certain other virtues appear sketched in and distant, while magnificence, liberality, courtesy itself, and modesty are done in the finest colors of the courtier's art—as though they were alive. The virtues of conversation—truthfulness, affability, and charm—are also presented in a lively manner.

G.M.   I see not only the outline of the courtier but his complete picture, his portrait in color. And if that other portrait, by Castiglione, was made for his time, the portrait you have made ought to be prized in these times when dissimulation is one of the most important virtues.

N.S.   But does an honest man dissimulate?

G.M.   Look at Socrates and Giotto. No false accusation, no calumny, no fraud, but only their excessive modesty could deprive them of their reputations for honesty.[10]

N.S.   Well now, do you believe that any mean can be excessive?

G.M.   I see what you wish to conclude. If something is excessive, it is neither a mean nor a virtue.

F.N.   Per aventura lo stringere altrui in questa guisa non s'appertiene a coloro che ragionano de la corte, ne la quale, se niuno eccesso è laudevole, questo co 'l quale si scemano le proprie laudi, oltre tutti gli altri merita lode e onore: come cortigiano dunque vi concederò facilmente, signor Lorenzo, che 'l simulare in questo modo sia virtù di corte, non solamente socratica.

G.M.   E di queste particolarmente che sono in fiore, de le quali io non ho molta certezza, ma pur n' ho sentito ragionar molte fiate.

F.N.   L'adattar le cose antiche a' tempi nostri è laudevol molto, purché si faccia acconciamente: nondimeno potrebbe parer a' cortigiani cosa odiosetta anzi che no, se alcun dicesse di non saper nulla e, riprovando sempre quel ch' è detto da gli altri, volesse rimaner al disopra in tutte le questioni: e l'uom si reca a minor vergogna di cedere a chi fa qualche professione di sapere, e può farla chi la può sostenere.

G.M.   E questi, che la possono sostenere, si veggono tutto dì ne le tavole de' principi.

F.N.   Ciò che voi dite è vero: nondimeno chi disputa ne le corti e aspira in tutti i modi a la vittoria e con tutte le persone egualmente senza risguardo e senza considerazion di tempi e di luoghi, è più tosto vago de la gloria che desidera il dialettico, che de l'onor cercato dal cortigiano, il qual non solamente ne le dispute, ma in tutte l'azioni de la vita dovrebbe contender, cedendo in quella guisa che fanno alcuni esperti lottatori, i quali, piegandosi a quella parte dove gli tira l'avversario, con questo pieghevole artificio più facilmente il gittano per terra.

G.M.   Assai piacevoli dunque saran que' contrasti d'ingegno che son convenienti a' cortigiani.

F.N.   Ma vogliam ritornare a quel che di sopra dicevamo, che la corte sia una ragunanza, come fanno

N.S.   Perhaps one should not be too strict on this point while discussing courts. For if no excess is wholly praiseworthy, yet the art of diminishing the praises one really deserves is more praiseworthy and honorable than any other excess at court. As a courtier, then, Signor Lorenzo, I readily confess that this kind of dissimulation is not only Socratic but also courtly.

G.M.   And it is especially necessary in the courts which flourish today. My knowledge is not very certain, but I have often heard about them.

N.S.   The adaptation of ancient things to our own times is very praiseworthy when it is done in the right way. Courtiers might find it rather exasperating, however, if one were to insist constantly upon one's ignorance while at the same time trying to win every debate by attacking the statements of others. It is less shameful to give in to a man who claims some knowledge of a subject and who can defend his claim.

G.M.   Men who can defend their claims to knowledge can be seen every day at the tables of princes.

N.S.   What you say is true. Nevertheless, the man who enters into discussions at court with a desire to win by any means and against everyone, without consideration of time or place, is more attracted by intellectual glory than by courtly honor. For not only in debate but in every activity, the courtier must compete by yielding, like certain expert fighters who give way when attacked and by a supple trick throw their opponents more easily to the ground.

G.M.   The courtier's witty encounters, then, ought to be pleasant.

N.S.   But do we want to go back, like men who have forgotten something or who are struck by some

coloro i quali hanno dimenticata alcuna cosa, o gli so-
pragiunge non pensata necessità?

G.M.   Come vi piace.

F.N.   Noi dicemmo che la corte è una congregazione d'uomini raccolta per onore.

G.M.   È vero.

F.N.   Ma questa congregazione vogliam presup-
porre che sia perfetta o imperfetta?

G.M.   Perfetta.

F.N.   E s'ella è perfetta, è bastevole a se stessa, o pur
non basta a se medesima?

G.M.   A bastanza contiene in se stessa tutto ciò che
l' è necessario.

F.N.   Ma tutte l'arti che son necessarie a la vita civile
son parimente necessarie al cortigiano?

G.M.   Parimente.

F.N.   Quelle ancora che si ricercano per ornamento,
come son la pittura e la scoltura: anzi forse tanto più
quanto, essendo la corte più risguardevole, deve abon-
dar di più nobili ornamenti.

G.M.   Così stimo.

F.N.   Tutti gli artefici dunque sono ne la corte?

G.M.   Sono.

F.N.   E gli artefici che son parte de la città son parimente de la corte?

G.M.   Parimente.

F.N.   Dunque il sartore sarà non solamente sartore
ma cortigiano, e 'l calzolaio e l'orafo e 'l pittore e lo
scultore e ciascun altro.

G.M.   In questo modo stesso.

F.N.   E gli artefici de la corte son più o meno
eccelenti?

G.M.   Più eccelenti senza dubbio.

F.N.   La corte dunque è una raccolta di tutte l'ecce-
lenze di tutte l'arti e tutte l'opere le quali sono fatture:

unforeseen necessity, to what we were saying before about the court being a gathering?

G.M. As you like.

N.S. We said that the court is a gathering of men for the sake of honor.

G.M. True.

N.S. But do we want to assume that this gathering is perfect or imperfect?

G.M. Perfect.

N.S. And if it is perfect, is it self-sufficient or not?

G.M. It contains in itself all that it needs.

N.S. Are all the arts that the citizen needs equally necessary to the courtier?

G.M. Equally.

N.S. Even those which are ornamental, like painting and sculpture, are necessary. The more considerable the court, perhaps, the more noble its many ornaments should be.

G.M. I agree.

N.S. Then the court contains every kind of craftsman?

G.M. It does.

N.S. And the kinds of craftsmen found in the city are also found in the court?

G.M. In the court too.

N.S. The tailor will be not only a tailor, then, but also a courtier, and so will the shoemaker, the goldsmith, the painter, the sculptor, and every other craftsman.

G.M. Exactly.

N.S. Are the craftsmen of the court more or less excellent?

G.M. Undoubtedly more excellent.

N.S. Then the court is a gathering of all that is excellent in the arts and in every kind of work. Some of

laonde parte de' cortigiani a contemplare, parte a l'operare, parte al fare saranno intenti.

G.M.   Nobilissima adunanza e bellissima raccolta è questa veramente.

F.N.   E i poeti e gli oratori e i musici e gli altri che fanno professione de la matematiche o pur de la filosofia naturale, son in quel modo cortigiani che son cittadini.

G.M.   In quel modo stesso.

F.N.   Ma propriamente cortigiano è colui ch'attende a l'azione e al negozio: e questo è il prudente al quale ne le corti s'appertiene il commandare intorno a tutte l'arti e tutte le scienze non altramente che faccia l'uom civile ne la città.

G.M.   Assai ragionevolmente mi pare che questi uffici in questo modo si corrispondano.

F.N.   Color dunque che son volti a la contemplazione de le cose grandi e sublimi, tutto che non siano cortigiani propriamente, tanto dovrebbono esser partecipi de la prudenza e de le maniere laudevoli de la corte, quanto bastasse a farli più cari al principe e a ciascun altro.

G.M.   Così mi parrebber assai graziosi.

F.N.   E quelli ancora ch'essercitano l'arti participano de la prudenza de' superiori.

G.M.   In questa maniera l'arti, quantunque ignobili, prendono qualità e gentilezza da la corte.

F.N.   Niuna maraviglia dunque è, signor Gianlorenzo, che voi siate invaghito di lei, che raccoglie il meglio, o quasi il meglio, non sol de la città ma de le provincie e de' regni, e, scegliendo il perfetto, s'alcuna cosa riceve di non perfetto, cerca d'aggiungerle perfezione.

G.M.   E io, con gli altri imperfetti avvicinandomele, posso acquistarla.

the courtiers will be devoted to contemplation, others to the active life, and others to labor.

G.M.   This is truly a most noble and beautiful gathering.

N.S.   Moreover, the poets, orators, musicians, and the professors of mathematics and natural philosophy can be courtiers just as they can be citizens.

G.M.   In the very same way.

N.S.   Properly speaking, however, the courtier is the active and prudent man who rules the arts and sciences in a court just as the prudent citizen does in a city.

G.M.   That the duties of the courtier and the citizen correspond in this way seems to me quite reasonable.

N.S.   Men who are devoted to the contemplation of high and sublime things, then, are not really courtiers, but they ought to possess at least enough of the courtier's prudence and praiseworthy manner to ingratiate themselves with princes and other men.

G.M.   Then I should find them full of grace.

N.S.   And even those who exercise the arts share in the prudence of their superiors.

G.M.   Thus even the most ignoble arts are elevated and take on the politeness of the court.

N.S.   It is no wonder, then, Signor Gianlorenzo, that you are in love with the court. It gathers to it the best, or nearly the best, of everything, not only from cities but also from whole nations and kingdoms. It seeks perfection and strives to make perfect whatever comes to it.

G.M.   I and other imperfect men can perfect ourselves by going to court.

F.N.   Potete agevolmente; né perché siate lucchese, vi sarà negato luogo fra' Lombardi, avegna che la corte sia adunanza di varie nazioni, le quali non usano una lingua solamente, ma con gli Italiani sono mescolati i Tedeschi, i Francesi, i Boemi, i Greci e quelli d'altre provincie, fra' quali è gran concordia nel servire al principe: e s'alcuna contesa è in questo, è contesa di gentilezza e di cortesia.

G.M.   Le vostre parole possono invaghir quelli ancora che n'avessero l'animo lontano.

F.N.   Anzi più tosto l'affabilità del principe dovrebbe confortarvi, il quale non dee far differenza fra le diverse nazioni, e se pur la fa giamai, è simile a l'agricoltore, il quale, avendo piantate ben mille maniere d'alberi, fa maggiore stima de' peregrini.

G.M.   Questa, o sia bontà de' principi o merito di chi serve, è certo accompagnata da molta grazia.

F.N.   Però non debbon in alcun modo diffidare i giovani cortigiani che vengono di lontane parti: e sì come il sol nascente e l'altre stelle matutine paiono aggrandirsi per la copia de' vapori, così per lo favore acquistato ne l'età giovenile sogliono essere in pregio maggiore, sì veramente che 'l valore o la diligenza porga occasione al favore.

G.M.   A raro valore non dovrebbono mancar rare occasioni.

F.N.   E 'l sole occidente ancora ha maggiore apparenza, e a questa similitudine tutte le cose accrescono la riputazione. I giovani dunque per la benevolenza, i vecchi per la riverenza sono più stimati; ma l'età interposita fra l'una e l'altra è riputata per l'operazione e

N.S.   You can, easily. And you will not be denied a place among the Lombards simply because you come from Lucca. The court includes many nations and uses more than one language. Germans, Frenchmen, Bohemians, Greeks, and other nationalities mingle with the Italians, and all are united in serving the prince. If there is any competition in their service, it is in politeness and courtesy.

G.M.   Your words have the power to attract even those who are not interested in courts.

N.S.   The graciousness of the prince ought to encourage you more than my words. He should not treat the courtiers from one nation any differently from those of another, but if now and then he does favor certain nationalities, he is apt to act like the farmer who has planted a thousand different kinds of trees and takes more care of the exotic ones.

G.M.   Whether such favor results from the goodness of the prince or from the merit of the servant, it is certainly full of grace.

N.S.   Therefore young courtiers who come from distant parts ought not to lack confidence in any way. Just as the rising sun and the morning stars appear swollen by the abundance of early vapors, so young courtiers usually rise to great esteem because of the favor accorded them in their youth—provided, of course, that courage and diligence seize the opportunities that favor offers.

G.M.   Rare courage ought not to lack rare opportunities.

N.S.   Furthermore, the setting sun appears enlarged, and like it all things in decline increase their reputations. Young men, then, increase their reputations as a result of goodwill, and old men as a result of respect. The age in between, however, is esteemed for its deeds and is perhaps more open to envy. Therefore

forse più sottoposta a l' invidia: però debbiam ricordarci di tutte quelle cose le quali sono atte a schivarla.

G.M.   Io ne farò conserva ne la memoria, quantunque sia lontano da questa età quanto da l'esser cortigiano.

V.M.   A mio figliuolo non manca il tempo, e ora dee pensare più a lo studio ch' a la corte: nondimeno questi ragionamenti li saranno stati in vece di studio, perché molte cose può avere apprese, ch'egli non sapeva.

F.N.   Più tosto le dovrebbe essere quasi uno sprone perch'egli prima impari le scienze, e poi di servirsene in quella guisa che si conviene a gentiluomo di corte, nel quale, non è tanto necessaria la eccelenza de le lettere, quanto la prudenza e l'accortezza di saperle a tempo manifestare; nondimeno l'una senza l'altra pare imperfetta.

we ought to keep in mind all the means of avoiding envy.

G.M.   I shall remember them, although I am as far from that age as I am from being a courtier.

V.M.   My son has plenty of time, and now he ought to be thinking more about his studies than about the court. Nevertheless, this discussion will have been a substitute for study because he may have learned a lot from it that he did not know.

N.S.   It should rather be a kind of spur to him to gain knowledge first and then to use it in the way that befits a gentleman at court. Excellence in letters is not as necessary there as the prudence and shrewdness to know how to make one's excellence known. One without the other, however, seems imperfect.

Minturno, or On Beauty

Minturno, or On Beauty represents Tasso's art
of the dialogue in its most developed and
complex form. Modeled on Plato's *Hippias
Major*, *Minturno* is a conversation between
the philosopher Antonio Minturno and
Geronimo Ruscelli, a colorful courtier and
dilettante. Its investigation of the nature of
beauty provides access to Tasso's mature
thought concerning the relation of art to
morality, religion, and philosophy.

Il Minturno
overo de la bellezza

Interlocutori:
ANTONIO MINTURNO, GERONIMO RUSCELLI

A.M.   Poche volte abbiam grazia di vedervi in questo nostro amenissimo lido, gentile e dottissimo signor Geronimo.

G.R.   Non m' è conceduto ozio di venirvi se non di rado, perché già l'occupazioni del marchese mio signore s'usurpavano la maggior parte di me medesimo: ora sono impiegato assai spesso in cose ch'appertengono a la maestà e a la gloria de l' imperatore, né si tratta di pace o di guerra o di lega, né si arma essercito, né si raccoglie armata, né si fortifica città senza il mio parere; laonde aviene ch' io soglia meno frequentare questa piaggia e questi colli, ne' quali solevano essere i miei diporti.

A.M.   In ciò si conosce ancora la vostra prudenza, con la quale vi sete seperato dal volgo e da le scuole de' fanciulli e congiunto con gli uomini di stato, inalzandovi a la cognizione de le cose del mondo e de' principi, anzi a la familiarità de' re e de gli imperatori. Però non so conoscere la cagione per la quale l'Aretino, il Dolce, il Clario, il Franco, il Muzio, il Fortunio, il Domenichi, il Flavio, il Corso, l'Atanagi e tanti altri nostri amici, i quali hanno in questa età fama di letterati, non abbiano voluto imitarvi.

G.R.   S' io non m' inganno, la cagione è stata debilezza d' ingegno, per la quale non hanno saputo trattare insieme le cose publiche e le private, e in un medesimo tempo acquistar gloria ne l'azione e nè la

Minturno, or On Beauty [1]

Interlocutors:
ANTONIO MINTURNO, GERONIMO RUSCELLI [2]

A.M.   It is not often that we have the privilege of seeing you in this delightful land of ours, [3] noble and most learned Signor Geronimo.

G.R.   Only rarely do I have the leisure to come here. The business of my lord the marquis used to take up the greater part of my time, and now I am almost always employed in matters concerning the majesty and glory of the emperor, [4] and no one treats of peace or war or an alliance, no army is equipped, no expedition assembled, no city fortified, without my having a say in it. This is why I have been coming less often to this shore and to these hills, where I used to find my amusements.

A.M.   Here too one recognizes that prudence which separates you from the vulgar and from the schools of boys and places you among men of state, elevating you to a knowledge of the things of the world and of princes, or even to a familiarity with kings and emperors. And I cannot understand why it is that Aretino, Dolce, Clario, Franco, Muzio, Fortunio, Domenichi, Flavio, Corso, Atanagi, and so many others of our friends who in this age have acquired fame as men of letters have been unwilling to imitate you. [5]

G.R.   If I'm not mistaken, the reason is a weakness of mind which has made them unable to deal at once with public and private matters and to win glory at the same time in action and in contemplation. Even

contemplazione. Anzi l'Ariosto medesimo, che fu assai adoperato da' suoi principi e poté avere esperienza eguale al sapere, ne l'azioni del mondo riuscì freddo anzi che no: e, vinto da pusillanimità, si ritirò da' servigi di quel suo magnanimo cardinale, il quale fu l'ornamento e la gloria di quell'età.

A.M. Adunque, s'egli rinascesse, sarebbe peraventura da noi schernito, quasi nuovo Dedalo da gli scultori che poi seguirono, i quali si beffavano de l'opere ch'a' suoi tempi parvero maravigliose e gli acquistarono gloria immortale.

G.R. Così averrebbe senza dubbio, signor Minturno; ma io soglio sempre e in tutte l'occasioni preporre gli uomini antichi a' moderni per ischivar l' invidia de' vivi e l' indignazione de' morti.

A.M. Buona è senza fallo la vostra opinione, e degne di fede e d'auttorità le vostre parole; e s' il mio testimonio può confermarle, io posso affermare senza bugia d'aver conosciuto in questa città il Bonfadio e il Flaminio e molti altri i quali se ne partirono quasi arrichiti co' doni, o almeno onorati con le ricchezze de' signori napolitani. Nondimeno il loro sapere e l' intelletto non mi pareva chi si potesse paragonare a l'acume e al sottile avedimento del quale sono forniti i più moderni, e voi oltre tutti gli altri, leggiadrissimo signor Ruscelli, al quale non si può tanto donare che più non meritiate.

G.R. Io sin ora son più ricco di favori e d'amicizia che di facoltà; e oltre quelli ornamenti che possono far riguardevole la persona e la casa, poche sono quelle cose che m'avanzino, o più tosto che mi bastino.

A.M. Grande sciagura è veramente di questi secoli, o più tosto di queste bellissime lettere di poesia e d'u-

Ariosto himself, who was frequently employed by his princes and was able to acquire experience equal to his knowledge, was more often than not unsuccessful in the actions of the world; yielding finally to his own timidity, he withdrew from the service of his cardinal, a man of great spirit who was the ornament and glory of that age.[6]

A.M.   If Ariosto were to come back to life, then, perhaps he would be mocked by us, as a new Daedalus would have been by the sculptors who succeeded him, men who ridiculed works which in his time had seemed marvelous and had won him immortal glory.

G.R.   That would certainly happen, Signor Minturno. But it is my practice always and on every occasion to set the men of former times before modern men, so as to avoid both the envy of the living and the indignation of the dead.

A.M.   Your view is certainly a good one, and your words carry conviction and authority, and if my testimony can confirm them, I can truthfully state that I have known Bonfadio, Flaminio, and many others in this city who left it, if not loaded with gifts, at any rate honored by the wealth of the nobility of Naples.[7] And yet it seemed to me that their knowledge and intelligence could not be compared with the keenness and the shrewd understanding of some of those of more recent times, and you beyond all others, most charming Signor Ruscelli, to whom it would be impossible to give so much that you would not merit more.

G.R.   Up to now I have been richer in favor and friendship than in means. And, apart from those ornaments which create respect for a man's person and house, there are few things that I can use, or rather that I need.

A.M.   It is surely a great misfortune for these times, or rather for our poetic and humane literature, that it is

manità, a le quali non si concede altro premio che quel de la gloria; là dove i leggisti, i medici, gli architetti, gli scultori e i pittori sogliono non solamente arrichire ma trarichire, come a' nostri tempi ha fatto Rafaello, Michel Angiolo e il cavaliero Pacciotto.

G.R.   I poeti sono pagati de l'istessa moneta, cioè de la gloria, la quale almeno devrebbe essere simile a la moneta di cuoio, che si spende a' tempi de la necessità e in miglior fortuna si ricompensa con l'oro e con l'argento; ma io veramente ho ceduto ad alcuno nel fare i poemi, ma nel darne giudicio a niuno: laonde volentieri fui ascoltato in Roma, in Toscana, in Venezia, in Napoli e in Sicilia: e da tutte le parti assai d'onore e di gloria ho riportato, e alcuna volta congiunta con molta utilità.

A.M.   O gentilissimo signor Ruscelli, ben si pare che la vostra sapienza è conforme a questa età, la quale è tutta gentilezza e cortesia; ma i letterati de' tempi a dietro erano rozzi anzi che no e sapevano poco accomodarsi a l'opinioni de' principi e del mondo: ma pur in qual parte la vostra virtù fu più onorata? in Roma forse?

G.R.   Non veramente, perch' in Roma ogni cosa più volentieri si soleva ascoltare che quelle de le quali io fo professione; ma s' io ragionava d'arme e d' imprese e de la bellezza di questa nostra lingua e de' nostri poeti, o pur di cortesia e di quel ch'appertiene al corteggiare e al cortesaggiare, era alcuna volta udito non mal volentieri: ma il premio de l'udienza era una simplice lode di virtuoso. Ne l'arti più secrete, com' è l'alchimia, non era chi mi prestasse credenza; ne le cose di stato molti discordavano da l'opinione e pochi per mio giudicio erano seguaci de le parti cesaree: ma grandissimi onori erano fatti a chi disputava se 'l papa avesse autorità sovra il concilio o se la residenza de' vescovi fosse *de iure divino*. Laonde io mi partii di quella città poco so-

granted no other reward than glory, while lawyers, doctors, architects, sculptors, and painters usually manage to make money and even to become rich, as in our own time has happened to Raphael, Michelangelo, and the noble Paciotto.[8]

G.R.   The poets are paid in the same currency—glory—which at any rate ought to resemble that currency of leather which is used in times of necessity and in better fortune is redeemed for gold and silver. As for myself, though inferior to some in composing poems, I will yield to none in the judging of them, and I have been well received by audiences in Rome, Tuscany, Venice, Naples, and Sicily, and have everywhere gained honor and glory, and sometimes considerable profit.

A.M.   Most noble Signor Ruscelli, it is apparent that your wisdom suits this obliging and courtly age. In earlier times, men of letters were of a rougher cast, and knew little how to accommodate themselves to the opinions of princes and of the world. But where was this talent of yours most honored? Perhaps in Rome?

G.R.   Far from it; in fact, almost anything is better received in Rome than the subjects I profess. When I spoke of arms and emblems[9] and of the beauty of our language and our poets, or even of courtesy and matters pertaining to courts and courtiership, what I had to say was sometimes well received, but the reward was merely praise for a man of talent. As for the more recondite arts—alchemy, for example—no one was prepared to believe me; in matters of state, most of them disagreed with my opinion, and few joined the imperial party out of respect for my judgment. But the greatest honors were given to those who would argue the question of whether the pope has authority over the council, or whether the residence of bishops is theirs by divine right.[10] I was rather dissatisfied with

disfatto di me medesimo, che non avessi atteso a cose più gravi; e me ne tornai a Napoli.

A.M.   In questa città senza dubbio la vostra virtù fu raccolta con maggiore cortesia.

G.R.   È vero: nondimeno erano in maggior pregio i musici e cantori, o pur i lottatori e gli schermitori e i maestri di cavalcare: laonde io fui costretto ad andarmene a Vinezia, dove per alcun breve spazio di tempo attesi a la correzione de le stampe e procurai ch' i libri da me stampati fossero i più belli e i meglio intesi di tutti gli altri; ma fui richiamato a questo regno da la cortesia del signor marchese, al quale aveva fatte alcune imprese bellissime che potrebbono esser scolpite co' trofei di Carlo Quinto. E bench' io ne' suoi servigi, essercitandomi ne l'officio di secretario, abbia atteso principalmente a le cose di stato, laonde ho fatto quasi una ferma scienza de' regni e de la republiche e de' costumi e de le leggi e de le mutazioni di ciascuna, nondimeno io non ho potuto dimenticarmi lo studio de le belle lettere, anzi di tutte le cose belle e de l'amore ch' io porto a la bellezza. Però, quando si pensa di fare uno essercito o di mettere in mare un'armata, io soglio pensare non solamente al numero e a la qualità de' soldati, de' cavalli, de' legni e de l'armi e degli instrumenti che sono necessari ne le guerre maritime e terrestri, ma a le divise, a l' insegne, a l' imprese de' principi e de' cavalieri, e sovra tutto al ben comparire e al far bella mostra, estimando ch'abbia gran parte de la vittoria colui il quale si mostra ne l'apparenza degno de l'essercizio de l'arme.

A.M.   Voi dunque vorreste vincer più tosto con la bellezza che con la virtù de' soldati: ma questo peraventura è impossibile, perché le ricche sopraveste e i cimieri e i padiglioni e gli altri impedimenti de l'essercito sogliono esser più tosto preda del nimico che spavento.

myself for not having paid attention to weightier subjects, and I left the city and returned to Naples.

A.M.   In this city, surely, your talent was given a
more courteous reception.

G.R.   True, but I found that musicians and singers
were held in higher esteem, and even wrestlers, fen-
cers, and riding masters. And so I was forced to go to
Venice, where for a short time I gave my attention to
the improvement of printing and succeeded in printing
books that were more beautiful and more legible than
any others. But I was called back to this kingdom by
the courtesy of the marquis, for whom I had made
some emblems which were quite beautiful and were to
be sculpted in the trophies of Charles V. And while I
was acting as secretary in his service, though giving
my attention mostly to matters of state—it was then
that I acquired a thorough knowledge of kingdoms,
republics, customs, laws, and their various muta-
tions—I never lost my concern for literature, or indeed
for all beautiful things, or the love I have for beauty.
And this is why, when someone is planning to raise an
army or send a fleet to sea, I usually think not only of
the number and quality of the soldiers, horses, ships,
and the arms and instruments that are necessary for
war on sea and land, but also of uniforms, standards,
the emblems of princes and lords, and above all of
making a good appearance and a beautiful display. I
consider it a great part of the victory when a man dis-
plays himself so as to appear worthy of the exercise of
arms.

A.M.   You would prefer to conquer, then, by the
beauty rather than by the virtue of your soldiers. But
perhaps this is impossible. Rich coats, plumes, pavil-
ions, and the other baggage of an army are more often
the spoils of the enemy than a terror to him.

G.R.   Non è sempre vero, anzi molte volte la bellezza de l'arme e de l'imprese è congiunta co 'l terrore; laonde io vorrei ch' i nostri esserciti fossero simili a quelli de' Cimbri, i quali, come si legge in Plutarco, portavano negli scudi orsi, lupi, leoni, cinghiali e altri animali feroci: laonde somigliavano uno essercito di fiere armate da la natura medesima a spavento de' nemici. Tanto importa per mio giudicio il terrore de l'armi congiunto con la bellezza.

A.M.   Io credeva che voi non ricercaste la bellezza, de la qual sete sì vago, ne gli esserciti e fra lo splendore de l'acciaio e il fumo e il rimbombo de l'artigliarie, ma più tosto ne' giardini e ne' palagi ornati di marmi e di pitture, i quali si veggono in questa fertilissima piaggia e in questi amenissimi colli, in cui peraventura non si contempla alcuna imagine così bene scolpita o dipinta come son quelle c' ha formate la natura medesima.

G.R.   La natura ha voluto dare i suoi angeli al suo paradiso, perché non era convenevole ch' in questo paese, il quale, curvandosi a guisa di luna, è quasi imagine del cielo, gli abitatori e l'abitatrici fosser d'altra natura che di celeste e d'angelica: anzi, s' è vero quel che dicono alcuni de' nostri teologi, ch' Iddio crei sempre nuovi angeli, mi pare che più in questa parte ch' in alcuna dimostri questi suoi miracoli. Ma io cercava la bellezza in tutte le cose e in molte: però ho creduta di trovarla negli alloggiamenti e fra l' imprese de' cavalieri.

A.M.   Peraventura, quando scriveste il vostro libro de le bellezze del *Furioso*, la cercavate più tosto fra l'arme che fra gli amori.

G.R.   In tutte le cose veramente io la ricercai, benché non la riconoscessi.

A.M.   Ancora ne la pazzia d' Orlando la raffiguraste, quando egli così lordo e pieno di brutture e orribile e

G.R. That is not always true; there are many times when the beauty of the arms and emblems causes fear. I would like to see our armies resemble those of the Cimbrians, who—as one may read in Plutarch[11]— used to carry shields decorated with bears, wolves, lions, boars, and other wild animals, which made them look like an army of beasts equipped by nature itself to be a terror to the enemy. So great is the importance, in my judgment, of the fear caused by arms together with beauty.

A.M. I imagined you would have sought that beauty of which you are so fond, not among armies and in the glitter of steel and in the smoke and crash of artillery, but in gardens and in villas adorned with marble and paintings, of the sort one sees along this fertile shore and in these delightful hills, where there are perhaps no images so well sculpted or painted as those which nature itself has formed.

G.R. And nature has been kind enough to supply its paradise with angels. For it would hardly be proper if in this country, which the moon-like crescent of its bay makes almost an image of heaven, the nature of the inhabitants were anything other than celestial and angelic. But if what some of our theologians say is true, that God is always creating new angels, it seems to me that these miracles of his are better attested here than in any other part of the world. But I was seeking beauty and in many things, and I believed I had found it in the camps and amid the emblems of nobles.

A.M. Perhaps you were seeking it in arms rather than in love when you wrote your book on the beauties of the *Furioso*.[12]

G.R. I really sought it in everything, though I may have failed to recognize it.

A.M. You recognized it even in the madness of Orlando, when he appears before his companions in a

spaventoso ne l'aspetto apparve a' suoi compagni ch'a pena il raffigurarono.

G.R.   Bellissima è senza dubbio l' invenzione.

A.M.   Ma in Rodomonte che, tutto sparso di sangue, si lavò nel fiume de la Sena, vi parve egli di vederla similmente?

G.R.   Mi parve, e forse prima che nel fiume; nondimeno alcuna volta dubbitai di non averla trovata.

A.M.   Se la bellezza è o si ritrova fra le cose del mondo, chi può meglio di voi averla ritrovata?

G.R.   Niuno peraventura la ricercò più di me; ma spesse volte quel ch' io giudicai bello non fu essistimato da gli altri o non da tutti, come aviene del *Furioso*.

A.M.   Possiamo di ciò assicurarci in modo alcuno? A me pare che, sì come tutti coloro che son savi son savi per la sapienza, e tutti i giusti son giusti per la giustizia, così tutti i belli o tutte le cose belle sian belle per la bellezza; e che la bellezza, o il bello che vogliam dirlo, sia quel che le fa quali esse sono. Però con questa osservazione e quasi regola cerchiamo di conoscer la bellezza in modo che niuna altra cosa sia presa in cambio, se pur altra cosa è quella che fa parer belle le figure orribil e mostruose, come sarebbono i serpenti o diavoli dipinti da Rafaello e da Michele Angelo, o pur le favole del Ciclopo e de l' Orco.

G.R.   È la bellezza de l' ingegno poetico per la quale si conosce senza dubbio c' hanno del terribile e del maraviglioso; nondimeno io la cerco più tosto in Marfisa e in Bradamante e in Olimpia, le cui bellezze furono descritte da l'Ariosto con tanta felicità di parole e di pensieri: laonde, s' io fossi costretto a dir quel che sia la bellezza, direi che fosse una bella ad Olimpia

condition so foul and ugly, so horrible and terrifying to look at that they barely recognize him.[13]

G.R.   The conceit is certainly very beautiful.

A.M.   What about Rodomonte, when he is completely covered with blood and then swims in the river Seine?[14] Did you think you saw beauty there too?

G.R.   I thought so—and even before he goes to the river. Still, there were many times when I doubted whether I had found it.

A.M.   If beauty exists or is to be found among the things of the world, who would be better able to find it than you?

G.R.   Possibly no one seeks it more than I do, but it has often happened that what I judged beautiful was not considered to be so by others, or not by everyone, as the *Furioso* is.

A.M.   Is there some way we can be sure of this? It seems to me that just as wise men are wise by wisdom, and just men by justice, so beautiful men, or all beautiful things, are beautiful by beauty, and that beauty—or the beautiful, as we may call it—is that which makes them what they are. With this observation and rule, as it were, let us try to recognize beauty in such a way that no other thing could be mistaken for it—if indeed it is some other thing that makes horrible and monstrous figures appear beautiful, as with the serpents or devils painted by Raphael or Michelangelo, or the fables of the Cyclops and the Orc.[15]

G.R.   It is the beauty of poetic genius which allows us to recognize with certainty what is terrible or marvelous in these things. Still, I'm more inclined to seek it in Marfisa, Bradamante, and Olimpia, whose beauties Ariosto has described with such felicity of language and thought, and if I were forced to say what beauty is, I would say it is a beautiful woman resembling Olimpia, at the moment when, without any robe

somigliante, la qual non coperta da alcun manto o d'alcun velo, ma ignuda si dimostrasse agli occhi de' riguardanti.

A.M.   S'a la bellezza togliete il velo, peraventura ella si troverà solamente ne l'anime separate; perch' i corpi sogliono esser quasi un velo de la bellezza de l'animo. L'Ariosto nondimeno, descrivendo la bellezza d'Angelica e d' Olimpia, fu simile a quel Dedalo che dianzi nominaste, anzi meno artificioso, perché Dedalo diede il moto a le statue e l'Ariosto il tolse a le persone vive; però si legge d'Angelica:

> Ed in quel suo dolor tanto penetra
> Che par cangiata in insensibil pietra.

E de l' istessa:

> Creduta avria che fosse statua finta,
> O d'alabastro o d'altri marmi illustri,
> Ruggiero, e su lo scoglio così avinta
> Per artificio di scultori illustri,
> Se non vedea la lacrima distinta
> Fra bianche rose e candidi ligustri
> Far rugiadose le crudette pome,
> E l'aura sventolar l'aurate chiome.

G.R.   È per mio parere eguale artificio il dare il moto a le cose inanimate e il toglierlo a l'animate: però l'Ariosto ne la sua Olimpia non è artefice men maraviglioso di Dedalo.

A.M.   Nondimeno io non vi dimandava una statua de la bellezza, ma quel che sia la bellezza, la qual può far belle l'altre cose non belle, come la balena e l'orca.

G.R.   La bellezza è la bella vergine che fa belli i pensieri e l'invenzioni del poema, belli i sospiri, belle le lacrime, i dolori e le passioni amorose, bella ancora la

or veil, she shows herself naked to the eyes of her beholders.[16]

A.M.   If you remove the veil from beauty, it will perhaps be found to exist only in souls separated from bodies, for bodies are, so to speak, a veil covering the beauty of the soul. But when Ariosto describes the beauty of Angelica and Olimpia, he resembles that Daedalus you mentioned earlier—or rather he is less artful, for while Daedalus gave movement to statues, Ariosto takes it away from living persons. As he says of Angelica:

> And had so far in sorrow gone
> She seemed turned to senseless stone.[17]

And of the same person:

> A statue would Ruggiero have thought her
>   Made of marble or of alabaster,
>   And to that rock so closely bound
>   By art of sculptors far renowned,
>   Had he not seen her tears distinct
>   Past roses white and whiter lily sink
>   To streak with drew her ripening breast,
>   And breezes move her golden tress.[18]

G.R.   It seems to me that no more art is required to give movement to inanimate things than to take it away from living things, and Ariosto, in his Olimpia, shows no less marvelous an art than Daedalus.

A.M.   All the same, I did not ask you for a statue of beauty; I asked what that beauty is which is able to make beautiful what is not beautiful in itself, such as the whale[19] and the Orc.

G.R.   Beauty is the beautiful virgin who makes beautiful the thoughts and conceits of a poem; who makes beautiful the sighs, tears, sorrows, and passions of love, and even death and the wounds received in

morte e le ferite che per lei si sostengono, bella l'aria, la terra, i fiumi, i fonti, i giardini, le selve, le valli, i monti, le spelunche e tutto ciò che le s'appressa: e a guisa del sole illustra con la sua luce tutte le cose vicine.

A.M.   Voi avete quasi descritta la figliuola del signor marchese vostro; ma se due sono le figliuole fra le quali è malagevole il far giudicio, due ancora sono le bellezze. Ma noi ricerchiamo una bellezza che faccia bella l'una e l'altra, e tutte le vergini che ne participano, né si perda con la virginità: altrimenti la bellezza sarebbe fior troppo caduco e simile a quella rosa descritta dal medesimo poeta, la qual perde l'onore con la stagione. Ma la bellezza, se non m' inganno, può fare ancora bella l'età matura: laonde ne l'onorato aspetto de la signora marchesa lor madre traluce un non so che di maraviglioso e di divino che n'empie di stupore e di piacere incredibile.

G.R.   Così è come voi dite: nondimeno ne la bellezza d'una bella vergine nulla più si desidera e nulla si può aggiungere; però io direi che la signora marchesa fosse bella come sua madre.

A.M.   La bellezza è quella di cui participando l'altre cose divengono belle e care; ma i figliuoli participano de la bellezza del padre e de la madre, non a l' incontro: dunque per questa ragione la bellezza sarà più ne la madre che ne la figliuola.

G.R.   Io estimo che la bellezza sia propiamente ne l'età giovenile come l'Amore.

A.M.   S'Amore nacque inanzi il principio del mondo, come dicono i poeti, conviene che sia antichissimo: e per questa ragione ancora la bellezza; perché l'amore è desiderio di bellezza. Ma lasciam ciò da parte, e ditemi, vi prego: di questa signora, che voi stimate la bellezza istessa, non vi paiono belli ancora i vestimenti?

her behalf; who makes beautiful the air, the earth, rivers, springs, gardens, woods, valleys, mountains, caves, and everything around her, and, like the sun, illuminates them with her light.

A.M.   You have almost described the daughter of your marquis. But as there are two daughters, and the choice between them is not easy, there must be two beauties, but we are seeking a beauty which makes both of them beautiful as well as every young girl who participates in it, and which is not lost with virginity. Otherwise, beauty would be too short-lived a flower—like the rose described by the same poet, which loses its glory as the season advances.[20] But beauty, if I'm not mistaken, can also make a mature woman beautiful. Consider the marchesa, the mother of these girls: in her dignified appearance there is a certain radiance, a marvelous and divine quality which never ceases to please and indeed to amaze.

G.R.   That is quite true. Still, in the beauty of a beautiful young girl there is nothing that is lacking or that one could add, and so I would say that the marchesa is beautiful insofar as she is the mother of this girl.

A.M.   It is through participating in beauty that other things become beautiful and dear, but children participate in the beauty of the father and mother, and not the other way around. By this argument, then, beauty would be more present in the mother than in the daughter.

G.R.   I consider beauty, like love, the proper possession of youth.

A.M.   If love came into being before the beginning of the world, as the poets say,[21] it must be very old indeed, and the same argument applies to beauty, for love is the desire for beauty. But leaving this aside, tell me, if you will: this lady, whom you consider beauty itself—do her clothes also seem beautiful to you?

G.R.   Anzi bellissimi.

A.M.   Per arte del sartore o del ricamatore, o per altro artificio?

G.R.   È bello tutto ciò ch'ella porta: perch'ella aggiunge bellezza a le cose portate.

A.M.   Ma 'l cavallo dal quale ella è portata e la carretta sono belli ancora?

G.R.   Si possono assomigliare a' carri del sole, tanto son belli.

A.M.   Ma che diremo de l' istesse cose, s'elle fossero altrui?

G.R.   Forse sarebbono belle e non belle.

A.M.   Perché potrebbono esser di tale a cui non converrebbono, o per altra cagione?

G.R.   Per questa che voi dite.

A.M.   Il convenevole dunque, o 'l decoro, è quello che fa bello ciascuno ornamento, perché gli istessi abiti in persona d'una Grabina non sarebbono dicevoli, e per conseguente non sariano belli; e 'l color de l'oro non è bello ne gli occhi: però Fidia fece ne la statua di Minerva gli occhi d'avorio e la pupilla di pietra.

G.R.   Così pare.

A.M.   L'abito dunque d' Onfale non era bello in Ercole, né la pelle del leone in Onfale: perché ne l'uno e ne l'altro era sconvenevole l'abito non propio.

G.R.   Assai vero mi pare quel che divisate.

A.M.   Dunque il decoro e 'l bello è una stessa cosa per vostra opinione, percioch' il decoro è quel che fa belle tutte le cose.

G.R.   Senza fallo.

A.M.   Ma l'abito pastorale non sarebbe bello ne la vostra donna, perch'a lei non converebbe, ma il reale più tosto.

G.R.   Anzi tutti gli abiti sono belli in lei; perch'ella fa belle tutte le cose, e non apparirebbe solamente bella in

G.R.   Extremely beautiful.

A.M.   Through the art of the tailor or embroiderer or of some other artisan?

G.R.   Everything she wears is beautiful—she adds beauty to whatever she happens to be wearing.

A.M.   Are her horse and carriage also beautiful?

G.R.   As beautiful as the chariot of the sun.

A.M.   But what would we say of the same things if they belonged to someone else?

G.R.   Perhaps they would be beautiful, perhaps not.

A.M.   Because they might belong to someone they were not suited to, or for some other reason?

G.R.   For the reason you mention.

A.M.   Then it is the suitable, or the fitting, which makes every ornament beautiful. The same clothes would not be suitable if worn by a Grabina,[22] and hence not beautiful, and it was because gold is not a beautiful color for eyes that Phidias made his statue of Minerva with eyes of ivory and pupils of precious stone.[23]

G.R.   So it seems.

A.M.   And Omphale's clothes were not beautiful when Hercules wore them, nor his lion's skin when worn by Omphale, because in both cases the other's clothes were unsuitable.[24]

G.R.   What you are saying seems to me very true.

A.M.   In your opinion, then, the fitting and the beautiful are the same thing, since the fitting is what makes everything beautiful.

G.R.   Certainly.

A.M.   But the clothes of a shepherdess would not be beautiful if worn by your lady, for they would not suit her as well as the clothes of royalty.

G.R.   No, all kinds of clothing are beautiful on her. For she makes everything beautiful, and she would look beautiful not only in the form of a queen but in

forma di regina, ma in quella di pastorella e di ninfa e di cacciatrice ne la quale Venere apparve al figliuolo.

A.M.   La vostra signora adunque non solamente è la bellezza, ma il decoro medesimo: poiché fa parer belle e convenevoli tutte le cose, quantunque non fossero tali per se stesse.

G.R.   Così è senza dubbio.

A.M.   Io dubbito nondimeno di due cose: l'una, che di lei avenga quel che de l'uomo sapientissimo, il quale, paragonato con gli dei, come stimò Eraclito, è quasi una scimia: similmente la bellissima donna, paragonandosi a la bellezza degli angeli, apparirà deforme anzi che no.

G.R.   Già ho detto per opinion d'alcun teologo che Dio fa novi angeli quando crea l'anime umane simile a la natura angelica.

A.M.   Lasciam questa opinione de parte, bench'ella non sia la medesima con quella d'Evagrio, che fu rifiutata per eretica, e concediamo a' poeti il dire:

Nova angioletta sovra l'ali accolta;

o pur:

Questa, angel novo fatta, al ciel sen vola,
    Suo propio albergo, e 'mpoverita e scema
    Del suo pregio sovran la terra or lassa.

E, se vi piace, solvetemi questo altro dubbio: s'egli è pur vero che 'l decoro faccia parer belle le cose che non sono, egli non sarà il bello, ma un inganno del bello; perché il bello fa le cose belle, ma il decoro le fa parer tali. Quella differenza adunque è tra 'l decoro e il bello, ch' è tra il vero e il falso e tra l'essere e l'apparere: laonde, se la vostra donna fa parer belle tutte le cose, io

that of a shepherdess, a nymph, or a huntress—the form in which Venus appeared to her own son.[25]

A.M.   Your lady is then not only beauty itself but fittingness itself, for she makes all things seem beautiful and suitable even if they might not be so in themselves.

G.R.   There is no doubt about it.

A.M.   All the same, I wonder about two things, and in the first place whether her case is like that of the very wise man who, as Heraclitus thought, is little better than an ape when compared to the gods.[26] In the same way, the most beautiful woman would appear ugly in comparison with the beauty of the angels.

G.R.   I said some time ago that in the opinion of certain theologians God makes new angels when he creates human souls that resemble the angelic nature.

A.M.   Let's leave this opinion aside—even though it differs from the opinion of Evagrius, which was condemned as heretical[27]—and allow the poets to speak of

A new angel, welcomed in its flight,[28]

or

An angel newly made, it flies to heaven,
Its proper home, and leaves the earth
Deprived of earth's most valued prize.[29]

But, if you don't mind, help me resolve the other question I was wondering about. If it is really true that the fitting makes things appear beautiful when they are not, then the fitting would not be the beautiful but rather an illusion of the beautiful—for the beautiful makes things beautiful, but the fitting makes them appear to be such. The difference between the fitting and the beautiful is, therefore, the same as that between the true and the false and between being and appearing. Accordingly, if your lady makes everything appear

direi ch'ella fosse ingannatrice o una incantatrice più tosto, da la quale devreste guardarvi non altrimenti che da la fraude.

G.R.   Non è inganno né fraude ne la bellezza di quella gentilissima signora: ma come il lume del sole scaccia gli inganni che fa la notte con le sue tenebre, e scopre le forme varie e i diversi colori de le cose, così la luce de la sua bellezza fa apparire quella mirabil maniera di costumi e di virtù ch'altrimenti starebbe ascosta. Laonde io non concedo che 'l decoro sia uno inganno de la bellezza, ma una sua luce, ne la quale chiaramente apparisce: fra 'l decoro adunque e l' inganno è quella differenza ch' è tra la notte e il giorno, e fra le tenebre e lo splendore.

A.M.   O dottissimo signor Ruscello, mi giova d'avere inteso da voi che 'l decoro non faccia parere ma apparir la bellezza: laonde si può conchiudere che, s'alcuna bellezza è congiunta co 'l decoro, non può essere occulta e, all' incontro, l'occulte non hanno bellezza. Ma s'occulta è la bellezza de la sapienza e occulta la beltà intelligibile, ne segue che siano senza decoro: il che par malagevole molto e duro d'affermare, se pur il decoro non è l' istesso che l' inganno, come parve a Socrate; perché l'altra opinione di Plotino, che sia quasi uno splendore per cui appaiono le virtù, è peraventura soggetta a l'opposizione ch'abbiamo fatta de le bellezze non apparenti a' sensi umani.

G.R.   Io non consentirei in modo alcuno che la bellezza o 'l decoro fosse un tacito inganno, come volle Teofrasto, o 'l decoro un inganno de la bellezza, come piacque a Ippia; ma più tosto mi pare che la bellezza sia una violenzia de la natura la quale sforzi gli animi ad amare in guisa che non si possa far difesa o resistenza: e

beautiful, I would have to call her an illusionist or rather an enchantress, and someone you ought to beware of no less than of any form of deception.

G.R.   There is no illusion or deception in the beauty of this most noble lady. As the light of the sun scatters the illusions created by the shadows of night and reveals the various forms and diverse colors of things, so the illumination of her beauty only makes apparent that charm of manners and those marvelous virtues which would otherwise remain hidden. And so I cannot agree that the fitting is an illusion of beauty; it is rather an illumination of beauty, through which beauty becomes clearly apparent. Between the fitting and illusion there is, then, the same difference as between night and day, shadows and brilliance.

A.M.   Most learned Signor Ruscelli, I am glad to hear from you that the fitting does not create the appearance of beauty but rather makes beauty apparent. One may infer that if any beauty is joined with the fitting, it cannot remain hidden, and conversely, that what is hidden cannot possess beauty. And yet if the beauty of wisdom—intelligible beauty—is hidden, it follows that it lacks the fitting. But this is a difficult and harsh thing to affirm, at least if, as Socrates thought, the fitting is not the same as illusion.[30] For the opinion of Plotinus, that it is a kind of brilliance through which the virtues become apparent,[31] is perhaps exposed to the objection we have made regarding those kinds of beauty which are not apparent to the human senses.

G.R.   I would not agree at all that beauty or the fitting is a silent illusion, as Theophrastus thought,[32] or that the fitting is the illusion of beauty, as Hippias believed.[33] But it seems to me that beauty is rather a violence of nature which forces the spirit to love in such a way that it is unable to defend itself or to offer any

chi chiamò la bellezza una tirannide di picciol tempo assai dimostrò de la sua natura. Né miglior definizione di questa mi sovviene d'aver letto o inteso giamai, perch' i belli son simili a' tiranni, e in quel modo istesso vogliono esser temuti e adorati: laonde non fu mai alcun re di Menfi o di Babilonia tanto superbo per l'ampiezza de l' imperio, quanto sono i belli per la forza de la bellezza, la quale astringe, costringe, rapisce, lega, infiamma e consuma, e a guisa di fuoco trasmuta gli animi in una altra natura. Direi adunque che la bellezza fosse una potenzia e una piacevol violenza e una graziosa tirannide de la natura, come volle Socrate, o un regno solitario, come estimò Carneade, perch' il bello non vuol compagnia nel regnare, ma regna solo come l'amore. All' incontra io chiamarei la bruttezza impotenzia, debilezza e servitù naturale, perché, s'alcuno è servo per natura, al brutto più ch'a ciascuno altro si conviene il servire; e se gli Etiopi o gli Indiani eleggevano i re bellissimi, ragionevolmente i bruttissimi devrebbono esser servi de' servi.

A.M.   Vorreste ancora ch' i servi de la vostra vergine fossero brutti o brutte le donzelle?

G.R.   Voi mi sforzate a concedervi e mi cacciate da la mia opinione quasi vinto, perch'ella meriterebbe d'esser servita da le Grazie e da gli Amori, quasi nova dea: ma il brutto e 'l bello è da me deffinito in comperazione e quasi in relazione; però le sue damigelle, che per rispetto de l'altre son bellissime, in sua comperazione sono brutte anzi che no.

A.M.   Voi riponete il bello ne l'ordine de la relazione come il bene, volendo che fra il brutto e il bello sia quella relazione ch' è fra il padre e il figliuolo; ma forse non fu vera l'opinione d' Ippocrate, che pose il bene nel

resistance, and the person who called beauty a short-lived tyranny understood its nature very well.[34] Nor can I recall ever having read or heard a better definition than this, for the beautiful resemble tyrants and want to be feared and worshipped in just the same way. And there was never a king of Memphis or Babylonia who was made so arrogant by the extent of his empire as are the beautiful by the force of their beauty, which constrains, compels, seizes, enchains, kindles, and consumes, and, like a fire, transmutes the spirit into a substance of another nature. I would therefore say that beauty is a power and a pleasing violence and a graceful tyranny of nature, as Socrates thought,[35] or the rule of a single king, as Carneades believed,[36] for beauty does not want to share its rule, but rules alone, like love. Ugliness, on the other hand, I would call lack of power, weakness, natural servitude, for if anyone is a servant by nature, it is more fitting for an ugly man to serve than for anyone else. And as the Ethiopians and the Indians chose as their kings the most beautiful men, it is reasonable that the ugliest ought to be the servants of servants.

A.M. Would you also prefer your lady to have ugly servants, or ugly waiting-maids?

G.R. You force me to yield and abandon my opinion, for she would deserve to be waited on by the Graces and Loves, as if she were a new goddess. But I define the ugly and beautiful by comparison and relatively: her waiting-maids, who in respect to others are very beautiful, are more nearly ugly in comparison with her.

A.M. You place the beautiful, like the good, in the category of relation, and suppose that there is the same relation between the ugly and the beautiful as there is between the father and the son, but perhaps Hippocrates was wrong in placing the good in the category of

predicamento de' relativi. Ma se 'l bello ha quella forza
e quella violenza che voi dite, è necessario che sia una
sostanza e una qualità efficacissima; ma come può esser
violenta e naturale, se tutte le cose violente sono contra
natura? E se la bellezza fosse violenza, come si tro-
varebbe alcuno amore volontario e per elezione? Tuttavolta noi sappiamo che molti non solamente vogliono amare, ma eleggono d'amare; e questa delibera-
zione da lungo consiglio è confermata. Né tirannide
adunque per questa cagione, né violenza direi che fosse
la bellezza, né regno solitario, perché del bello come
del bene è propio il far parte di se medesimo a molti.

G.R.   Ma chi può negare ch'ella sia una potenza?
Perché bellissima cosa è nel regno e ne la republica l'esser possente: ma nel regno d'Amore, s'Amore ha regno come si crede, il bellissimo è il potentissimo; e
qual potenza si può aguagliare a quella di Cleopatra,
che vinse Cesare, vincitore del mondo, e di lui quasi
trionfò? Onde si legge:

> Quel ch' in sì signorile e sì superba
>   Vista vien prima, è Cesar, ch' in Eggitto
>   Cleopatra legò tra i fiori e l'erba.
> Or di lui si trionfa, ed è ben dritto,
>   Se vinse il mondo ed altri ha vinto lui,
>   Che del suo vincitor si glorii il vitto.

A.M.   Questa potenza nondimeno, così nel regno
che voi chiamate d'Amore, come negli altri, può far le
cose buone solamente o pur le ree e le scelerate? Per
mio aviso malvagia potenza fu senza fallo che Cleopatra costringesse Cesare prima e poi M. Antonio a
cosa indegna de la virtù romana, e al fine a la vergognosa fuga, de la quale niuna cosa è più indegna a chi
desidera di signoreggiare. Ma la bellezza a me non pare

relative things. If the beautiful has the force and the violence that you say it has, it must necessarily be a substance and a quality of very great power.[37] And yet how can it be both violent and natural, if everything violent is contrary to nature? And if beauty were violence, how could there be any voluntary or freely chosen love? In any event, we know that there are many who not only wish to love but freely choose to love, and this deliberation is strengthened by judgments formed over a period of time. For this reason I would say that beauty is neither tyranny nor violence nor the rule of a single king, for it belongs to the beautiful as to the good to give of itself to many.

G.R.   But who can deny it is a power? To be powerful in a kingdom or a republic is a very beautiful thing, but in the kingdom of Love—if, as is generally believed, Love has a kingdom—the most beautiful is the most powerful. What power can equal that of Cleopatra, who conquered Caesar, the conqueror of the world, and, as it were, triumphed over him? For we read that

> The one who first came to try the powers
>   Of Egypt's proud queen was Caesar:
>   Cleopatra bound him in chains of flowers.
> Now she has her triumph, and it is fair,
>   If he who won the world is by another won,
>   That the conquered glory in his conqueror.[38]

A.M.   Does this power lead then only to good deeds, whether in the kingdom you call the kingdom of Love or in others, or to vicious and criminal deeds as well? In my opinion it was an evil power by which Cleopatra compelled first Caesar and then Mark Antony to deeds unworthy of Roman virtue, and finally to shameful flight, and nothing is so unworthy of one who desires to rule. But it seems to me that beauty

che possa esser cagione de le cose non buone: laonde non è l' istessa con la potenza, da la quale, come abbian già detto, soglion procedere le male operazioni e le pessime, come incendi, essilî, rapine, omicidi, guerre e distruzione de le città e degli imperi.

G.R. Se ciò fosse vero, Elena non sarebbe stata bella, perché ella mosse l'Asia e l' Europa a guerreggiare, e fu la fiamma e la ruina de l'antichissimo regno troiano; e se i rapti non son buoni, non potevano esser cagionati da la sua bellezza, la qual costrinse Teseo e Alessandro a l'una e a l'altra rapina; ma a me sovviene d'aver letto tutto il contrario, ch' Elena per la sua bellezza fu degna d'eterna gloria a giudicio prima di Teseo, poi d'Alessandro, che poté giudicar de la divina, non solamente de l'umana.

A.M. Potrei peraventura rispondere ch' i rapti non sempre sono mala cosa, come non fu quel de le Sabine, co 'l quale crebbe e multiplicò la generazione de' Romani; ma risponderei più tosto che la bellezza per sé non sia cagione di rapine, ma d'onor e di riverenza. Però si legge:

> Quella ch'amare e riverire insegna,
> E vuol che 'l gran desio, l'accesa spene,
> Ragion, vergogna e riverenza affrene,
> Di nosto ardir fra se stessa si sdegna.

Ma l' incontinenza de gli uomini e l' impudicizia de le donne può dare occasione a le rapine e a le guerre; laonde forse, s' Elena fu impudica, non fu bella, perché la bellezza è sempre congiunta con l'onestà, e con la voce greca τὸ καλόν altrettanto il bello quanto l'onesto è significato. E se ciò è vero, si potrebbe affermare ch' il bello fosse il giovevole e quel ch' è utile, e ch' il bello

cannot be the cause of things that are not good. And so it is not the same as that power which, as we have already said, gives rise to wrong actions and to things yet worse—to arson, exile, plunder, murder, war, and the destruction of cities and empires.

G.R.   If that were true, Helen would not have been beautiful, for she incited Asia and Europe to war, and she was the fire and ruin of the ancient kingdom of Troy, and if plundering and the carrying off of women is not good, then the cause of it could not have been her beauty—which compelled Theseus and Alexander to act as they did. But I recall having read just the contrary, that Helen was judged worthy of eternal glory on account of her beauty, first by Theseus, then by Alexander, who was able to judge not only of human but of divine beauty as well.[39]

A.M.   I could perhaps reply that the carrying off of women is not always something bad, as for example that of the Sabine women, through which the generation of the Romans increased and multiplied.[40] But I would reply instead that beauty by itself is not the cause of the carrying off of women, but rather of honoring and revering them. As one may read:

> She who to love and reverence trains,
>> Who wants desire and kindled hope made
>>> tame
>> By check of reason, reverence and shame,
>> Our passion in her heart disdains.[41]

But the incontinence of men and women's lack of chastity can give rise to the carrying off of women and to war, and if Helen was not chaste, she was perhaps not beautiful, for beauty is always joined with decency, and the Greek word τὸ καλόν signifies both the beautiful and the decent. If this is true, one could affirm that the beautiful is the advantageous and that which is use-

avesse quasi l' idea di padre per rispetto del bene; percioch' il bello è quasi cagione, il bene quasi effetto:
laonde sogliam estimar bella cosa la prudenzia e la sapienza, perché son causa di grande utilità ne la vita de
gli uomini. Che ne dite, signor Geronimo?

G.R.   A me pare assai buona questa opinione.

A.M.   Ma s'ella è pur vera, non è vera quell'altra che
da tutti è ricevuta, ch' il bello sia il bene e il bene all' incontro il bello: perché il padre non è figliuolo né il
figliuolo è padre, né l'una persona può mutarsi ne l'altra, variandosi fra due il rispetto o la relazione, com'a-
viene a colui ch' è destro, il qual può divenir sinistro, e
il sinistro da l'altra parte può divenir destro: oltre acciò
la bellezza è una di quelle cose che s'ama per se medesima, ma le cose utili e le giovevoli non sono amate per
se stesse. Che diremo adunque che sia la bellezza, o
signor Geronimo? Poich'ella non è la bella vergine,
non è decoro, come parve ad Ippia; non inganno, come
esistimò Teofrasto; non tirannide, come disse Socrate;
non violenzia né potenzia, come fu opinione del medesimo Sofista, anzi pur de molti Platonici; non regno
solitario, come giudicò Carneade; non quel che giova,
come Socrate mostrò di credere con Ippia disputando:
ma poi non fu costante ne la sua opinione.

G.R.   Diciamo che bello sia quel che piace.

A.M.   Dunque il bello sarà piacevole e il piacevol sarà
bello a l' incontro.

G.R.   Senza dubbio.

A.M.   Ma quel che piace a l'uno rade volte suol piacere a gli altri, perch'alcuni lodano in una leggiadra
donna

ful, and that the beautiful is related to the good as a father, as it were, for the beautiful would be in the nature of a cause, the good of an effect. It is for this reason that we are accustomed to consider prudence and wisdom a beautiful thing, for they are the cause of much that is useful in the life of men. What do you say to this, Signor Geronimo?

G.R.   This opinion seems very good to me.

A.M.   But if it is indeed true, then that other opinion, which is accepted by everyone, is not true—namely, that the beautiful is the good and the good the beautiful. For the father is not the son nor the son the father, nor can the one be changed into the other by a change that is simply relative to them, as would be the case with a change of position, where the one on the right could become the one on the left, and the one on left the one on the right. In addition to this, beauty is one of those things that are loved for their own sakes, but the things that are useful and advantageous are not loved for themselves. What, Signor Geronimo, are we then to say is beauty? Since it is not a beautiful young girl, it is not the fitting, as it seemed to Hippias; it is not an illusion, as Theophrastus thought; it is not tyranny, as Socrates said; it is not violence or power, as was the opinion of the same sophist, and of many Platonists as well; it is not the rule of a single king, as Carneades believed; it is not what is advantageous, as Socrates seemed to believe in arguing with Hippias—but then Socrates was not constant in his opinion.[42]

G.R.   Let's say that the beautiful is what pleases.

A.M.   Then the beautiful will be pleasing, and conversely, the pleasing will be beautiful.

G.R.   Without a doubt.

A.M.   But what pleases one person rarely pleases others, for some praise as the mark of elegance in a woman

Un pallor di viola e d'amor tinto;

altri il candido insieme co 'l purpureo colore; altri s' invaghiscono de gli occhi azzurri; ad altri sogliono piacere i negri maggiormente; a molti la severità diletta, a molti la mansuetudine: né la umiltà e la alterezza piacciono a tutti egualmente; laonde ad un uomo istesso in diversi tempi sogliono piacere diverse cose. Però disse il poeta:

> Ed in donna amorosa ancor m'aggrada
> Ch' in vista vada altera e disdegnosa,
> Non superba, ritrosa.

E altrove più loda la gentilezza e la cortesia, come in que' versi:

> Chinava a terra il bel guardo gentile,
> E tacendo dicea, come a me parve:
> Chi m'allontana il mio fedele amico?

e ne' precedenti. Però il bello sarà trasmutabile, e a guisa di camaleonte prenderà diversi colori, diverse forme e diverse imagini e apparenze; ma io crederei più tosto ch' il bello paresse bello a tutti e facesse belle tutte le cose: perch' io non ricerco quel ch' è bello par alcuno uso, il quale suole essere ancora soavissimo, ma quel che per sé è bello.

G.R.   Diciamo adunque ch' il bello sia quel ch'a tutti piace, sì come il bene è quel che da tutti è desiderato.

A.M.   Ma di qual piacere vogliamo intendere, di quel che piace a tutti i sentimenti o di quel che piace a la vista e a l'udito solamente? Perché, se bello è ciò che piace al gusto e al tatto e a l'odorato, come Aristotele mostra di credere ne' suoi *Problemi* e il Nifo in quel libro ch'egli scrisse de la bellezza, le cose dolci in

A pallor of the shade of the violet and love,[43]

while others praise a coloring of white and vermilion;
some are enamoured of blue eyes, others are more
pleased by black; many are charmed by severity, many
by complaisance. Nor is everyone equally pleased by
pride or humility, and indeed the same man may be
pleased by pride or humility, and indeed the same man
may be pleased by different things at different times.
As the poet says:

> It gladdens me still in a lady who loves
> That she walk disdainful and proud,
> Though not arrogant, not cold.[44]

And elsewhere he gives greater praise to obliging manners and to courtesy, as in these verses:

> She lowered her pretty and obliging glance
> And spoke silently, as it seemed to me:
> Who takes from me my faithful friend?[45]

and in the ones preceding them. And so the beautiful
will be changeable, and like a chameleon will take on
different colors, different forms, and different images
and appearances. But I should rather believe that the
beautiful appears beautiful to everyone and makes
everything beautiful, for I am not looking for what is
beautiful according to some usage or convention—
though that too can be most delightful—but for what
is beautiful in itself.

G.R.   Let's say then that the beautiful is what pleases
everyone, just as the good is what everyone desires.

A.M.   But what kind of pleasure do we mean, that
which pleases all the senses, or that which pleases only
sight and hearing? For if what pleases taste and touch
and smell is beautiful, as Aristotle seems to argue in his
Problems and Nifo in his book on beauty,[46] then sweet
things will be beautiful by the fact that they are sweet,

quanto dolci e le morbide in quanto morbide saranno belle, e belli saranno gli odori de l'ambra e del muschio e del fumo de gli incensi.

G.R.　Così avrei creduto senza dubbio.

A.M.　Né vi sarebbe forse dispiaciuto il parer d'Aristotele, il quale ne la medesima parte de' *Problemi* afferma che quello suol parer bello ch' è più soave al congiungimento, e che le bevande ancora paiono belle a l'assetato per la soavità che se n'aspetta nel bere.

G.R.　A me certo non dispiace.

A.M.　E peraventura non è falsa opinione, s' intende di quelle cose che sono belle per alcuno uso; ma il servire a l'uso è propio de le cose utili, non de le belle o de le piacevoli: e noi ricerchiamo quel che per sé è bello, senza aver risguardo al modo co 'l qual si possa usare o abusare. E perché la bellezza è veramente cosa divina, estimo sconvenevole molto ch'ella sia sottoposta al giudizio di sensi materiali come sono il gusto e 'l tatto; e a pena può esser giudicata da la vista e de l'udito, sensi assai più spirituali, riserbandosi nondimeno il pieno giudicio de la bellezza a l' intelletto, essercitato ne la contemplazione de le forme separate da questa mescolanza e quasi feccia de la materia.

G.R.　Il bello adunque sarà una parte del piacevole: perch'essendo quel che ci suol dilettare obieto di tutti i sentimenti, quella sola particella che da' sensi più nobili è giudicata merita il nome di bello: belli adunque sono non solamente i colori e gli splendori e le varie imagini de le cose, ma i canti e i suoni e la musica suole parer a gli orecchi ben purgati bellissima armonia. Ma mi pare ch'a questi sensi ancora appertenga tutto ciò

and bitter things by the fact that they are bitter, and the smell of amber and musk and the smoke of incense will be beautiful.

G.R.   I would certainly have thought so.

A.M.   And perhaps you would not have found displeasing the view of Aristotle, who states in the same part of the *Problems* that what is smoothest to the touch usually seems beautiful, and that liquids seem beautiful to one who is thirsty on account of the smoothness anticipated in drinking.

G.R.   It is certainly not displeasing to me.

A.M.   And possibly it is not a false opinion, if it is understood of those things that are beautiful according to some usage. And yet to be subordinate to usage is a property of useful things, not of things beautiful or pleasing, and we are looking for what is beautiful in itself, without regard to the manner in which it can be used or abused. And because beauty is truly something divine, it seems to me very unfitting to make it subject to the judgment of the material senses of taste and touch; indeed, it can barely be judged by the more spiritual senses, sight and hearing, which reserve the full judgment of beauty for the intellect—a judgment exercised in the contemplation of forms which are separate from this mixture and residue, as it were, of matter.

G.R.   The beautiful will then be a part of the pleasing, for as that which gives delight is the object of all the senses, only that small part of it deserves to be called beautiful which is judged to be so by the nobler senses. Not only, therefore, will colors and lights and the various images of things be beautiful, but also songs and the music of instruments, which provide a most beautiful harmony for ears that are suitably refined. But it seems to me that to these senses belongs as well everything that has been written of customs,

che si scrive de' costumi, de le leggi e de le scienze, le quali rinchiudono quasi nel seno bellezze maravigliose.

A.M. Vero è senza fallo quel che voi dite: nondimeno i sensi giudicano del colore e del suono in un modo, e in uno altro de le proporzioni o delle cose ch'appertengono a le scienze: perché di queste non possono i sensi far giudicio che vero sia, ma, quasi ministri e messaggieri de l'intelletto, portano a la mente quel che di fuori s'apprende; laonde non pare ch'una sia la bellezza che noi andiamo ricercando, perché gli oggetti de' sensi materiali deono esser corruttibili, come è il senso medesimo, ma la mente divina e immortale non fa giudicio se non di cose a lei somiglianti: Non è dunque uno il genere de la bellezza, o univoco, come dicono i filosofi e com' esistimò il Nifo; ma come lo splendore de le lucciole e de' funghi putridi, che suol di notte apparire, è diverso dal lume de le stelle o da la luce del sole, così ancora la bellezza de le cose terrene è assai dissomigliante da quella che si contempla ne le forme eterne e divine. E se ciò è vero, quel che per sé è bello non piacerà a' sensi perché non potranno essi darne giudicio.

G.R. Se non è bello quel che piace a' sensi de l'udito e de la vista, qual altra definizione trovaremo de la bellezza, che tanto ci piaccia?

A.M. Non ci sia grave ancora di ricercarne.

G.R. Io ho letto assai spesso che la bellezza è proporzione di parti ben composte: e questa opinione, come approvata comunemente da molti, malagevolmente può esser ripresa.

A.M. La proporzione si considera ne le parti dissimili; ma se la bellezza fosse proporzione de le parti dissomiglianti, non sarebbe alcuna bellezza ne le cose semplici: ma bello è l'oro e l'argento al giudizio de' miseri mortali, belli i diamanti, i rubini e l'altre pietre

laws, and the sciences—things which yield many marvelous beauties.

A.M. What you say is undoubtedly true. Still, the senses judge in one way of color and sound, and in another way of proportions or the things that belong to the sciences, for of the latter the senses are unable to make a judgment that is true, and act instead as ministers or messengers to the intellect, bringing to the mind what they learn from the world outside. And so it seems that the beauty we are in the process of seeking is not one and the same, for the objects of the material senses must of necessity be corruptible, as must the senses themselves, but the mind, which is divine and immortal, judges only of those things that resemble it. The genus of beauty is not, then, one or univocal, as the philosophers say and as Nifo believed, but just as the light of the glowworm or of rotting mushrooms appearing at night differs from the light of the stars or the sun, so the beauty of the things of this world is very different from that beauty which may be contemplated in the eternal and divine forms. If this is true, that which is beautiful in itself will not be pleasing to the senses, for they will not be able to judge of it.

G.R. If the beautiful is not what is pleasing to the senses of hearing and sight, what other definition can we find that is equally satisfactory?

A.M. Let's not abandon the search for one.

G.R. I have often read that beauty is a proportion between parts that are well arranged. This opinion, which many have shared, is not easy to dismiss.[47]

A.M. There is proportion only where there are dissimilar parts. But if beauty were a proportion between parts that do not resemble each other, there would be no beauty in simple things, but gold and silver are beautiful, in the judgment of miserable mortals, as

preziose, belli i colori e bellissima la luce, ne la quale non è alcuna proporzione: oltre acciò alcune volte rimane la proporzione de le parti, come ne' corpi già vecchi e languidi, ma non rimane la bellezza, ch' è perduta co 'l fior de la gioventù. Però di questa diffinizione ancora non rimango sodisfatto.

G.R.   Io non so quale altra addurne che più vi piaccia; ma vi deono pur sovvenire quelle di Plutarco e di Plotino: l'una è che la bellezza sia un ornamento o vero un onore de l'animo che risplenda nel corpo; l'altra che sia una vittoria che la forma vittoriosa riporta de la materia. A queste si potrebbe aggiungere che la bellezza sia uno sembiante overo una imagine del bene, sì come la bruttezza è una oscura faccia del male.

A.M.   Già mi sovviene d'averne udito ragionare e letto alcuna cosa; ma io m'avolgo ne' medesimi dubbi: perché, se la bellezza è ornamento de l'animo compartito al corpo o vittoria de la materia sovra la forma, ella pur è ne le cose corporee e materiali, ne le quali peraventura non è alcuna bellezza, o non quella che noi ricerchiamo. Laonde io mi maraviglio del Nifo e de gli altri Peripatetici che riposero la bellezza nel corpo e ne la materia, perch'ella è per sua natura brutta e deforme oltra modo, anzi è la bruttezza istessa: laonde il bello si troverebbe nel brutto quasi in propio soggetto; il che pare molto sconvenevole, perch' il bello dee germogliar nel bello quasi fiore in fiore. Oltre acciò, se vera fosse l'opinione di coloro che in questo modo l' hanno definita, gli angeli non sarebbono belli, perché ne la natura angelica la materia non è superata da la forma e non si trova corpo a cui sia participato l'onore de l'animo. Lasciamo adunque ne le cose basse e terrene questa vittoria e quasi trofeo de la forma: ne le cose, dico, ne le quali la materia quasi ribella, fa mille muta-

well as diamonds, rubies, and other precious stones; colors are beautiful, and light, in which there is no proportion at all, is very beautiful indeed. Besides, there are times when the proportion between the parts remains—as in bodies grown old and feeble—but not beauty, which is lost with the flower of youth. For these reasons I am not satisfied with this definition either.

G.R.   I do not know if I can produce any other that will satisfy you more. But you must recall the definitions of Plutarch and Plotinus. The first is that beauty is an ornament or glory of the soul which irradiates the body, the other that is a victory of form over matter.[48] To these one could add another: that beauty is an appearance or an image of the good, as ugliness is a darkened face of evil.

A.M.   I remember having read something of these things and heard them spoken about, but I find myself with the same doubts. For if beauty is an ornament of the soul imparted to the body or a victory of form over matter, then it must exist in bodily and material things, in which there is perhaps no beauty at all, or not the kind we are seeking. And I wonder at Nifo and the other Peripatetics, who have located beauty in the body and in matter, because by its nature matter is ugly and deformed in the extreme, or rather is ugliness itself, so that the beautiful would be found to exist in the ugly as its proper medium, which is not at all fitting, for the beautiful should issue from the beautiful as flower issues from flower. Besides, if the opinion of those who have defined it in this way is true, the angels would not be beautiful, since in the angelic nature matter is not overcome by form, and there is no body to which the soul's quality can be imparted. Let us leave to low and earthly things, then, this victory of form—to things in which rebellious matter makes a thousand

zioni d'una in altra sembianza e, dispogliandosi de
l'antiche forme, de le nuove si riveste, rimanendo sempre in lei un perpetuo desiderio di trasmutarsi in tutte a
guisa di città o di republica male ordinata, che faccia
mille mutazioni, variando leggi, governi e costumi.
Ma ne le cose celesti, ne le quali la materia è obbediente
a la forma e non fa mai ribellione o contrasto, o in
quelle dove non è alcuna materia, qual vittoria può esser quella de la forma o de l'arte divina? Niuna, se non
m' inganno. Dunque, s'a voi ancora così pare, diremo
che la beltà sia in que' soggetti fra' quali, non essendo
guerra o discordia, non via fa d'uopo di vittoria: e per
l'avenire non cercheremo la beltà fra le armi discordi
de' regi e degli imperatori, ma più tosto fra' pacifici
studi de le scienze, s'ella può ritrovarsi in modo alcuno. E a voi che ne pare, signor Ruscelli?

G.R.   Io non so ricercarne con altra guida che con
questa de' sentimenti, co' quali posso ancora inalzarmi
a la contemplazione del sole e de le stelle e de l'ordine
loro, ch'oltre tutti gli altri è bellissimo.

A.M.   Ditemi, vi prego: credete voi che la bellezza,
s'ella pur si ritrova, sia fra le cose false o fra le vere più
tosto?

G.R.   Fra le vere.

A.M.   Ma quali vi paiono vere, quelle che si mutano
o si rimutano, o quelle che durano sempre in uno stato
medesimo? Io estimo senza fallo che l' instabile e l' in-
costante sia simile al bugiardo: però l'uomo che fa
mille mutazioni d'aspetto, di costumi, d'età, non è
vero uomo, né 'l fanciullo è vero fanciullo, né 'l giovine è vero giovine, né 'l vecchio è vero vecchio; ma
l'uomo è più tosto una imagine e una fantasia de l'umana essenzia, come afferma Mercurio Trimegisto, e una
grandissima bugia. Solo è vero quel che mai non si
muta né si varia né patisce augumento o diminuzione,

changes of appearance, stripping away the old forms and clothing itself in new ones, and in which there remains always a perpetual desire to change every form for another, like a badly ordered city or republic which makes a thousand changes, altering its laws, governments, and customs. But in celestial things, where matter is obedient to form and never rebellious or contrary, or in those things where there is no matter at all, what kind of victory of form or of divine art could there be? None, unless I am mistaken. Accordingly—if you are of the same opinion—we shall say that beauty exists in those things in which, there being neither war nor discord, there is no need of victory, and in the future we shall seek beauty not in the discords and the arms of kings and emperors, but rather, if we are to find it anywhere, in the peaceful study of the sciences. What is your view of this, Signor Ruscelli?

G.R.   I do not know how to seek it except through the guidance of the senses, by which I can raise myself to the contemplation of the sun and the stars and their order, which is beautiful beyond anything else.

A.M.   Tell me, if you will: do you think that beauty, if it is to be found anywhere, exists in false things or rather in true things?

G.R.   In true things.

A.M.   But which seem to you true—those that change, or those that remain always in the same state? I think there can be no doubt that what is unstable and inconstant resembles a lie. The man who makes a thousand changes of appearance, of manners, of age, is not a true man, nor is the child a true child, the youth a true youth, or the old man a true old man. Man is rather an image and a phantasm of the human essence, as Mercury Trismegistus says,[49] and a very great lie. Only that is true which never changes or varies or increases or diminishes, but remains always within itself

ma sempre rimane in se stesso e simigliante a se medesimo. Però tutte le cose generabili e corruttibili sono
false; e 'l sole, del quale disse il nostro poeta:

> . . . . Solem quis dicere falsum
> Audeat?,

per le mutazione ch'egli fa, contiene in se stesso un non
so che di bugia: e gli altri corpi celesti similmente.

G.R.   L'uomo adunque è imagine e bugia; e i cieli e i
pianeti sono buggiardi anzi che no.

A.M.   Così mi pare che si possa conchiuder per questa ragione: laonde non solamente si può conoscere
quanto sian vani e fallaci i giudìci de gli astrologi, ma
quanto inganni l'apparenza di quelle cose le quali da'
miseri mortali son giudicate belle: e quelle particolarmente che chiamiamo feminili bellezze sono fraudi e
inganni de le cose de la natura, ombre di luce, larve e
simolacri di bellezza, e in somma somma e manifesta
bugia, a pena non conosciuta da' ciechi.

G.R.   Non è dunque la bellezza nel sole e ne le stelle
e ne le sfere celesti, perch'elle contengono qualche
parte di falsità, e molto meno ne le cose caduche e
mortali.

A.M.   Non è; ma dove sarà ella? forse ne la natura
angelica, o pur ne l'anima umana, signor Geronimo?

G.R.   Ne l'una e ne l'altra per mio parere.

A.M.   Ma se l'anima, come si scrive, è composta di
quel ch' è indivisibile e di quel che si può dividere, la
parte divisibile è soggetta a le mutazioni e a l'altera-
zioni e per consequente assai meno capace di bellezza;
l'altra che non si può partire è, s' io non m' inganno,
assai bella, ma la bellezza in lei non è tirannide, non
regno, non inganno, non violenza, non proporzione,

and identical to itself. Accordingly, all things subject to generation and corruption are false, and the sun, of which our poet said

> That the sun is false,
> Who would dare say?[50]

contains in itself, on account of the changes it undergoes, a certain lying element, and the same is true of the other celestial bodies.

G.R.   Man, then, is an image and a lie, and the heavens and planets are liars for the most part.

A.M.   So it seems one can conclude from this argument. And it is from this that one can recognize not only how vain and illusory are the judgments of the astrologers, but also how deceptive is the appearance of those things that are judged beautiful by miserable mortals. And, in particular, those we call feminine beauties are fraudulent illusions of natural things, shadows of light, masks and simulations of beauty—in short, a complete and manifest lie, and something that a blind man would be hard put to recognize.

G.R.   Beauty does not exist, then, in the sun and the stars and the celestial spheres, since they contain some element of falsity, and much less in things that are transitory and mortal.

A.M.   It does not. But where then would it be? Perhaps, Signor Geronimo, in the angelic nature, or even in the human soul?

G.R.   In both, in my opinion.

A.M.   But if, as has been written, the soul is composed of that which is indivisible and that which can be divided,[51] the divisible part is subject to changes and alterations and in consequence is much less capable of beauty. The other, the part that cannot be divided, is indeed very beautiful, but its beauty is not a tyranny; not a kingdom; not illusion, violence, proportion, or

non misura, non vittoria de la materia, non onore participato al corpo: e quantunque io non nieghi ch'ella sia un non so che d'eterno e divino, non so però quel che sia, perché, si potesse definirsi, potrebbe aver termine; ma la bellezza de l'anima peraventura non patisce d'esser descritta o circoscritta dal luoco, dal tempo, da la materia o da le parole, e 'l ricercarne più oltra è peraventura ardire e presunzione o fede troppo animosa e simile a quella di coloro che, passando dentro al velo del tempio, entrano in *sancta sanctorum*. Ivi si conosce, ivi si contempla, ivi solamente si può sapere quel che ella sia; ma noi altri fuor del velo andiamo rimirando le colonne e le travi di cedro e di cipresso odorifero, gli archi, la testudine, il vaso e l' imagini da le quali è sostenuto, chiamando bello quel ch'appare, o che pare più tosto e lusinga i nostri sentimenti: però non v' ingannaste, signor Geronimo, quando consacraste a la gloria immortale de la signora donna Giovanna d'Aragona il *Tempio*, perché nulla cosa è più simile a la bellezza che 'l tempio.

G.R.   Io veramente fui l'architetto di quel maraviglioso magistero; ma tante furono l'imagini, tanti i pittori, tanti gli scultori di tutte le nazioni i quali ivi dimostrarono quanto avevano d'ingegno e d'artificio, ch'a me toccò la minor parte de la fatica e de l'onore similmente.

A.M.   O voi glorioso, e gloriosi i poeti a' quali fu conceduto di celebrarla, perché ne le sue laudi furono simili a coloro i quali cantano le laudi divine; ma ella oltre tutti gli altri è gloriosissima, ch'a voi fece parte de la sua gloria: e direi bellissima com' è descritta dal Nifo, s' io devessi a guisa di peripatetico in questa materia scrivere e ragionare.

G.R.   Bellissima almeno è l'anima sua, quantunque

measure; not a victory over matter; not a quality imparted to the body; and though I would not deny that it is something eternal and divine, I do not for that reason know what it is. For if it could be defined, it would have a limit, but perhaps it is impossible to describe or circumscribe the beauty of the soul in place, time, matter, or in words, and to seek more than this is perhaps too daring and presumptuous, or a sign of too audacious a faith, as with those who go beyond the curtain in a temple and enter the *sancta sanctorum*. There one may recognize the soul's beauty and there contemplate it; there only may one know what it is. But those of us on the outside of the curtain walk about admiring the columns and the beams of cedar and scented cypress, the arches, the vault, the capitals and the statues that support them, and call beautiful whatever we see, or rather what seems beautiful to us and flatters our senses. So you were not mistaken, Signor Geronimo, in consecrating your *Temple* to the immortal glory of the Lady Giovanna of Aragon, since there is nothing that resembles beauty so much as a temple.[52]

G.R.   I was indeed the architect of that marvelous enterprise. But so many were the statues, so many the painters and sculptors of every nation who there demonstrated their talents and their art, that I had a lesser share both in the work itself and in the honor.

A.M.   It was glorious for you and for the poets who had the opportunity to celebrate her, for in praising her they were like those who sing the praises of God, but she who made you share in her glory is glorious beyond all the others. And I would say she is most beautiful as she is described by Nifo[53]—if I were to speak and reason in these matters as a Peripatetic.

G.R.   At any rate her soul is most beautiful—and

la lunga età non abbia tolta al corpo la grazia e la maestà.

A.M.   Questo è così creduto da tutti, bench' il velo de l'umanità sia impedimento a la contemplazione; ma in qual modo crediamo, signor Girolamo, che l'anima divenga bella?

G.R.   Ciò meglio si può apprendere da l' imitazione di questa signora che da niuna altra ragione o artificio.

A.M.   Assomigliam dunque il suo intelletto medesimo a lo scultore il quale, volendo fare una bella statua, parte ne taglia, parte ancora ne drizza e ne rade per nettarla, parte ne liscia e ne polisce insino a tanto ch'appaia ne la statua una bella faccia espressa co 'l suo artificio: così potranno l'altre co 'l suo essempio, togliendole il soverchio, dirizzando quel ch'appare distorto e obliquo, illustrando le cose oscure, essercitarsi ne la propia statua e non cessar prima che risplenda una divina luce de la virtù, con la quale si veda la temperanza sedere in maestà.

G.R.   Maravigliose scultrici sono quelle che sovra le colonne de la propia nobiltà hanno polite le statue d'eterna bellezza.

A.M.   Dicono ancora che l'anima non si fa bella per acquisto d'alcuna cosa esteriore, ma purgandosi a guisa di fuoco ne la fiamma: laonde le umane virtù, che paiono così belle, altro non sono che purgazione de l' impurità appresa in loro per la compagnia del corpo. Sono dunque le virtù naturali ne l'anima e nativa è la bellezza; ma la bruttezza è straniera e derivata da la contagione del corpo, e sciocco è senza fallo il giudicio di coloro i quali cercano la bellezza in queste membra terrene: e mi paiono simili a quelli che rimirano l' imagini e l'ombre ne l'acque, come si favoleggia di Narcisso, e, mentre abbracciano l'onde e i fuggitivi simolacri, restano sommersi senza avedersene. Però al-

yet a long life has not robbed her body of its grace and majesty.

A.M.   This is certainly everyone's belief, though the veil of humanity prevents the contemplation of it. But in what way, Signor Girolamo, do we believe the soul becomes beautiful?

G.R.   That can better be learned from an imitation of this lady than through any other art or reasoning.

A.M.   Then we shall liken her intellect itself to a sculptor who, wishing to make a beautiful statue, cuts away a part, planes and scrapes off more, and polishes and rubs away still more, until there appears in the statue a beautiful face fashioned by his art. In this way others too can occupy themselves with their own statues, removing what is superfluous, planing what appears crooked and distorted, illuminating what is dark, and not ceasing until they radiate a divine light of virtue, with which temperance is seen to sit in majesty.[54]

G.R.   They are marvelous sculptresses who have polished statues of eternal beauty on the columns of their own nobility.

A.M.   They also say that the soul does not become beautiful through the acquisition of anything external to it, but by purifying itself as the fire is purified in the flame, and the human virtues, which seem so beautiful, are nothing other than a purgation of the impurity which has fastened onto them as a result of their being accompanied by the body. The virtues are then natural to the soul, just as beauty is native to it, but ugliness is foreign, and derived from contact with the body. And it is certainly the case that those who seek beauty in these earthly limbs judge very foolishly: they seem to me to resemble those who admire images and shadows in a pool, as Narcissus is supposed to have done in the fable, and while embracing the water and the fleeting images manage to drown themselves while being

cuno potrebbe sgridarci: «Fuggiamo, amici, da questi fonti e da queste acque ingannatrici, e ne la dolce patria facciamo ritorno. Ma qual ragione è nel fuggire? O per quale strada fuggiremo gli incanti e le malie di Circe? Benché la favola d' Ulisse, oscura anzi che no, ci dimostri la vi de la fuga, schivando que' piacevoli oggetti i quali ci si fanno quasi a l' incontro e allettano i sentimenti. Ma dove è la nostra patria, donde venimo, là debbiamo ritornare. Qual sarà dunque la fuga? Qual l'armata che ci conduca? Già non si può fuggire a piè, perch' i piè portano in una altra terra assai lontana: né per questa cagione debbiamo apprestarci cavalli da cavalcare o navi da navigare; ma tutte queste cose a dietro si debbiano tralasciare, anzi non si dee pur riguardarle, ma fuggir con gli occhi del corpo, usando in quella vece gli occhi de la mente, i quali hanno tutti, ma da pochi sono usati». Però accortamente disse quel nostro giovine poeta, anzi ancora fanciullo, di cui molti fanno alto e maraviglioso presagio: piaccia a Dio che l' infelicità de la fortuna non perturbi la felicità de l' ingegno. Udiste mai questi versi?

> Io, che forma terrena in terra scorsi,
>   Rinchiusi i lumi e dissi: Ahi, com' è stolto
>   Sguardo ch' in lei sia d'affisarsi ardito.
> Ma de l'altro periglio or non m'accorsi,
>   Che mi fu per gli orecchi il cor ferito,
>   E i detti andaro ove non giunse il volto.

G.R.   Sono i versi, se non m' inganno, di Torquato, figliuolo del signor Bernardo Tasso, ch' in anni giovenili ha mossa di sé molta espettazione.

A.M.   Sottile senza dubbio è l'avedimento del giovine, co 'l quale ci ammonisce a fuggir non solamente con gli occhi rinchiusi ma con gli orecchi: ma egli, incappato ne le reti d'Amore e punto da' suoi strali, non è presto a la fuga.

scarcely aware of what they are doing. And so someone might cry out to us: "Friends, come away from
those springs and those deceiving pools, and let us return to our own country. But what point is there in
fleeing? By what path shall we flee the charms and
spells of Circe? The fable of Ulysses shows us, though
perhaps obscurely, the way of flight—in the avoiding
of those things that please and as it were welcome us
and engage our senses. But we must return to our
country, to the country we left. Where then is our
flight? Where the army to escort us? It is too late to flee
on foot, for our feet will carry us to another land far
away, nor ought we to provide ourselves with horses
to ride or ships for sailing. All these things must be
abandoned; we must not even think of them, and
should avoid them with the eyes of the body. We must
use instead the eyes of the mind, which all men have
but few use." [55] And that young poet of ours, or rather
that youth, of whom many foretell a high and marvelous future—please God that unhappy fortune may
not mar a happy talent—spoke very wisely. Have you
heard these verses?

> I, who saw on earth an earthly form,
>> Shut my eyes and said: To look
>> On her is foolish daring. But
> I never sensed the greater harm.
>> Through the ears my heart was struck:
>> Words went where a glance did not. [56]

G.R.   If I'm not mistaken, the verses belong to Torquato Tasso, Signor Bernardo's son, who at an early
age has shown much promise.

A.M.   The young man's insight, his warning to flee
with the ears shut as well as the eyes, is certainly fine,
but he is not about to flee himself, being caught in the
toils of love and a target for its arrows.

G.R.　Io sono omai attempato anzi che no, ma non ho ancora molto sospetto de le cose belle e piacevoli: anzi alcuna volta vorrei mille occhi e mille orecchi per mirare e per udire a pieno la bellezza e l'armonia de la mia signora, la qual a guisa di sole ci dimostra una obliqua via di salire al cielo e di tornare a noi medesimi. Ma voi, signor Minturno, sete troppo severo ne l'opinioni e ne' pensieri, e quasi dimenticato de' vostri amori e del vostro amore innamorato. Io nondimeno soglio prestar credenza a coloro i quali vogliono che la bellezza sia proporzione e misura de le cose c' hanno parti dissimili: laonde né la terra né l'acqua né l'aria né 'l foco né 'l cielo medesimo è bello, perch'egli non ha parti dissomiglianti di figura e di natura, bench'egli sia scolpito e adorno; e però, se crediamo a Plinio, è detto *caelum*. Non parlo de gli angeli e d' Iddio, il quale per opinione d'alcuno non è bello né perfetto, perché non è fatto: ma se gli angeli son belli in cielo, niuna cosa in terra è più bella di quella signora, ch' è di costumi e di natura veramente angelica.

A.M.　Io non voglio con voi di ciò più lunga contesa: credete dunque a vostro senno, sol che non ve ne privi questa vostra cortese opinione, la qual v' è ficcata ne la testa

Per maggior chiodi che d'altrui sermone:

per la liberalità, dico, del signor marchese suo padre, in cui la prudenza, il valore e tutte l'arti civili e militari sono bellissime virtù e degne di lode immortale.

G.R.   I am fairly well along in age, but I have not yet
become suspicious of beautiful and pleasing things.
On the contrary, there are times I wish I had a thousand eyes and a thousand ears in order to see and hear
fully the beauty and the harmony of my lady, who like
the sun shows us an oblique path by which to ascend to
heaven and return to ourselves.[57] But you, Signor Minturno, are too severe in your opinions and thoughts, as
if you had forgotten your loves or indeed your "Love
in Love."[58] As for me, I am inclined to the belief of
those who understand beauty as a proportion or measure of things that have dissimilar parts, so that neither
earth, water, air, fire, nor heaven itself is beautiful, for
it does not have parts dissimilar in shape or nature,
even though it is sculpted and adorned—for this is
why, if we are to believe Pliny, it is called *caelum*.[59] I
will not speak of the angels and of God, who in the
opinion of some is neither beautiful nor perfect because He is not made,[60] but if the angels are beautiful in
heaven, nothing on earth is more beautiful than my
lady, who in her manners and nature is truly angelic.

A.M.   I do not want to prolong our dispute about
this. Believe, then, as your own judgment dictates, so
long as you are not deprived of it by this courtly opinion of yours, which is fixed in your head

By nails stronger than another's speech,[61]

by, that is, the liberality of her father the marquis, in
whom prudence, courage, and all the civil and military
arts are virtues of great beauty and worthy of immortal
praise.

Notes

Discourse on
the Art of the Dialogue

1. The *Discourse on the Art of the Dialogue* seems to have been written during the early months of 1585. On the date and early editions of the *Discourse*, see Torquato Tasso, *Prose*, ed. Ettore Mazzali (Milan: Riccardo Ricciardi, 1959), p. 331, and Guido Baldassarri's introduction to his critical edition, "Il discorso tassiano 'Dell'arte del dialogo,'" *Rassegna della letteratura italiana* 75 (1971): 93–119. The following notes to the *Discourse* owe much to the work of both Mazzali and Baldassarri.

2. Don Angelo Grillo, a Benedictine monk and poet from Genoa, had sent Tasso two sonnets in 1584, and a copious exchange of letters followed (see Mazzali, *Prose*, p. 332, n. 1).

3. The dialogues referred to here are the *Cavaletta, or On Tuscan Poetry* and the *Rangone, or On Peace*. On the dates and early history of these works, see Torquato Tasso, *Dialoghi*, ed. Ezio Raimondi, 3 vols. (Florence: Sansoni, 1958), 1:39–40 and 44–46.

4. On Giotto's possibly blameworthy modesty, see Giovanni della Casa, *Galateo* (Turin: Einaudi, 1975), p. 26. Cf. Boccaccio *Decameron* 6. 5.

5. See Aelius Aristides *Orations* 46. 294. Tasso follows Aristides in including Cinesias, an Athenian poet, in this list, but Cinesias was in fact satirized not by the philosopher Plato but rather by the comic poet of that name (see Plato Comicus fr. 184 in J. M. Edmonds, ed. and trans., *Lyra Graeca*, Loeb Classical Library, 3 vols. [Cambridge, Mass.: Harvard University Press, 1940], 3:248. Plato the philosopher mentions Cinesias at *Gor-*

gias 501e. Plato's reference to himself as a tragedian occurs in *Laws* 817a–b.

6. In "L'arte del dialogo in Torquato Tasso," *Studi tassiani* 20 (1970): 8–9, Guido Baldassarri argues that the modern author referred to here is Lodovico Castelvetro (see Castelvetro's *Poetica d'Aristotele vulgarrizzata, et sposta* [Basel, 1576], p. 12b). A similar division into three kinds, however, can be found in Carlo Sigonio's *De dialogo* (Venice, 1562), pp. 12a and 17a; and behind both Castelvetro and Sigonio lie Diogenes Laertius's life of Plato (*Lives of the Philosophers* 3. 50) and Proclus's commentary on Plato's *Republic* (1. 196 [Kroll]).

Tasso's sources are often difficult to determine, especially in his works of literary theory. Sometimes he appears to be using an ancient source directly; at other times he probably depends upon a Renaissance restatement of commonplace ancient ideas. As Mazzali and Baldassarri make clear in the notes to their editions (*Prose*, pp. 331–46; "Il discorso tassiano 'Dell'arte del dialogo,'" pp. 120–34), Tasso's *Discourse* seems to borrow heavily from the treatise by Sigonio, his former teacher, as well as from Castelvetro's commentary on the *Poetics*. Nevertheless, the *Discourse* as a whole amounts to a personal and original statement of Tasso's aims and practice as a writer of dialogues; in constructing that statement, Tasso did not copy any source slavishly but rather made free use of ancient material that was the common heritage of learned men in the sixteenth century. The notes to this edition confine themselves mainly to identifying the relevant passages in classical literature and call attention only to Renaissance sources and analogues that seem especially striking.

7. Dramatically.

8. On this distinction and the view that Homer wrote tragedies, see Plato *Republic* 392d–394c, 598e, and Aristotle *Poetics* 1460a7–8. Cf. Sigonio, *De dialogo*, p. 3a.

9. Plato *Symposium* 185c–d, 212c ff., *Menexenus* 236b ff.

10. The first of these is the subject of debate in Plato's *Protagoras*, the second in his *Crito*. On the distinction be-

tween infinite and finite subjects of debate, see Cicero *Partitiones oratoriae* 18. 61.

11. Tasso alludes here to the treatise "On Style" formerly attributed to the fourth century (B.C.) Athenian philosopher and statesman, Demetrius of Phalerum. See Pietro Vettori, *Commentarii in librum Demetrii Phalerei de elocutione* (Florence, 1562), p. 172.

12. Here Tasso seems to have in mind Aristotle's derivation of "drama" (Greek: δρᾶμα) from the Greek verb "to do" or "to act" (δρᾶν); see *Poetics* 1448b1–2.

13. The author to whom Tasso refers as "most prudent Cyrus" is Theodorus Prodromus, a Greek who lived at Constantinople during the first half of the twelfth century (see Karl Krumbacher, *Geschichte der Byzantinischer Literatur von Justinian bis zum Ende des Oströmischen Reiches (572–1453)* [Munich, 1891], pp. 359–68). His *Dialogus de exilio amicitiae* appears in Johannes Stobaeus, *Sententiae ex thesauris Grecorum delectae* (Zurich, 1543), pp. 529a–535a. Mazzali's attribution of this dialogue to Ctesias of Cnidos (late fifth century B.C.) is incorrect.

14. Cf. Aristotle *Poetics* 1449b36 ff. and Sigonio, *De dialogo*, pp. 18a and 36b.

15. Aristotle *On Interpretation* 20b12–26.

16. Aristotle *Prior Analytics* 24a22–25.

17. Aristotle *Posterior Analytics* 77a36–40.

18. Aristotle *Posterior Analytics* 78a6–13.

19. Aristotle *Sophistical Refutations* 165a38–b11.

20. *The Litigant* is given as a subtitle for the *Euthydemus* in Diogenes Laertius *Lives of the Philosophers* 3. 59.

21. Cf. Sigonio, *De dialogo*, p. 40b.

22. Plato *Hipparchus* 225a. The Athenian Stranger is the central character in Plato's *Laws* and *Epinomis*. The *Hipparchus*—"the first dialogue"—is placed first in Ficino's translation of the Platonic dialogues.

23. Xenophon *Oeconomicus* 1. 1, *Hiero* 1. 2.

24. Cicero *Partitiones oratoriae* 1. 2.

25. Tasso is probably referring to Giovanni Battista Possevino the Elder (1520–49), author of the *Dialogo dell'onore* (Venice, 1553).

26. Cicero *Tusculan Disputations* 1. 5. 9 and 4. 7–8. Cf. Sigonio, *De dialogo*, pp. 29b–30a.

27. Cf. Sigonio, *De dialogo*, pp. 23b and 42a–b.

28. Plato *Gorgias* 523a ff., *Phaedrus* 274c ff., *Republic* 614b ff.

29. See Vettori, *Commentarii*, pp. 196–197. Cf. Sigonio, *De dialogo*, p. 14a.

30. Cf. Aristotle *Poetics* 1454b8–14.

31. See Vettori, *Commentarii*, pp. 20–21.

32. This praise of Plato's style echoes many ancient and Renaissance writers; see, for example, Vettori, *Commentarii*, pp. 77–78, and Quintilian *Institutio oratoria* 10. 1. 81.

33. Plato *Protagoras* 312a.

34. Plato *Protagoras* 314c–315d.

35. Plato *Rivals* 132a–b.

36. Plato *Charmides* 155b–c.

37. Plato *Crito* 43a–b.

38. This passage and the one referred to in the next sentence are actually to be found in Plato's *Phaedo*; see 60b and 89a–b.

39. Tasso refers here to the settings in Plato's *Phaedrus* and *Laws*.

The Father of the Family

1. *The Father of the Family* was completed in September 1580. See Tasso, *Dialoghi*, 1:29–30, and Mazzali, *Prose*, p. 75. The notes to this translation are indebted to those of Mazzali.

2. On Scipione Gonzaga, one of Tasso's oldest and most constant friends, founder of the Accademia degli Eterei, patriarch of Jerusalem, and a cardinal, see Mazzali, *Prose*, p. 75, n. 1.

3. *The Father of the Family* appears to be based on an experience that Tasso had while traveling to Turin in 1578. See Angelo Solerti, *Vita di Torquato Tasso*, 2 vols. (Turin: Loescher, 1895), 1:293–99.

4. The river mentioned here is the Sesia. Mazzali points out, however, that the boundaries of Piedmont (the

Duchy of Savoy) in fact extended beyond the Sesia (*Prose*, p. 76, n. 11).

5. On Tasso's earlier trip to France (October 1570–March 1571), see Solerti, *Vita*, 1:135–54.

6. On Cardinal Vercelli and the effort to identify the model for the father of the family in the dialogue, see Solerti, *Vita*, 1:109, 297–99.

7. Virgil *Georgics* 4. 133.

8. Petrarch *Rime* 50. 21–24.

9. The father's classification of agricultural activities reflects both the fourfold division of Virgil (*Georgics* 1. 1–5) and the threefold division of an earlier Roman writer on farming, M. Terentius Varro; see his *Res rusticae* 1. 1. 11.

10. Lucretius *De rerum natura* 4. 1256.

11. Homer *Iliad* 2. 371–74, *Odyssey* 12. 325–88; Lucian *The Parasite* 44–45.

12. Virgil *Aeneid* 1. 180–93.

13. Virgil *Aeneid* 1. 215.

14. Catullus 27. 2.

15. The father refers here to Tasso's father, Bernardo, and to Girolamo Muzio, author of an *Arte poetica* published in 1551. On Muzio's critical theories, see Bernard Weinberg, *A History of Literary Criticism in the Italian Renaissance* (Chicago: University of Chicago Press, 1961), pp. 729–31. The letters of both men can be found in Bernardo Tasso, *Lettere* (Padua, 1733), pp. 5 ff.

16. Within the Hebrew and Christian traditions, the view that the world was created in the autumn rests mainly on certain passages in Exodus. See, for example, the commentaries on Exodus 12:2 in *The Interpreter's Bible*, ed. Arthur Buttrick et al. (New York: Abingdon-Cokesbury Press, 1952), and *The Oxford Annotated Bible with the Apocrypha*, ed. Herbert G. May and Bruce M. Metzger (New York: Oxford University Press, 1965).

17. Cf. Plato *Timaeus* 33b, 34a, 43b.

18. Cf. Plato *Timaeus* 39b–c, 33c–d; *Republic* 509b.

19. Plato *Timaeus* 41a–d.

20. Cf. Dante *Inferno* 34. 112 and *Purgatorio* 2. 1–3.

21. Cf. Petrarch *Rime* 128. 63–64.

22. The Emperor Charles V retired in order to live near the monastery Yuste in 1556. He gradually relinquished his titles in a series of abdications that began in 1555 and continued until 1558.

23. Petrarch *Rime* 214. 35. *Consort* (Italian *consorte*) derives from the Latin *consors* and means literally "one who shares the same fate."

24. Dante *Convivio* 4. 3. 121–24.

25. The doctrine of transmigration of souls was taught by the Pythagoreans and figures in the work of Plato, Plotinus, and other Platonists. A revival of interest in the doctrine occurred in the Renaissance: see S. K. Heninger, Jr., *Touches of Sweet Harmony: Pythagorean Cosmology and Renaissance Poetics* (San Marino, Calif.: The Huntington Library, 1974), pp. 267–69.

26. Virgil *Aeneid* 4. 24–25 and 27–29 (Tasso omits 26).

27. Hesiod *Works and Days* 695–705.

28. Aristotle *Politics* 1260a30 and 1277b23. The remark attributed to Aristotle's daughter can be found in Stobaeus *Anthology* 3. 31. 8.

29. Euripides *Helen* 1187–88.

30. Homer, *Iliad* 3. 172.

31. Boccaccio *Decameron* 3. 6.

32. Homer *Iliad* 15. 153–351.

33. A technical term used by Aristotle to describe imparted motion or compression; see *Physics* 267a2–20, *On Sleep and Waking* 457b1–3, *Meteorology* 348b2 ff.

34. Aristotle *Politics* 1236a15–22.

35. Virgil *Aeneid* 9. 603–6.

36. Virgil *Aeneid* 9. 614 and 616–20 (Tasso omits 615).

37. [Aristotle] *Economics* 1344a–b.

38. For this derivation of *servant* from the Latin *servare* see Isidore of Seville *Etymologies* 9. 4. 43, and St. Augustine *The City of God* 19. 15.

39. Servants in plays by Terence. Davus is a character in *The Lady of Andros*, Syrus in *The Self-Tormentor*, Geta in *Phormio*.

40. In what follows *family* (Italian *famiglia*) sometimes refers

to servants only, sometimes to the servants and to the father's wife and children. This ambiguity may be intended to suggest an irony: the father's rule over his wife and children resembles the rule of a prince over subjects.

41. Petrarch *Rime* 34. 126–28. Tasso has altered the lines slightly. In fact, they are spoken not by the poet but by Love, who is here trying to defend himself against Reason for having caused the poet to fall in love.

42. Hesiod *Works and Days* 405–7.

43. Dante *Inferno* 17. 90.

44. Cicero *Pro Milone* 29, Valerius Maximus *Facta et dicta memorabilia* 6. 8.

45. Herodotus *Histories* 4. 3.

46. Petrarch *Rime* 50. 18.

47. Virgil *Georgics* 1. 160.

48. Virgil *Aeneid* 1. 177–78.

49. Aristotle's principal discussion of friendship is in the *Nicomachean Ethics* 1155a1–1172a16. Of the several kinds of friendship discussed there, the highest—the only one really praised—is friendship between equals who are also virtuous (1156b7–35).

50. See Terence *Adelphi* 15–21.

51. Marcus Tullius Tiro, freed by Cicero in A.D. 53, had been his secretary and confidential adviser. A grammarian and inventor of a system of shorthand, Tiro also wrote a life of his former master.

52. Giovanni della Casa, *Trattato degli uffici comuni tra gli amici superiori e inferiori*, in *Opere*, 4 vols. (Milan, 1806), 1: 265–314.

53. [Aristotle] *Economics* 1344a2–3, 1344b23–25.

54. Strabo *Geography* 16. 2. 24.

55. See Suida *Lexicon* s.v. νόμος.

56. Aristotle *Politics* 1259a6–21.

57. Virgil *Aeneid* 8. 407–13. The father omits the last part of 411 and the first part of 412.

58. Pietro Bembo *Stanze a madonna Lisabetta Gonzaga duchessa d'Urbino per il carnevale del 1507* 37. 5–6.

59. Virgil *Aeneid* 7. 14.

60. On Penelope, see Homer *Odyssey* 2. 93–95, 19. 137 ff., 24. 128 ff.; on Circe, 10. 220–23; on Nausicaa, 6. 20 ff.

61. See Livy *Early History of Rome* 1. 57–58.

62. The notion of the universe as an ordered harmony of disparate parts is of Greek origin; the philosophical term for the universe so understood—*kosmos*—means simply "order" (see, for example, Plato *Timaeus* 27a ff., *Laws* 821a ff.). Compare Xenophon *Oeconomicus* 8.

63. Tasso visited France during 1570–71 in the entourage of Cardinal Luigi d'Este. See Tasso, *Lettere*, 1:27–46. The hospital referred to is almost certainly the well-known hôtel-Dieu built between 1443 and 1451 by the Burgundian chancellor, Nicholas Rolin.

64. Terence *Eunuchus* 4. This reference to a flattering parasite who organizes the servants of his master's household into an army in order to carry off a young slave girl in another household picks up earlier imagery comparing the tools of servants to arms and suggests that the family is a kind of army, formed to take advantage of other families. The family, Tasso suggests, is a structure formed for protection against nature and man.

65. Thucydides *Peloponnesian War* 1. 5.

66. Virgil *Aeneid* 9. 612–13.

67. Cicero *De officiis* 1. 42. 151.

68. See, for example, Cicero *In Verrem* 2. 2. 3. 7, *Pro Plancio* 26. 64. Note that the concept of a two-leveled style, addressed to both civil and speculative men, might be derived from these remarks about Cicero.

69. Cicero *De officiis* 1. 8. 25.

70. Money changing in the sixteenth century involved two kinds of related activities: exchanging coins of one origin for those of another and dealing in bills of exchange—devices for making payments at a great distance without incurring the risk of shipping gold and silver. While both activities met an important economic need, both could be, and apparently frequently were, performed in a manner that at least bordered on fraud. The money-changer was open to the often justified sus-

picion that through the use of debased, sweated, or clipped coins he was cheating his clients. And because he purchased bills of exchange at a discount that was in fact a thinly disguised form of interest, he also acquired some of the odium of the usurer. We are indebted to Professor James A. Gherity of Northern Illinois University for this explanation. Cf. Raymond de Roover, *L'Evolution de la lettre de change: XIVe–XVIIIe siècles* (Paris: A. Colin, 1953).

71. This discussion of formal and material numbers is derived from Aristotle *Metaphysics* 1085b24–1086a19.

72. That is, money changing practiced for the sake of facilitating international trade and not as a form of usury.

73. Aristotle's condemnation is to be found in *Politics* 1258a38–b8. Cf. Thomas Aquinas *Summa Theologica* 2. 2.Question 78. The key Biblical texts on usury are Exodus 22:25, Deuteronomy 23:19, Psalms 15:5, Ezekial 18:8, Matthew 5:42, and Luke 6:34 ff. On the hardening attitude toward usury taken by the Roman Catholic Church in the latter half of the sixteenth century, see "Usury (Christian)," in *Encyclopedia of Religion and Ethics*, ed. James Hastings (New York: Scribners, 1922).

74. Dante *Inferno* 11. 101–11. Virgil is speaking to Dante. The *Physics* mentioned is that of Aristotle. The passage referred to in Genesis is 3:17, where God tells Adam: "Because you have listened to your wife and have eaten from the tree which I forbade you, accursed shall be the ground on your account. With labour you shall win your food from it all the days of your life" (*The New English Bible*). The "two" referred to in 107 appear to be art and nature (the subject of Aristotle's *Physics*). Dante's "art" seems to correspond to the "labour" of Genesis, and his "nature" to "the grounds" (see the notes on these lines in *La divina commedia*, ed. Attilio Momigliano, 3 vols. [Florence: Sansoni, 1945], 1:84–85).

75. Plato *Symposium* 223d.

76. [Aristotle] *Economics* 1345b.

77. In the latter part of the sixteeth century, Asti and Ver-

celli were ruled by Savoy, Modena and Reggio by Ferrara, and Monferrato (Montferrat) by Mantua.

78. [Aristotle] *Economics* 1346a.

Malpiglio, or On the Court

1. The *Malpiglio* probably dates from early 1585. On the circumstances connected with its composition, see Tasso, *Dialoghi*, 1:40–42.

2. Vincenzo Malpiglio, originally from Lucca, was in charge of the treasury at the court of Ferrara. His son, Giovanlorenzo, a young man who aspires to become a courtier, is the Neapolitan Stranger's main interlocutor in *The Second Malpiglio, or On Fleeing the Multitude*.

3. Paolo Sanminiato, a wealthy and learned gentleman from Lucca, appears as one of the interlocutors in Tasso's dialogue *Cataneo, or On Erotic Disputations*. See also Solerti, *Vita*, 1:128–31.

4. See Castiglione *The Courtier* 2. 3.

5. Tasso himself seems to have suffered from a stammer (see Solerti, *Vita*, 1:131, and Tasso, *Dialoghi*, 2:798).

6. Why Tasso refrains from naming a particular prince at this point is not clear. Is he challenging the reader to think of a prince who took power "for the sake of the public good"?

7. The Flaminius mentioned here is probably the Roman consul Gaius Flaminius, who fell into Hannibal's trap at Lake Trasimene in 217 B.C. (see Polybius *Histories* 3. 80–84 and Livy *Early History of Rome* 22. 4–6). Minucius must be Marcus Minucius Rufus, another Roman general, who nearly lost his life and his army in 216 B.C. when his impatience with the cautious strategy of Fabius led him into an ill-considered attack upon Hannibal (see Polybius *Histories* 3. 90–106 and Livy *Early History of Rome* 22. 24–30). Regulus is almost certainly the famous Marcus Atilius Regulus, who attacked the Carthaginians on disadvantageous ground in 255 B.C. and was defeated and captured. According to tradition

he was later sent to Rome to negotiate peace or an exchange of prisoners. Upon his arrival, however, he urged the senators to refuse the offered terms and then returned to Carthage where he was tortured to death. (See Polybius *Histories* 1. 33–35 and Cicero *De officiis* 1. 39 and 3. 99–115.) Paullus is less easy to identify, but since the other examples in this passage are all Roman generals from the Punic Wars, perhaps Tasso was thinking of Lucius Aemilius Paullus, one of the Roman commanders in the disastrous attack upon Hannibal at Cannae in 216 B.C. Nevertheless, while Paullus no doubt shares some of the responsibility for that defeat, Polybius and Livy agree in putting most of the blame on the other Roman general, Varro, and in presenting Paullus primarily as the voice of reason and prudence (see Polybius *Histories* 3. 107–18 and Livy *Early History of Rome* 22. 38–51).

8. Hephaestion was one of Alexander's most trusted lieutenants. Parmenion was also an important figure at the Macedonian court, but when his son, Philotas, was convicted of treason in 330 B.C., Parmenion himself came under suspicion, and Alexander had him murdered (see Plutarch *Life of Alexander* 47–49).

9. See Plutarch *Life of Cato the Younger* 14.

10. Socrates' "modesty"—his insistence upon his own ignorance—is famous. On Giotto, see p. 245, n. 4 above.

Minturno, or On Beauty

1. Although there is no direct evidence as to the date of its composition, the *Minturno* is now generally agreed to have been written toward the end of Tasso's life, in 1593 or 1594. See *Dialoghi* 1:59–63. The notes that follow are indebted to those of Mazzali.

2. Antonio Sebastiani (?–1579), called Minturno from the name of his native town, pursued a career in the Church, eventually becoming bishop of Crotone in southern Italy. He was the author of two influential treatises on lit-

erary theory, *De poeta* (Venice, 1559) and *Arte poetica* (Venice, 1564), and is said to have studied philosophy under Agostino Nifo. For a brief account of him see Croce, *Poeti e scrittori del pieno e del tardo Rinascimento*, 3 vols. (Bari: Laterza, 1952-58), 2:85-102. Much of the career of Geronimo (or Girolamo) Ruscelli (?-1566) is presented in the *Minturno* itself. Ruscelli was or had been at various times an editor, translator, printer, poet, and critic; patronized by a Neapolitan aristocrat active in the service of Spain, Ruscelli increasingly flourished in the role of courtier and eventually attached himself to the emperor, Charles V. Tasso's portrait of him appears to draw particularly on a work entitled *Lettura di Girolamo Ruscelli sopra un sonnetto dell' illustriss. signor marchese della Terza alla divina signora marchesa del Vasto* (Venice, 1552). The dramatic date of the *Minturno* would appear to fall between the death of Ruscelli's patron Alfonso d'Avalos in 1546 and the abdication of Charles V some ten years later (see n. 4 below).

3. Naples.

4. Alfonso d'Avalos, marquis of Vasto (1502-46), a Neapolitan noble of Aragonese descent, held a number of important political and military posts in Italy under the Emperor Charles V; he was also a patron of artists and men of letters, including such figures as Titian and Pietro Aretino.

5. Pietro Aretino, Lodovico Dolce, Isidoro Clario, Niccolo Franco, Girolamo Muzio, Gianfrancesco Fortunio, Lodovico Domenichi, Rinaldo Corso, and Dionigi Atanagi (the identity of Flavio is uncertain) were contemporary men of letters, many of them friends of Tasso or his father. Aretino and Domenichi had written works attacking courts and courtiers.

6. Ludovico Ariosto (1474-1533), the author of *Orlando Furioso*, was secretary to Cardinal Ippolito d'Este from 1503 to 1517, when he was discharged for refusing to accompany the cardinal to Hungary after d'Este had been made bishop of Buda. Ariosto subsequently entered the service of the cardinal's brother Alfonso, duke

of Ferrara, eventually becoming governor of a district of Ferrara before retiring to devote himself entirely to poetry.

7. Iacopo Bonfadio had been secretary to some important ecclesiastical figures in Rome and Naples during the 1530s; later professor of philosophy and the official historian of Genoa, he was executed by the Genoese in 1550 on suspicion of religious heterodoxy. Marcantonio Flaminio (1498–1550) was an important poet of Latin verse and author of commentaries on parts of the Bible and the Aristotelian corpus. During their stay in Naples both men had frequented the reformist religious and literary circle of Juan de Valdes, which also included Alfonso d'Avalos, his wife Maria of Aragon, and her sister Giovanna.

8. Francesco Paciotto of Urbino (1521–91), a famous military architect.

9. Emblems (*imprese*) were the personal symbols—usually composed of a picture accompanied by a motto—that were popular among the nobility of sixteenth-century Italy. Tasso devotes a dialogue to this subject (*The Count, or On Emblems*); Ruscelli had written a treatise on it (*Discorso intorno all' invenzioni delle imprese, dell' insegne, de' motti e delle livree* [Venice, 1556]).

10. The movement for a general council of the Church had gained in strength with the rise of Protestantism and resulted in the convening of the Council of Trent in 1545. Those who held the view that the residences of bishops belong to them by divine right denied that the pope had authority over the bishops in council; this was the position particularly of the Spanish bishops.

11. Plutarch *Life of Marius* 25. 10.

12. *Le Bellezze del Furioso*, originally intended as an introduction to Ruscelli's edition of *Orlando Furioso*, was in fact never published. See the preface to that edition (Venice, 1556) as well as Ruscelli's *Del modo di comporre in versi nella lingua italiana* (Venice, 1558), p. xix.

13. Ariosto *Orlande Furioso* 39. 36–38, 44–47.

14. Ariosto *Orlando Furioso* 18. 18–25.

257

15. The Orc is the sea monster killed by Orlando, *Orlando Furioso* 11. 28–45. In his *Arte poetica*, Minturno argues that Ariosto's genius "makes what is barbaric in its nature and devoid of grace seem beautiful by his style" (Naples, 1725, p. 30).

16. Ariosto *Orlando Furioso* 11. 67–69.

17. "Ed in quel suo dolor tanto penetra / che par cangiata in insensibil pietra." The reference is evidently to *Orlando Furioso* 1. 39, where Ariosto says of Sacripante, who is being observed by Angelica: "Ed in un gran pensier tanto penetra / che par cangiato in insensibil pietra" ("And had so far in thought gone / He seemed turned to senseless stone").

18. Ariosto *Orlando Furioso* 10. 96.

19. Ariosto *Orlando Furioso* 6. 37.

20. Ariosto *Orlando Furioso* 1. 42.

21. See particularly Hesiod *Theogony* 116–22 (cf. Plato *Symposium* 178a–c).

22. A reference to the character Gabrina (the name is misspelled in the text); see Ariosto *Orlando Furioso* 20. 115–16.

23. Cf. Plato *Hippias major* 290a–d.

24. See Ovid *Heroides* 9. 54 ff.

25. See Virgil *Aeneid* 1. 314–20.

26. Heraclitus fr. B83 (Diels-Kranz; cf. Plato *Hippias major* 289a–b).

27. Evagrius Ponticus, a Greek theologian of the fourth century, was anathematized by the early ecumenical councils as a follower of Origen. The writings of Evagrius and Origen on angels have not survived, but they evidently argued that angels or angelic souls have been sent by God to inhabit human bodies as punishment for their sins—a view which the orthodox seem to have regarded as a relic of Platonism (see, for example, St. Jerome *Epistles* 124). The view advanced by Ruscelli seems to lack theological authority of any kind.

28. Petrarch *Rime* 106. 1. The text of Petrarch has *accorta* ("observant") for *accolta* ("welcomed"); the reference is to Petrarch's Laura.

29. Giovanni della Casa *Rime* 37. 9–11. The poem is an elegy addressed to Venice on the death of Pietro Bembo, the "new angel" being Bembo's soul.

30. Plato *Hippias major* 294b–c.

31. Plotinus *Enneads* 1. 6. 3–4.

32. Diogenes Laertius *Lives of the Philosophers* 5. 19.

33. Plato *Hippias major* 293e–94a and ff.

34. The remark is attributed to Socrates by Diogenes Laertius (*Lives of the Philosophers* 5. 19). A similar saying was associated with the philosopher Bion (Plutarch *Amatorius* 770b, Stobaeus *Anthology* 4. 21. 23).

35. The definition or definitions attributed to Socrates appear to represent a combination of Diogenes Laertius *Lives of the Philosophers* 5. 19 with Plato *Phaedrus* 250d–52a. Tasso's immediate source is evidently Agostino Nifo, *De pulchro* (Rome, 1531), Sections 14 and 20.

36. Diogenes Laertius *Lives of the Philosophers* 5. 19. Instead of "rule of a single king" (*regno solitario*) Diogenes' text actually has "kingdom without bodyguards": the point of Carneades' remark is that beauty brings voluntary obedience. According to Stobaeus *Anthology* 4. 21. 15 (cf. Diogenes Laertius *Lives of the Philosophers* 6. 63), Diogenes the Cynic "called beautiful courtesans queens, because there are many who do what they command."

37. "Relation," one of Aristotle's ten categories or modes of being, describes terms whose meaning can only be stated with reference to something else, like "father" or "half" (see, for example, *Metaphysics* 1020b26–1021b11). Minturno's point is that Ruscelli treats beauty as something entirely relative rather than as an inherent quality or a substance. The reference to Hippocrates is perhaps to the beginning of the treatise *On Breaths*.

38. Petrarch *Trionfo d'Amore* 1. 88–93.

39. Alexander (Paris) is supposed to have been appointed by Zeus to judge a beauty contest between Aphrodite, Athena, and Hera, which Aphrodite won by promising to deliver Helen to him. Many legends also connected Helen with Theseus, king of Athens.

40. An account of this event of early Roman history may be found in Livy *History of Early Rome* 1. 9–10.

41. Petrarch *Rime* 140. 5–8. But the first line of Petrarch's text reads: "Quella ch' amare e sofferir ne 'nsegna" ("She who to love and its suffering trains").

42. Plato *Hippias major* 303e; cf. 296e–297c.

43. Petrarch *Rime* 224. 8. In Petrarch's poem, the phrase describes a despairing lover.

44. Petrarch *Rime* 105. 8–10.

45. Petrarch *Rime* 123. 12–14.

46. [Aristotle] *Problems* 10. 52. 896b10–28; Nifo *De pulchro* 28, 39–40, 63.

47. It was the opinion of the Stoics in particular. See Plotinus *Enneads* 1. 6. 1, Nifo *De pulchro* 19.

48. The definition ascribed to Plutarch is a combination of two remarks attributed to him by Stobaeus, 4. 21. 12 and 13 (cf. also 22). For Plotinus's definition see *Enneads* 1. 6. 3–4.

49. Probably a reference to the Hermetic treatise *Pimander* (*Corpus Hermeticum* 1) 14.

50. Virgil *Georgics* 1. 463–64.

51. Aristotle *On the Soul* 430a26–b31.

52. Cf. Plotinus *Enneads* 1. 6. 7. Minturno is alluding to a work edited by Ruscelli, *Il tempio alla divina signora donna Giovanna d'Aragona fabricato da tutti i piu gentili spirti e in tutte le lingue principali del mondo* (Venice, 1565), a poetic anthology honoring Giovanna of Aragon (1502–75), the sister-in-law of Alfonso d'Avalos.

53. Nifo's treatise is dedicated to Giovanna and gives a very full description of her physical beauty (*De pulchro* 5, 18).

54. Cf. Plotinus *Enneads* 1. 6. 9.

55. This passage largely derives from Plotinus *Enneads* 1. 6. 6 and 8.

56. Tasso *Rime d'Amore* 3. 9–14.

57. Ruscelli had once argued that women are "capable of separating and cleansing us from earthly things and lifting us to the way of heaven, and from them we derive the fullest contentment and happiness in this world" (*Lettura*, p. 30r).

58. An allusion to Minturno's *Amore innamorato*, a composition in prose and verse in celebration of love, published in his *Rime et prose* (Venice, 1559) with a dedication by Ruscelli.

59. Pliny *Natural History* 2. 3. 8.

60. Consider Nifo *De pulchro* 37.

61. Dante *Purgatorio* 8. 138.

Selected Bibliography

AQUILECCHIA, GIOVANNI. "Nota sulla prosa del Tasso." *Cultura neolatina* 9 (1949):154–63.

———. "La prosa del Tasso e la tradizione stilistica medievale." *Cultura neolatina* 11 (1951):130–50.

BAIARDI, GIORGIO CERBONI. "I *Dialoghi* di Torquato Tasso: Linee di storia della critica." *Studi urbinati di storia, filosofia e letteratura* 42 (1968):113–42.

BALDASSARRI, GUIDO. "L'arte del dialogo in Torquato Tasso." *Studi tassiani* 20 (1970):5–46.

———. "Il discorso tassiano 'Dell'arte del dialogo.'" *Rassegna della letteratura italiana* 75 (1971):93–134.

BANFI, ANTONIO. "Etica e religione in Torquato Tasso." In *Torquato Tasso*, edited by the Comitato ferrarese per le celebrazioni di Torquato Tasso, pp. 1–28. Milan: Marzorati, 1957.

BIANCHINI, GIUSEPPE. *Il pensiero filosofico di Torquato Tasso.* Verona-Padua: Drucker, 1897. See especially pp. 18–40.

BRAND, C. P. *Torquato Tasso: A Study of the Poet and of His Contribution to English Literature.* Cambridge, Eng.: Cambridge University Press, 1965. See especially pp. 179–88.

CHIORBOLI, EZIO. "L'eredità di Platone in Torquato Tasso." *La Romagna* 3 (1906):328–36, 372–82, and 418–30.

CROCE, BENEDETTO. "Libri sulle corti." In *Poeti e scrittori del pieno e del tardo Rinascimento*, 3 vols., 2:198–207. Bari: Laterza, 1952–58.

———. "La teoria del dialogo secondo il Tasso." In *Poeti e scrittori del pieno e del tardo Rinascimento*, 3 vols., 2:118–24. Bari: Laterza, 1945.

DA POZZO, GIOVANNI. "La prosa dei *Dialoghi* del Tasso." *Lettere italiane* 9 (1957):371–95.

DONADONI, EUGENIO. *Torquato Tasso.* 1920–21. Reprint. Florence: La Nuova Italia, 1936. See especially pp. 487–511.

FIRPO, LUIGI. "Il pensiero politico di Torquato Tasso." In

Studi in onore di Gino Luzzato, pp. 176–97. Milan: Giuffrè, 1950.

———. "Tasso e la politica dell'età sua." In *Torquato Tasso*, edited by the Comitato ferrarese per le celebrazioni di Torquato Tasso, pp. 29–54. Milan: Marzorati, 1957.

GETTO, GIOVANNI. *Interpretazione del Tasso*. Naples: Edizione scientifiche italiane, 1951. See especially pp. 79–111.

LEO, ULRICH. *Torquato Tasso: Studien zur Vorgeschichte des Secentismo*. Bern: Francke, 1951. See especially pp. 177–242.

LORD, CARNES. "The Argument of Tasso's *Nifo*." *Italica* 56 (1979):22–45.

MAZZALI, ETTORE. "Tradizione retorica e tradizione poetica nella poesia del Tasso." In *Torquato Tasso*, edited by the Comitato ferrarese per le celebrazioni di Torquato Tasso, pp. 115–65. Milan: Marzorati, 1957.

MORO, DONATO. "Note al discorso 'Delle'arte del dialogo' di Torquato Tasso." *Quaderni del Liceo Classico P. Colonna* 1 (1973):17–27.

RAIMONDI, EZIO. "Il problema filologico e letterario dei dialoghi." In *Torquato Tasso*, edited by the Comitato ferrarese per le celebrazioni di Torquato Tasso, pp. 478–502. Milan: Marzorati, 1957.

SOLERTI, ANGELO. *Vita di Torquato Tasso*. 2 vols. Turin-Rome: Loescher, 1895.

SOZZI, BORTOLO TOMMASO. "Nota sui *Dialoghi* del Tasso." *Studi tassiani* 4 (1954):67–76.

TASSO, TORQUATO. *Dialoghi*. Edited by Ezio Raimondi. 3 vols. Florence: Sansoni, 1958.

———. *Lettere*. Edited by Cesare Guasti. 5 vols. Florence: Le Monnier, 1854–55.

TORTORETO, ALESSANDRO. "Il tasso ovvero dell'arte del dialogo." *Aevum* 47 (1973):512–17.

TRAFTON, DAIN A. *Tasso's Dialogue on the Court*. English Literary Renaissance Supplements, no. 2. Amherst, Mass.: Dartmouth College and *English Literary Renaissance*, 1973.

Designer: Wolfgang Lederer
Compositor: G&S Typesetters, Inc.
Printer: Thomson-Shore, Inc.
Binder: John H. Dekker & Sons
Text: Linotron 202 Bembo
Display: Linotron 202 Bembo